170448

50/-

Adolescent Behavior in Urban Areas

Adolescent Behavior in Urban Areas

A Bibliographic Review
and Discussion of the
Literature

DAVID GOTTLIEB
and JON REEVES

THE FREE PRESS OF GLENCOE
COLLIER-MACMILLAN LIMITED, LONDON

Contents

Adolescent Behavior in Urban Areas

Introduction

Youth is a universal phenomenon. In all societies, be they primitive or highly complex, certain roles and behavior limits are assigned along an age and sex dimension. As the youngster moves from one stage of biological growth to another, adult expectations as to what behavior is proper and "good" will change. Behavior tolerated in a five-year-old, for example, may not be considered acceptable in a fifteen-year-old. Similarly, evaluation of behavior will vary with the sex of the actor. What we accept as "normal" for girls differs from what we accept as "normal" for boys.

When adult expectations are fulfilled by youth, conflict between generations is kept at a minimum; there is little anxiety about the transmission and continuity of cultural values, little concern for the future of the society. When, however, the system of beliefs held by youth is not in harmony with attitudinal and value expectations of the adult governing body, there may be serious consequences for the functioning of the society.

Recently we have seen sufficient evidence to suggest that there is a very real lack of harmony between the values held by youth and those held by adults. There seems to be a growing feeling that we are no longer in contact with our young and a general recognition that we are unable to understand why they behave the way they do. Numerous explanations have, of course, been presented. Some suggest that our entire society is undergoing a moral devaluation and youth are merely reflecting this downfall. Others prefer the more individual psychoanalytical interpretation. Still others—taking an existentialistic outlook—propose that our youth are reacting to a world filled with uncertainty. The multitude of possible explanations is clearly expressed by the Jets, a fictional youth gang in the popular musical play and film West Side Story, who point out that for every profession concerned at least one interpretation can be advanced for why adolescents behave the way they do.

1

This lack of clarity and the presentation of such a variety of definitive answers may be attributed in part to two factors: First, investigators, for the most part, have taken a narrowly specialized approach in their study of adolescent behavior. There seems to be little familiarity and concern with the work carried out in other behavioral sciences. Often, there is even no attempt to assess the work done by colleagues in the same field. Second, and this factor cannot be detached from the first, few attempts have been made at a systematic compilation and review of our current stage of knowledge in this important area.

This bibliographic review provides an overview of the major lines of research on adolescent behavior, summarizes their major findings, and indicates their implications for further research. It is intended to provide those who work with youth some understanding of the variables which play an important part in determining the behavior of adolescents. To sum up our goals, we hope this document will serve at least three basic purposes: first, that it serve as a bench mark giving some indication of what is now known about adolescent behavior; second, that it be a source book for both those who study and work with young people; finally, that it may suggest areas deserving of further empirical research.

Although the bibliography that follows covers a good portion of the considerable body of published materials, the review stresses mainly research dealing with adolescent behavior (as a cultural, social, or psychological phenomenon) as observed in American urban communities.

Bibliographic research is ordinarily cumulative, resting heavily on bibliographic work of the past; this report is no exception. A major initial source of references was J. M. Seidman's The Adolescent: A Book of Readings. Two other initial sources which have proved consistently valuable were Sociological Abstracts and Psychological Abstracts.

In addition to the initial sources noted above, a number of professional journals were examined for relevant material. The following list includes only those journals which proved to be of greatest value in the collection of titles. These 27 journals account for over two-thirds of the references noted in the General Bibliography. Those most valuable are starred (*).

* American Journal of Sociology
* American Sociological Review
* California Journal of Educational Research
* Child Development
  Dissertation Abstracts
* Education
  Educational and Psychological Measurement
  Genetic Psychology Monographs
* High School Journal
  Journal of Abnormal and Social Psychology
  Journal of Applied Psychology
* Journal of Educational Psychology
* Journal of Educational Research
* Journal of Educational Sociology
  Journal of Experimental Education
  Journal of Genetic Psychology
  Journal of Human Relations
  Journal of Social Casework
  Marriage and Family Living
  Review of Educational Research
  Rural Sociology (comparative studies)
  School and Community
* School and Society
  School Forces
  School Review
  Sociology and Social Research
* Sociometry

This report is based upon an extensive search through published materials. Obviously, however, it cannot cover that considerable body of work which has not appeared in print. An appreciable amount of research on adolescent behavior has been undertaken by manufacturers, advertising firms, and market research agencies. While some of this work may be irrelevant or of indifferent quality, it is likely that some portion would be of great value for a better understanding of how changes occur in adolescent consumption patterns.

This bibliographic review was sponsored by the Special Study Committee on 4-H Clubwork in Non-Farm Areas. The authors are indebted to the members of this committee and are especially grateful for the continued cooperation by Russel G. Mawby and members of his staff. Funds for the study were provided by the Sears-Roebuck Foundation of Chicago. Of particular importance to the success of the project, were the special efforts of Judith Cutler, Diane Moore, Carol Killebrew, and Jane Reeves.

Existing literature in the area of adolescence ranges from highly speculative discussion to narrowly empirical investigations, from the newspaper commentary on adolescent behavior to refined scientific investigations in specific areas. There have been psychological, sociological, physiological, and philosophical investigations into the various aspects of adolescence. Considering the purposes of this report and the volume of existing literature, it has been necessary to limit the scope of our survey.

We have decided to limit our selection to empirical studies of adolescent behavior. This removes from consideration speculative and popular media discussions. Full discussions of delinquent behavior data have been avoided since there already are numerous publications on them available to the interested reader. (See for example, The Annals of the American Academy of Political and Social Science, Vol. 261, January, 1949, and Vol. 322, March, 1959; also O. Moles, R. Lippitt, and S. Withey, A Selective Review of Research and Theory on Delinquency, Ann Arbor, Michigan: Institute for Social Research, September, 1959.) The listing was further limited to selection of articles concerning adolescents in urban areas, thus eliminating the research involving rural communities.

Discussions of the research findings, Part I which follows, have been classified into six sections. The first section (A) concerns the adolescent as consumer and includes research involving the adolescent and mass media, clothing, grooming, recreation, and the use of leisure time. The second section (B) deals with adolescent behavior within the context of the social institutions of the family and the school. The third section (C) is on the adolescent and his peers. The emphasis here is on prestige evaluation and the development and nature of peer relationships. The fourth (D) discusses research on occupational and educational expectations and the development of the self-image— the adolescent's preparation for adulthood. Adolescent values, attitudes, and sentiments about the world in which he lives are discussed in the fifth section (E); the final section (F) is briefly concerned with deviant behavior among adolescents. The bibliographic reference symbols (e.g., B.1, C. 12, etc.) in the discussions direct the reader to pertinent sections and numbers in the Annotated Bibliography (Part III), where a short summary of the research—including a statement of the problem, methods employed, and conclusions drawn—will be found for each selection discussed. Because the number of studies which could be included in the annotated bibliographies is necessarily limited, we have also provided a General Bibliography (Part IV)—an unannotated, alphabetic listing primarily of references not cited in the discussions and annotations; the General Bibliography also lists all the annotated references (followed by the appropriate location symbols) by way of an index.

Part II consists of a compilation and discussion of comments which we have solicited from a number of leading sociologists in the field of adolescent behavior on the subject of the possible validity and theoretical implications of the notion of "an adolescent subculture."

Finally, the reader should recognize that in itself the term "adolescent" holds different meanings for different investigators. For some, the age of "adolescence" is limited to the high-school years; for others, it is the period between "puberty and the taking of adult roles"; and for yet others, it is any period up to the time of marriage. A few investigators attempt to avoid the problem by not defining the term. We were not dismayed by this lack of consensus; our criterion for the selection of studies dealing with "adolescents" was a simple one: Whenever an investigator stated that he was dealing with a sample of adolescents (regardless of the criteria he used to identify this sample), his work was eligible for inclusion in this review.

I. Discussion of the Literature

A / ADOLESCENT AS CONSUMER

There are, of course, a number of ways in which the adolescent plays the role of consumer. He is a consumer of learning in our educational institutions; he is a consumer of food, clothing, and the mass media within the structure of our economic institutions; he is a consumer of recreation and athletic activities within the dimensions of his own leisure time. His impact on merchandizing and advertising has been so great that credit-card-carrying adolescents seem to be the order of the day (A.7).

Young people in our society are a potent economic market, and many manufacturers look to this age group for economic survival. While the published reports of the motivational and marketing researcher are difficult to come by, there is every reason to believe that large sums of money have been spent in order to determine efficient strategy in attacking this market. From personal experience the senior author of this review can recall investigations sponsored by recording firms, food manufacturers, department stores, magazine publishers, and the movie makers. Manufacturers recognize (and here they seem to be ahead of educators, parents, and youth workers) that adolescents are very much influenced by their peers and the social system in which they function. Through knowledge of current adolescent values and preferences and how these vary by socio-economic background, residence, community, education and so forth, the manufacturer is better able to decide what products should be introduced, who should introduce them, and what diffusion processes should be employed. He knows that while rock and roll is popular in the rural regions, it may already be passé in large metropolitan areas, and hence, it is best to launch the campaign in Allentown, New Jersey, not Chicago. Similarly, he recognizes that adolescents outgrow certain popular heroes and, therefore, it is important to know just who should sing the song, wear the dress, eat the cereal, or author the book. The middle-aged, middle-class American housewife may prefer a Como or Crosby, but the adolescent's tastes run toward something less dependable, such as a Paul Anka or Bobby Darin, or perhaps, when under adult pressures, a Pat Boone.

It would be pointless at this time to deal with the part played by these manufacturers in keeping the adolescent subculture alive. Obviously the adolescent does not always get what he needs and wants. Adults, be they manufacturers or not, certainly help in setting the current adolescent normative system. For our present purposes, it is sufficient to point out that representatives of the business world are very much concerned with the adolescent as a consumer.

Leaving the sphere of economics to move into the area of recreation, leisure time, and mass media, we find an emphasis in the research on descriptive studies of adolescent preferences in mass media (A. 13, A. 17, A. 19, A. 21, A. 25) and recreation and leisure-time activities (A. 1, A. 12, A. 16, A. 18, A. 22, A. 26, A. 27). A second line of investigation involves the impact of mass media on the behavior of adolescents (A. 3, A. 6, A. 9, A. 10, A. 30). An interest is also seen in adolescent clothing and grooming attitudes and practices (A. 2, A. 8, A. 24, A. 28).

Regarding the adolescent's preference in type and content of media, there is evidence to support the notion that educational and other "serious" content is preferred much less than entertainment or "light" content. Lyness (A. 17) notes a content preference among girls for love, glamor, and private life, while the boys have a strong preference for "light" material reflected in the newspaper reading interests of a group of high-school students. Among British adolescents, this preference is noted by McKellar and Harris (A. 19) with regard to selection of radio programs. This 1952 study, conducted with 1400 British adolescents and children also revealed a three-to-one ratio in preference for radio over movies.

Popular music is widely recognized as an important
area of adolescent interest, or at least the number of disc
jockeys and popular music programs directed to the adolescent would lead one to conclude that this music plays
an important role in the adolescent's life. Johnstone and
Katz (A. 13), investigating the role of dating behavior and
peer group relationships in the formation of adolescent
girls' preferences in popular music, have found that preferences varied according to the neighborhood in which
a girl lived and her popularity with her peers. While they
were unable to establish a direct peer group influence on
preferences, they noted that the peer group did influence
the listening habits to the extent that a given disc jockey
was consistently preferred, thus limiting the music to
which the group members listened.

The relationship between the type of media preferred
and the specific content interest of the adolescent has been
studied by Sterner (A. 25). Regarding adventure, humor,
and love as major interests of adolescents, Dr. Sterner
investigates the media preferences of 372 high-school
students and concludes that a preference for specific content rather than type of media attracts most adolescents
to the media. In addition, she was unable to establish a
relationship between the interest or media preference of
the group and their age, sex, intelligence, or socio-economic status. This study offers a valuable source of information in the annotated bibliography dealing with studies
on adolescent interest in various media.

Adolescence is commonly regarded as the age of ir-
responsibility, a time of freedom from adult cares, a time
remembered by many adults as "the best years of our
lives"—a time of relative leisure. The investigation
of the development and variety of leisure pursuits has
assumed increasing importance in recent years. The development of commercialized recreation and voluntary
social organizations, as well as the attention given leisure
activities in the mass media, suggest an increase in leisure
time within the population as a whole. Sociologists have
been interested in the social implications of increased
leisure, and various social organizations serving differing
age groups have investigated leisure activities in connection with program planning and implementation.

Generally, the investigations of adolescent leisure

pursuits have been of a descriptive nature. Within the adolescent group, comparisons have been made between age groups (A. 31) and social classes (A. 20, A. 31).

In 1929, Lynd and Lynd (A. 16) illustrated the changes in leisure pursuits. In an industrial community of approximately 35,000 inhabitants, they found increasing formalization and standardization of leisure activities. New problems were arising in connection with the acceptance of new inventions such as the radio and the automobile. They also note a widening of the differences in leisure activities between the working and middle classes.

More recently, Sullenger, investigating the leisure interests of grade-school boys, has found that sports and creative activities have a strong appeal in the 11-16 year age group (A. 26). A 1955 survey reveals, for the 14-16 year age group, a strong preference for swimming, hunting, working on cars, and team sports (A. 31). In at least one urban area (A. 22), a strong need was felt by adolescents for organized and formalized recreational facilities. By the time the adolescent reaches college his interests have changed. This is partly due to a general increase in available funds. Young adults as well as adolescents emphasize group activities, but the older adolescent and the young adult are better able to afford many of the group activities which involve relatively large expenditures (A. 11). Interests among college students have also expanded to include leisure activities involving work with people, service work, and preparation for professional careers (A. 27). The results of several studies indicate a strong desire among adolescents for leadership and direction in these organized leisure activities (A. 22, A. 26, A. 31).

In considering group membership in voluntary organizations and social class differences in leisure activities, a number of interesting points have been made. Mac-Donald, McGuire, and Havighurst (A. 20) note systematic differences between four social classes in a sample of 241 students. They found that family participation and reading interests increases as socio-economic level increased. They also note a significant number of lower-class children participating in middle-class activities. Keislar, on the other hand, indicates that the distinctive characteristic of members of adolescent clubs where memberships is by invitation was comparable grade-point average rather than intelligence or father's occupation (reflecting socio-economic status) (A. 14).

In 1955, an extensive examination of adolescent group membership was published by the Boy Scouts of America (A. 31). This study, conducted by the Survey Research Center, Ann Arbor, Michigan, investigated a representative sample of 1045 scout-age boys (14-16 years old) and collected information concerning principle leisure activities, amount of leisure, and needs and concerns of adolescents, the importance to them of group membership, the characteristics of nonjoiners, and the types of groups most attractive to boys. Among the significant findings reported, we see: (1) Among adolescents, leisure activities and organizational membership are infrequently mentioned as sources of either satisfaction or concern; (2) half of the sample works part time and most of them have had experiences with a variety of leisure pursuits; (3) of the boys questioned, three out of ten belonged to no clubs or organizations. Lack of time or other external pressures are the most often mentioned reasons for nonmembership. Of the boys who did belong to organizations, the largest proportion were in national activity organizations; (4) those boys who do belong to organized groups were generally from higher status groups and engaged in a greater variety of leisure pursuits than did the nonmembers. Considering the heterogeneity of the adolescent population, it is doubtful if any organization, regardless of the scope of its program, can hope to appeal to even a majority of the adolescents in a given area.

From the amount of discussion in the popular press on the impact of television and radio on the behavior of adolescents, one would expect to find the professional literature revealing support for unfavorable evaluations of the mass media. Contrary to this expectation, the studies examined indicated that the school work of adolescents is not appreciably affected by television (A. 3, A. 30). There is an indication that television viewing does affect the amount of time spent in other leisure activities (A. 6), but there is no indication that television can be considered as a primary source of adjustment and behavior problems (A. 30). In at least one case (A. 9), evidence is found to support the notion that certain radio programs

designed for adolescents attract a sizable audience and
have a greater influence on behavior than primary groups
and other sources of advice. Riley and Flowerman (A. 23)
note that adolescents who are integrated in a peer group
have different activities, interests, and reactions to a
given communication than adult-oriented adolescents.

The adolescent is often seen as a slave to fad and
fashion, and vulnerable to the slightest variation in clothing and grooming trends. In effect, in the case of the
adolescent girl this may be regarded as an integral part
of her desire for approval and for a consistent and satisfy-
ing self-image (A. 28). While a considerable amount of
conformity can be found in the clothing and grooming
practices (A. 24) of adolescent girls, a certain amount of
differing opinion on what constitutes proper practices can
be seen between girls of different social classes and
between girls and their mothers. For most girls, however,
the motivating desires in clothing and grooming are the
desire for approval, the desire for sexual attractiveness,
and the inner feelings of poise, self-confidence, and happiness (A. 24).

B / ADOLESCENT AND SOCIAL
INSTITUTIONS: SCHOOL
AND FAMILY

In past years, a heavy research emphasis has been
placed on the study of adolescent behavior within our social
institutions. Two major institutions which have received
most attention are the family and the school. The family is
especially important in the childhood development of the
adolescent, since it is the first agency in the social structure which the child contacts and it has the responsibility
of the initial socialization and preparation of the child for
future contact with the external world. By the time the
child reaches high school, he has entered the period of his

life and development which has been characterized as transitional or interstitial (B.28), the period of rapidly increasing physical and mental maturity between childhood and adulthood—adolescence.

While research on the development of the child can profitably focus on the physiological, psychological, and sociological implications of various child-rearing practices, the research examined for this report, which studies the relationship between the adolescent and the family, appears to emphasize the attitudes, conflicts, and relationships which characteristically arise between adolescents and their parents. Several studies examine the relationship between the adolescent's personality development, social acceptability, and his particular family environment (B.4, B.14, B.19, B.51, B.52, B.83, B.97); but the major interest seems to be the description of various aspects of the parent-child relationship and the examination of attitudes held by the parents and the child (see especially, B.7, B.8, B.11, B.16, B.26, B.30, B.43, B.45, B.57, B.64, B.80, B.92).

The reaction of adults to adolescents is often one of insistance on the adolescent's immaturity, while demanding that he behave in a mature manner (B.33). This situation, together with the lack of status offered to the adolescent by the adult world and the increasing length of time during which the adolescent is unable to be productive in our society, has led, in the opinion of some, to an increase in the importance of the school as a training ground for the adolescent years (B.34, B.90). The growing interest in the status system of the adolescent is reflected in much of the research reported in this section, as is the interest in the relationship of social class position to behavior in the school setting (B.1, B.5, B.9, B.13, B.20, B.22, B.23, B.25, B.35, B.39, B.40, B.46, B.53, B.93, B.95, B.98, B.100). The educator reveals an interest in predicting the success of students and developing more efficient methods of teaching (see especially, B.17, B.29, B.47, B.56, B.62, B.77, B.79, B.86, B.91, B.96). Other areas of investigation involve the teacher's knowledge of her pupils (B.3, B.12, B.63, B.65, B.70, B.74, B.99), the study of leadership (B.54, B.58, B.68, B.89, B.101), ethnocentrism and prejudice (B.59, B.60, B.66, B.85), and the dropout of students from school (B.10, B.21).

In the investigation of the relationship between family environment, personality formation, and social acceptability, one notion seems to run through all the examined research. Hollingshead (B.41) finds that the influence of the social class culture permeates the behavior of the adolescent in his relation to the school, the church, the family, and the peer group. While social class undoubtedly plays an important role in the value system and personal relations of the adolescent, the type of family relationship enjoyed by the adolescent has repeatedly been shown to influence his personality and social acceptability. Landis (B.51, B.52), Cavan (B.19), Peck (B.83), and Warnath (B.97) all note that the adolescent who comes from a democratic family, as opposed to an authoritarian family, has a better chance to adjust favorably to his life situation. Cavan, investigating problem and nonproblem children, reports that socially well adjusted children are a product of good home environments. Peck shows that adolescents who come from warm, democratic homes reveal more positive personality traits than those who come from disapproving authoritarian homes. Analysis of 142 interviews leads Warnath to conclude that adolescents coming from affectionate, democratic families are better able to adjust to the social structure of the adolescent peer group. Going beyond the democratic-authoritarian dichotomy, Landis (B.52), in an analysis of data from questionnaires applied to 5500 high-school seniors, finds not only that adolescents from democratic families are better adjusted and have fewer problems, but also that children from larger families reveal fewer problems than only children. The only child had fewer friends, was more introspective, and was more active outside the home.

With regard to affection seeking, Bartlett and Horrocks (B.4) find that children from broken homes reflect a greater need for affection in their approval-seeking behavior toward the opposite sex.

On the subject of the attitudes of parents and adolescents toward each other, we note first the study by Butler (B.15, B.16) concerning mothers' attitudes toward the social development of their adolescent children. The mothers' attitudes to the early stage of adolescent development reflected their confusion over the lack of well-defined cultural roles for the mother at this stage. They were generally unprepared for their children's new attitudes toward the family, the home and the neighborhood, and they had little comprehension of the rebellious attitudes of their children. By the period of late adolescence, the children had developed sufficiently to allow a move by the parents toward accepting them as adults. The late adolescents' demonstration of ability in the economic sphere made for increased consideration of their preferences. Mothers at this stage also reported greater satisfaction in marital relations and a greater self-awareness in the mother role.

Some aspects of adolescents' attitudes toward their parents are reported by Johannis and Rollins (B.44) in their investigation of 1400 tenth-grade students. They found that 80 per cent of the students rated their parents' marriages as happy, and 82 per cent were happy with their home life; there was no difference between boys and girls in the way parents' marriages were rated; and the students had more positive attitudes toward their mothers than toward their fathers. Among adolescents who do not live with their parents, however, Johnson (B.45) finds significantly more positive feelings toward parents and family in general than among adolescents who live with their parents.

In the specific relationship between the adolescent boy and his father, Payne and Mussen (B.82) found that boys who identify strongly with their fathers felt that their parental relationships in general were warm and rewarding. These boys also felt that their fathers were warm, friendly, and more rewarding than their mothers, and these boys were rated as more calm and friendly than those who did not identify strongly with their fathers. Cava and Raush (B.18) report similar results.

The idea that conformity in adult life is a generalization of conformist behavior learned in childhood is supported by Mussen and Kagan (B.76) in a study which revealed that a group of college students who were rated as conformists regarded their parents as harsh, punitive, rejecting, and restrictive.

Liccione (B.57) proposed that during the pubertal period, the relationship between daughter and mother would exhibit more conflict than that between the girls and their fathers in the same period. He found that at all ages there was a greater amount of both conflicting and nonconflicting interaction between the girls and their mothers than between girls and their fathers. This is explained in terms of the greater interaction between mothers and daughters. This factor of greater interaction between girls and their mothers may help to explain the finding of Ellis (B.31), drawn from the analysis of questionnaire responses of 500 college girls, that the girls felt more love for their mothers and sisters than they did for their fathers and brothers.

Following Hollingshead's notion that the social class culture influences the behavior and adjustment of the adolescent, Nye (B.80), in a study of 1472 high-school students in Michigan, finds that socio-economic level influences parent-child adjustments in differing degrees at different levels.

One of the central ideas in the notion of an adolescent subculture is a value and behavior system among adolescents which consistently deviates from the values and behavior of the adult culture. In disputing the existence of an adolescent subculture, Elkin and Westley (B.30) maintain that in order to speak of a subculture, one must establish the widespread and dominant presence of the phenomenon. In their study of 40 middle-class, white adolescents living in a relatively homogeneous suburb of Montreal, they were unable to find many sharp conflicts between the children and parents. In addition, they found little discontinuity in the socialization process and no youth culture pattern which prevailed over the family guidance pattern. On the basis of the findings from this relatively small and selective sample, they question the validity and the existence of an adolescent subculture.

Other, less significant, results indicating a similarity of attitudes and interests between adolescents and parents are presented by Berg (B.7) and Johannis (B.43). Berg has investigated the similarities between the attitudes of parents, students, and teachers with respect to their judgment of suitable behavior in a variety of school situations. These seven situations include, for example, the class, playing on a school team, class trips, behavior between classes, and behavior on a public vehicle. While they were able to establish significant agreement between the three groups on the appropriate behavior in these situations, there was disagreement between the students and the parents on the methods by which these standards might be obtained.

Johannis (B.43) found a great deal of family participation in several selected social activities when he investigated a sample of 1027 high-school sophomores in Tampa, Florida. In fact, in eight of the ten activities selected, it was found that over 78 per cent of the families participated as a group.

In an excellent article on the problem of parent-youth conflict, Davis (B.26) contends that the conflict between generations found in Western society arises from the interaction of certain universals in the parent-child relationship and certain cultural variables. These universals include the difference in age between the parent and the child, the factor of decreasing socialization with increasing age, and the physiological, psychological, and sociological differences between the age groups. These universals interact with the following variables: the rate of social change, the complexity of the social structure, the degree of integration in the culture, and the force of vertical mobility.

One of the important functions of the adolescent period is to develop increasing independence from the family. It is possible that one measure of increasing independence may be found in the individual's attachment to and attitude toward his neighborhood. In a study of 420 adolescents, Bernard (B.8) notes the influence of age and socio-economic level in the child's emancipation from the home neighborhood. She finds that the greatest relative decline in attachment to the neighborhood comes at age 17 for the middle-class child and at age 15 for the lower-class child. It was also found that initially the lower-class child was more attached to his neighborhood than was the middle-class child.

In a comparison of American and Swiss children between the ages of 6 and 16, it has been shown that the American child develops independence from the family at an earlier age than the Swiss child. Americans also develop independence of thought at an earlier age (B.11).

One possible explanation for the rapid evolution of independent attitudes on the part of the adolescent may be seen in the influence and support of the peer group. A study by

Kinch and Bowerman (B.49) has shown that increasing age leads to increased activity and contact with the peer group. As the peer group contact expands, there will be a complete shift from a family orientation to a peer orientation unless the family is able to maintain a satisfactory adjustment.

An illustration of the cross pressures between the peer group and the parents can be seen in the study of the observation of the Kosher meat laws between Jewish adolescents and their parents (B.92). In both conflict situations (peers observant—parents nonobservant and vice versa), it was found generally that the attitude of the peer group influenced the adolescent's choice to a greater degree than did the parents' attitudes.

The influence of social class position is seen also in the area of attitudes of prejudice toward Jews and Negroes (B.64). This longitudinal study of adolescent attitudes concludes that although prejudice among lower-class boys is often based on the acceptance of a cultural stereotype of the ethnic group and is not related to specific personality needs or family environments, the middle-class adolescent's prejudice is likely to reflect his personality needs and experiences in the family environment.

A growing problem in recent years has been the increase in high-school age marriage. One possible explanation for this rise has been investigated by Burchinal (B.14). He hypothesized that: (1) early marriage is directly related to dissatisfaction with parental relations; (2) early marriage is directly related to the amount of heterosexual involvement of the girls; (3) early marriage is a result of adult role deprivation and is desired for its expected satisfactions anticipated in a change of roles. Analysis of the comparison of 60 married and 60 unmarried high-school girls, matched for grade, age, father's occupation, parents' educational level, religion, and size of family, failed to support either the first or the third hypothesis but did find that these girls who were married prior to graduation had had more heterosexual involvement that the girls who had not married.

The inconsistent attitudes and policies of school authorities in dealing with this problem is noted in a survey study by Landis (B.103).

Regarding the school situation, a particular interest of

the educator, psychologist, and sociologist concerns achievement and prediction of success in educational pursuits. The following studies are included to illustrate the type of research which has been conducted. It is felt that this area of research, while undoubtedly of great significance, is of minor importance for this report.

One point of perennial interest is the comparative success of public and private high-school boys in the college situation. An article summarizing the results of several investigations in this area has found: (1) With I.Q. held constant, the public school boy tends to outperform the private school boy and his grades may be more easily predicted; and (2) the two groups reflect different social values and childhood experiences in Thematic Apperception Tests (B.62). It has also been shown that performance on the Rorschach Test is a fair indication of how a student will perform in certain areas (B.78).

In connection with the psychological approach to performance, the differences between the academic performance of children with above-average intelligence has been associated with personality characteristics. The gifted children with high grades tend to come from superior home environments and are rated high on such favorable personality traits as dependability, originality, and self-reliance, while the gifted children with poor performance generally come from less favorable home environments and manifest less favorable personality traits (B.56). This relationship does not seem to hold true in the area of creative writing, however. Neals (B.77) has shown that, among seventh-grade students, those who had higher intelligence and came from better homes were not as creative in their writing as were those from poor home environments.

Other findings from various areas of interest include:

1. Establishment of a negative correlation between intelligence and performance on the Taylor Manifest Anxiety Scale (B.17).

2. A relationship between delinquency proneness and school achievement which indicates that, in an area of high delinquency, those boys who are not delinquent have better performance in reading and mathematics (B.48).

3. Among superior readers, the majority could read before the first grade. Few of these superior readers

18

credit teachers or school with much influence in the development of their reading skills (B.47).

4. Support for the hypothesis that interest in science in general is correlated with performance in high school chemistry courses (B.29).

5. Support for the use of the Miller Analogies Test as a predictor of achievement in the junior college situation (B.86).

6. Support for the use of tests, previous grades, and performance in the prediction of success in such topics as high-school algebra (B.67) and high-school shop training (B.88).

7. Study habits, at least in the subject of general science at the ninth-grade level, are not any more responsible for performance than are intelligence, reading ability, or aptitude (B.79).

Of somewhat more interest to this report are the studies concerned with the evaluation of the extent of the teachers' knowledge of the friendship patterns and popularity of their students. In the school situation, where so much of the teacher's time is spent in contact with the adolescent, it would normally be expected that the individual teacher would have acquired relatively complete information on her pupils and be able to judge which of them were the most acceptable to their peers. Contrary to this expectation, a study by Baker (B.3) presents us with some interesting observations. This analysis was made on the questionnaire response of 27 teachers and 250 students from varying high schools who were asked for information on the extent of the teachers' knowledge of behavior and background differences among their students. It was found that, while there was a great variation between teachers in the amount of accurate knowledge held, most of the teachers knew less than one-fourth of the facts regarded as necessary by school counselors in the educational guidance of individual students. In this particular study, and most likely in similar situations, the quantity of teachers' knowledge was related to such factors as the size of the class, the amount of association between teacher and student outside of the classroom environment, and the amount of time the teacher devoted to conferences with her students.

The teachers did not fare much better in their evaluations of the number of friends possessed by the individual students. In a study conducted at North Texas State College (B.12), Bonney found that teachers were not very accurate in their estimations of the number of friends a given adolescent would have. This was true even in the cases where the teacher was evaluating students who were fairly well known by her. It is possible here that the criteria used by the teacher in her estimation was not equivalent to the criteria utilized by the adolescents in the determination of the members of their peer groups who would be acceptable friends.

Parallel to these findings, the study by Marshall (B.70), an examination of the accuracy of adult leaders' judgments of the social acceptability of 263 girls in 22 4-H clubs, offers somewhat different results. In general, it was found that the accuracy of the adult judgments increased as the popularity of the individual girl increased. The adults were better able to rate the acceptability of the older girls than the younger girls. Accuracy in judgment also depended on the number of girls in the group, adult judgments of the larger groups being less accurate.

Contrary to the teacher's knowledge of her pupils, Witryol (B.99) notes that there is a considerable agreement, increasing with the age of the student, between student attitudes on what they feel the teachers would consider as socially appropriate behavior and teachers' statements of what they hold as socially acceptable behavior. Among the students, the girls seem to be better than the boys at estimating the teachers' attitudes.

Two studies report on the value of using sociometric techniques in the classroom (B.63, B.74). These techniques enable the teachers to gain important information on the acceptability of their students and offer them aids in planning the activities of the group. In one instance (B.74), the investigators found that the students would have organized the room differently if they had been allowed to do so. Their organization would have seen the development of groups and leaders in the classroom and the exclusion of the undesired peers from group activities. A more extensive investigation of a stratified tenth-grade class is presented by Cook (B.22). This study, conducted over a two-year period, notes an increase of 100 per cent in the number of "best friend" choices made by the students as a result of increased interaction in the group. Three-fourths of these choices were made within the tenth-grade class. In spite of the increased interaction, or perhaps because of it, the upper-class children tended to be overchosen as friends while the lower-class children tended to be under-chosen.

An area of major importance in the school situation is the reaction of the school to the social class membership of the students. Recalling Hollingshead's notion of the pattern of class values of the various social strata which influences the behavior and attitudes of the adolescent and the fact that the majority of teachers are of middle-class background and training, we find that the reaction of the school to the adolescent becomes important. Havighurst and Neubaur (B.39) point out that the values of the school and the adolescent peer culture, which permeates the school environment, are predominantly middle-class values. Likewise, the "character-building" organizations such as the Boy Scouts, Hi-Y, and 4-H operate on middle-class values and appeal to the middle-class adolescent. Weckler (B.98) associates the character reputation of the adolescent with his social class position, noting that the reputation of the individual depends to a great extent on his conformity to the school culture, which is predominantly middle-class. Langworthy (B.53) finds that in the areas of ethnic choice and preference, the status system of the school reflects that of the community. In addition to the similarity between the community and the school in terms of class status and values, an age ranking of status was operative whereby students in the higher grades had more status than those in the lower grades.

In a descriptive study of the attitudes of 60 teachers in the Chicago school system, Becker (B.5) finds variations in the teachers' reactions to students of different classes in the areas of teaching procedures, discipline, and moral acceptability. These teachers felt that the lower-class adolescent is more difficult to discipline and teach and often displays behavior which is morally unacceptable to the teacher. More specific disparities are cited in two studies which compare the rewards and behavior of the middle- and lower-class adolescent (B.1, B.23). These studies maintain that: (1) middle-class students receive a disproportionate share of the high grades in class work; (2) middle-class students fill most of the elective offices in the class and in the school; (3) middle-class students engage in more school and extracurricular activities; and (4) middle-class students go to church more often, continue their educations more often, and win the American Legion Award more often than do lower-class adolescents.

Recognizing the adjustment difficulties and the lack of understanding which meet most lower-class or "socially underprivileged" youth in the school, at least one author has recommended that a separate educational program be organized for these students (B.13). Such a program would not only help the lower-class adolescent to adjust to the world around him, but it would also benefit the more acceptable student by removing from the school situation a major source of conflict and educational mediocrity.

One approach to the class differences in adolescent behavior is to consider the adolescent a member of a social class, outside of the school system, which socializes its junior members along certain lines to achieve the desired end products. The results of this differential socialization lead to behavior which varies when various social strata are compared. Thus, a lower-class and a middle-class adolescent boy may react differently to the school situation, but these reactions are essentially reactions to differences in perceptions rather than different reactions to the same situation. The lower-class boy may be well socialized in terms of lower-class standards, but may appear to be totally unsocialized when seen through middle-class eyes in a middle-class setting (B.25).

With the adolescent spending a great part of his time in the school situation, the question arises as to the source of adolescent status in the school environment. The school would naturally like to feel that academic achievement and competence play an important role in the peer group status structure, for education of the young is the avowed goal of the school. Several recent studies indicate that the role of academic performance in the adolescent status system can only be understood in terms of the values of the adolescent groups in a given school environment. Gordon (B.35), in an investigation of the behavior of adolescents in relation to their position in the general social structure of the school, finds that the individual adolescent is likely to seek roles in the school environment which afford him prestige in the informal peer group structure. Specifically, Gordon states that successful participation in student activities is more indicative of the general status of an individual than is success in academic pursuits.

Grades, however, may in a given environment earn the adolescent a certain amount of prestige. This finding is noted by Ryon and Davie (B.93) in their investigation of 326 students in a suburban high school. They were able to establish a significant positive relationship between grades and social acceptance. Two-thirds of the students tested, however, were taking college preparatory courses and it would be expected that such a group would reflect greater interest in the academic areas.

An excellent examination of the status systems of a series of high schools has been reported by Coleman (B.20). In this study of the status systems of ten midwest high schools of varying composition, the author utilized school grade records, I.Q. test results, and questionnaires asking, among other things, how the student would most like to be remembered in his school. The results indicate that in all the schools investigated, the majority of students would rather be remembered as a star athlete, a leader in activities, or a popular person than as a brilliant student. These results varied slightly according to the composition of the school but the general tendency was present in all cases. The explanation offered for this phenomenon centers on the values of the adolescents themselves. In the cases investigated, the adolescent group awarded status and prestige to success in nonacademic areas. The emphasis placed by the school and the adult population on interscholastic athletics and extracurricular activities is seen as a potent influence in the determination of adolescent values. Coleman also notes that in the schools in which the adolescents stress nonacademic achievement, those who are regarded as the intellectuals or "brains" are actually not the most capable students. The most able are more likely to expend their efforts in areas which offer them the most status and prestige among their peers, leaving the area of academic excellence to those who are unable or unwilling to compete for the highest prestige and status positions.

An earlier study by Biddulph (B.9) also notes the importance of athletics in the world of the adolescent. An investigation of 461 high-school boys found that those who were more active in athletics also revealed a greater degree of personal and social adjustment than did the boys who were inactive in athletics.

In an attempt to isolate the factors which influence an individual's participation in the social life of the school, Jones (B.46) compared two groups of students on ten points, including behavior ratings, intelligence, reputation, physical abilities, socio-economic status, attitudes, and self-concept. While she was able to establish significant differences in the areas of behavior ratings, reputation, and socio-economic status, they were not considered conclusive in determining who would be most active in the social life of the school.

Two points of view on the presence of cliques and sororities in the high-school situation are presented in studies B.40 and B.95. On the one hand, Heaton (B.40) feels that the presence of cliques and sororities reflects a lack of planning on the part of the school for the needs of the students. The unsatisfactory group life of the school results in the formation of cliques and sororities. On the other hand, Spaulding and Bolin (B.95) feel that membership in cliques facilitates adjustment to the high-school situation. They found that girls who entered the high-school situation with no clique affiliations established them shortly after entering high school. The emphasis here lies in the clique as a device for social adjustment rather than as a reaction to unsatisfactory group life in the school.

An early study by Reals (B.89) finds only slight differences in the home backgrounds of leaders and nonleaders in the high school. A later study by Latham (B.54), investigating the relationship between physical maturity and leadership, finds that in three areas of leadership (elective, appointive, and athletic), only the area of athletic leadership consistently preferred physically mature boys. In the other two areas, no relationship could be found between maturity and selection.

Studies conducted in 1952 by Lundberg and Dickson (B.59, B.60) reveal interesting findings on the relations between ethnic groups in a high-school population. Examination of a sample of 1544 students in different ethnic groups revealed that all the ethnic groups became progressively more ethnocentric as their choices progressed from desired leaders to work-partners and dates to friends. While a preference was shown for ethnic group members in all areas, outsiders were accepted as leaders more often than as friends. The authors conclude that prejudice is not restricted to the majority group but that the minority groups often feel strong antagonistic feelings toward the majority group. In these situations, the expressed ethnocentrism is related more to specific interpersonal relationships than to sentiments of prejudice in general.

The change in ethnic reaction in high school between the tenth and the twelfth grades has been investigated by McNeil (B.66). In this longitudinal study of 50 high-school students, it was found that the number of negative responses to ethnic and racial stereotypes more than doubled between the tenth and the twelfth grades. Those who were found to be the most prejudiced in the tenth grade were also the ones who were the most prejudiced in the twelfth grade.

Investigations into the problem of school drouput are illustrated by two items of research (B.10, B.21). In the first study, Bledsoe notes three main factors associated with school dropout: low intelligence, dissatisfaction with the school program, and financial need. He also finds that the level of the parents' education and occupation influence the adolescent's level of aspiration. Cook (B.21) in a comparison of withdrawals and nonwithdrawals, finds that those who drop out of school are older than their classmates and are educationally retarded. They were found to have lower levels of intelligence and to achieve considerably less in school than did those who remained in school. Many of those who withdraw prior to graduation have poor family relationships and are likely to have made poor adjustments to the school situation.

C / ADOLESCENT AND HIS PEERS

Granting that the adolescent is involved in several of the institutions of the community such as the school, the family, the church, and the authority structure, it is important to remember that he (or she), quite often relates to these institutions as a member of a formal or informal group of his age-mates. This group can take the form of a social club, a gang, or an apparently nonstructured group of friends. In his family contacts, his behavior can hardly be understood solely in terms of the family environment but requires an understanding of the influence of the attitudes and norms of his peers. Likewise, his leisure pursuits and interests are influenced by his association with his age-mates or peers.

Research into this area has ranged from discussions of the structure and function of the adolescent peer group (C.4, C.8, C.43, C.48, C.54) through investigations of dating behavior and the development of appropriate sex roles (see especially C.12, C.14, C.23, C.24, C.30, C.35, C.46, C.56, C.58), to extensive work on peer acceptance, popularity, and status (see especially B.20, C.1, C.2, C.3, C.9, C.15, C.20, C.26, C.32, C.40, C.47, C.51, C.62).

Discussions of the functions of the peer group in the life of the adolescent characteristically note the role of the peer group as an aid in the adolescent's emancipation from his family (C.4, C.43, C.48, C.54). The support gained by the adolescent from the peer group encourages him in his struggle against parental authority and adult control. Phelps and Horrocks (C.48) have shown in an intensive study of 200 adolescent boys and girls that the most important over-all reason for the formation of informal groups among adolescents is the desire to achieve freedom from adult control.

Aside from its specific support in the struggle with adult authority, the peer group is seen as an insulator against the frustrations and anxieties in the shift from adolescence to adulthood (C.4, C.48). The peer group supports the adolescent by offering him a source of status (C.4) and a training ground where he can experiment with personal relations, gain heterosexual experience, and develop social contacts which will be of future use to him. Several writers note the influence of the peer group in the later formation of personality characteristics (C.4, C.8, C.52, C.60). Seidler and Ravitz (C.52), investigating a Jewish peer group, reveal that the values and norms of the group were so internalized by the subjects that the peer

26

group took on the function of a primary group and replaced the respective families. They support this conclusion on the basis of the number of out-group marriages, nonconformist ideas, and the trend away from business occupations and toward professional and service occupations. This study illustrates how the peer group may, with intense solidarity and long duration, influence the personality of its members. Bossard (C.8) notes that the experience of involvement in a peer group is a basic influence in the shaping of the adult personality but that the nature of the contact with a peer group or groups depends on length of membership and the individual's need for peer group activities.

Cameron (C.10), in a study of 200 young adolescents, has characterized the "in-group" as being concerned with acceptance by its peers, approval from the opposite sex, and social activities. The desired image involved a combination of physical and social maturity, friendliness, good looks, and high popularity. In spite of this characterization, one would expect the peer group values and behavior to vary with the social class and age of its members. Variation in the manifest behavior of adolescent groups seems to appear in many areas. The behavior of the adolescent street gang is in direct opposition to the behavior of an organized supervised youth group. The social class differences in the factors influencing the formation of informal groups is discussed in the study by Phelps and Horrocks mentioned earlier (C.48). They found that informal groups were formed by the lower-class adolescents in reaction to the predominantly middle-class orientation of the school. In this case, the informal groups offered the lower-class students status and a form of recognition which they were unable to attain in the middle-class school situation. The middle-class adolescents formed informal groups for a variety of reasons, as pressure toward social conformity, opportunities for unchaperoned activities, and a desire to escape the moral code of home and school. From a different point of view, but still comparable, Pope (C.49) finds that early adolescents in the upper social classes place a higher value on conforming to adult standards and conventional codes of conduct than those in the lower socio-economic classes, who emphasize self-assertion and aggression.

Despite the variations in peer group behavior, Tyron (C.54) feels that the adolescent peer groups reflect the form and purposes of their adult counterparts. She sees a definite similarity of general characteristics between the adult peer groups and the adolescent groups. Whyte (C.59), writing in 1941, noted the characteristic relationships of small groups as reflected in the clique behavior of a group of Italian male adolescents in a slum area in Boston. He observes that the clique has (1) a hierarchial structure as the basis of group organization, (2) mutual obligations as the basis of all group relationships, (3) behavior determined by the status position of the member, and (4) a leader who represents and directs the group's activities.

One example of the influence of the peer group in the setting of adolescent norms has been offered by Neiman (C.44). In an examination of 322 adolescents between the ages of 11 and 24 (this age span is indicative of the lack of agreement among investigators as to just how old an "adolescent" is) with regard to their attitudes toward feminism, he finds that as adolescents grow older there is a significant lessening of the importance of family norms and an increasing influence of peer group norms.

Dating behavior and sex role behavior are two areas of adolescent peer relations which have received appreciable attention in the literature. The work on dating is mainly descriptive of dating practices, attitudes toward dating, and selection of dating partners. Who makes a good date, what are accepted activities, when do adolescents start dating, what is the attitude toward going steady, are the types of questions which have generally been asked in connection with dating. The investigation of sex roles has been concerned with the development of appropriate behavior patterns and the problems of adjustment to contradictory situations.

Heterosexual activity and experience is an important part of the period of adolescence. This is the period when the individual is becoming more aware of the opposite sex, is experimenting with interpersonal relations, and is rapidly gaining physical maturity. Dating patterns and behavior also reveal significant norms and values operating within and between adolescents and adults.

The influence of the peer group in the development of dating behavior is seen in the choice of dating partners and preferred activities. The peer group is also important in the development of interest in dating. Crist (C.14), reporting on the dating behavior of high-school students, notes that the dating of the investigated students was generally controlled by their parents, but activities and date partners were approved by peers. Crist also finds that early dating is usually a result of group expectations and that, in fact, many students date solely because they wish to be accepted by their group, not because they are particularly interested in dating as such.

The selection of dating partners is not a random process. Not all adolescents are judged equally in terms of their acceptability as dates. Adolescents from different social strata behave differently and have different criteria for the selection of acceptable dates. In general, these criteria are similar to those used in the evaluation of peers in general and friends in particular. These characteristics will be discussed later in connection with peer group status, prestige, and acceptance.

In 1937, Waller (C.55) recognized the presence of what he calls the " rating and dating complex" in the dating behavior of college students. He notes that there is a definite class system or gradient of dating desirability among college students. The rating complex is not unique to a given school, but is found among all college students. Between schools a great deal of variation in the component parts of the rating complex can be seen, but regardless of the form taken, the system is clearly recognized and adjusted to by the students. The general characteristics usually found in the rating for boys includes: fraternity standing, activities, money, clothes, and access to a car. The rating of girls generally involves the factors of popularity as a date, clothes, and dancing well.

Variations in rating and dating patterns are also to be found among different student cliques or interest groups. Obviously the criteria used by the " beatnik" or deviant will be different from that endorsed by the " collegiate" or " rah-rah" type. Similarly, high-school students will reflect different views based on their own position within the activity structure of the school. Membership on the varsity football or basketball team may, for example, greatly alter the appeal of a boy even though he does not possess a car or fraternity membership. Among the same lines, a girl who is a cheer leader in her high school may find her dating currency up even though she possesses certain characteristics which are considered unacceptable by her peers. Each of these examples points out the need for research that not only studies the individual but also takes account of the total institution in which the individual is being observed.

The influence of class position on dating patterns is discussed in a study by Hill (C.23). In an investigation of 229 high-school students from several socio-economic levels in Florida, he found that the majority of students dated within their own social and school classes. Students in the upper social classes had more dating partners while the lower classes tend to date outside of their social and school class. Christensen (C.12) supports the idea of distinct dating patterns for boys and girls.

Why adolescents date and what their attitudes are toward dating has received some attention from investigators. It has been noted (C.46) that girls, as might be anticipated, generally are much less liberal than boys in their attitudes toward dating and related practices. Boys seem to be more interested in having a good time on dates while girls often emphasize that the dating situation is one where they can learn and practice certain social skills. The necessity of mate selection and the preparation for marriage are important factors to consider in the evaluation of dating behavior (C.39). In considering dating as a type of preparation for marriage, one would reasonably expect attitudes toward marriage roles to increase in accuracy from the predating to the postmarriage stage. Hobart (C.24), however, has shown that unrealistic romantic ideas follow a cyclical pattern with adolescents being most unrealistic at the beginning of their courtships and most realistic at the end. Those close to marriage appeared to hold the most unrealistic attitudes toward marriage roles. He attributes this situation to the operation of a youth subculture in which unrealistic and romantic attitudes are associated with going-steady and engagement.

In the area of sex activity the male is usually seen as the aggressor (C.12). The prevalence of sexual activity is often associated with socio-economic class levels, with the lower classes being considered as the most lax and the middle and upper classes having more restrictive codes.

30

It is important to note here that a number of studies dealing with the aspect of social class and behavior leave much to be desired in terms of methodological sophistication. Too often the investigator has failed to move beyond a three variable analysis once a relationship has been found to exist between social class and some dependent variable. There is some evidence to indicate that perhaps we have been making too much of social class and too little of other salient factors in our analysis of human behavior. With regard to male aggression, Kanin (C.30) has investigated alcohol, place of occurrence, and family environment as relevant factors in the explanation of aggression. He finds that the length of involvement in the relationship, and the season of the year (spring and summer) are more important factors in determining the reasons for male aggression.

Whyte, writing in 1943, indicates the existence of very strict and complicated sex codes in slum areas (C.58). Rather than an absence of sex mores, we see the classification of women into several categories, each of which has an acceptable form of sexual behavior and accessibility which is sanctioned and furthered by the mores of the group.

Research in the area of sex roles has emphasized the psychological aspect of sexual maturation and the development of sex role conflict. The main interest in the development of sex roles is found in the writings on the psychology of adolescent personality development. The papers by Jones discussed in the following section (D) illustrate some of the social implications of maturity.

It is commonly noted in the popular literature that the female matures at an earlier age than the male. Hildreth (C.22) notes, in addition, that girls also mature earlier than boys in social interests associated with heterosexual activities. In an examination of 87 boys and 105 girls in the 10-14 year age group, variation in social interests are found which account for apparent social incompatibility of like-age boys and girls in junior high school. Sex appropriate behavior has been shown to increase significantly among girls between the ages of 15 and 17, while boys in this period have shown no comparable increase. Although variations in behavior exist at all age levels, girls appear to be more stable from year to year than boys (C.61).

Variations in maturity play an important role in the social development and prestige ratings of adolescents. Jones (C.28), reporting some results of a continuing study of physical maturity and social behavior, concludes than in an urban American culture, girls seem to have a greater problem than boys in adjusting to changing social requirements. While the development of male sex roles in early adolescence appears fairly consistent, by age 15, girls' roles have shifted from an emphasis on quiet, "lady-like" behavior to active, aggressive and talkative behavior. Early-maturing girls seem to be at a disadvantage in their peer relationships due to an interest in boys which far exceeds that of their age-mates. The late-maturing girls, with a longer period of development and adjustment to new impulses and interests, are more favorably received by their peers. Among boys the opposite relation prevails with the early-maturing boy in a more favorable position with regard to peer acceptance.

Komarovsky (C.35, C.36) points out a significant area of sex role conflict among college girls, resulting from discrepancy between the traditional feminine role of homemaker and the modern role of potential career girl. Conflicting pressures from male friends and family result in uncertainty and insecurity which seem to be centered on academic performance, social life, and vocational plans. In an approximate replication of Komarovsky's study, Wallin (C.56) also finds conflict arising from discrepant expectations of family and friends, but holds that, while the problem of contradictory role expectations is widespread, the majority of college girls either do not take it seriously or are easily able to resolve the problem.

A considerable amount of the research on adolescents has been concerned with popularity, status, social acceptability, and friendship patterns. The most cursory examination of newspaper articles and books by popular authors reveals the apparent preoccupation of the adolescent with the maintenance of a socially acceptable pattern of behavior. Considering the function of the adolescent period as a training ground for the development of interpersonal relationships and a period of experimentation with various self-images, the adolescent's concern with acceptance and popularity seems not unnatural.

The research on social acceptance, status, and prestige

factors in the years of adolescence has been concerned with the description of these factors in terms of social class, age, sex, and personality trait differences. Anastasi and Miller (C.1) investigated a group of 100 male and female high-school students matched for sex ratio, age, and grade level, but sharply differentiated by scholastic achievement and socio-economic level. They note distinct differences in the prestige factors listed for the precollege group (high in socio-economic status and scholastic achievement). Factors listed by all the students as important fell into the stereotype of the friendly, popular, well-dressed, conformist to group ideals. The precollege group, in addition to the above, included serious-mindedness, talkativeness, creativity, and enthusiasm as important traits. The noncollege group emphasized such traits as being athletic, a good listener, a good fellow, having a good sense of humor, a neat appearance, and being " grown up."

Sex and age differences in personality characteristics associated with social acceptability have been investigated by Kuhlen and Lee (C.37). They found a progression in acceptability characteristics from the sixth to the twelfth grades. The higher the grade, the more acceptability characteristics reflected interest in heterosexual activities. By the twelfth grade, girls were less aggressive in heterosexual social activities and boys had increased in activity, social aggression, and extroversion. In addition to the general characteristics of popularity, being friendly, enthusiastic, and the initiator of activities as criteria of acceptability among twelfth graders, boys reflected an interest in the opposite sex, and the most acceptable girls were sociable and had a good sense of humor.

Another approach to acceptability in adolescence is illustrated by Bretsch (C.9). On the basis of sociometric tests, he divided 696 high-school students into three levels of social acceptance: high, middle and low. These same students also rated themselves on level performance in eight social skills and, in addition, checked a frequency list of 49 different social activities in which they participated. On the basis of these measures, Bretsch found that the more acceptable students participated in a slightly, but significantly, greater number of social activities. He also found that members of the highly acceptable group felt themselves to be more adept in the social skill than those of the low group. In the list of activities, 39 out of the 49 activities listed showed differential participation by sex, and over half showed significant differences between the well accepted and the poorly accepted groups. This type of study emphasizes the behavioral manifestations of acceptability rather than the personality characteristics of acceptable individuals. In an attempt to link declared adolescent interests to social acceptability, Marks (C.41) found that accepted girls expressed more interests that can be considered sociable, heterosexual, and provocative of adult disapproval and they had considerably fewer intellectual-cultural interests, while the accepted boys had few mechanical and constructional interests.

With regard to social acceptability and personality characteristics, one author states that although socially acceptable children possess a large number of desirable traits in common, it is impossible to classify popular and unpopular children on the basis of their personality traits. It is the total personality configuration rather than specific traits which operate to determine an individual's acceptability (C.7). Wardlow and Greene (C.63) also indicate the difficulty of determining what personality characteristics are significantly related to peer status. While they do find some significant characteristics, they note that sociometric research involving the correlates of peer status must recognize that peer status is situational or specific in character. On the other hand, it is quite possible that the specific traits common to socially acceptable adolescents are sufficient to distinguish and classify accepted and rejected individuals. Gronlund and Anderson (C.16), in an investigation of acceptability and personality characteristics, have found that strong, positive personality characteristics are associated with social acceptability among junior high school students. For both boys and girls, the socially accepted revealed traits including: good-looking, tidy, friendly, likable, enthusiastic, cheerful, quiet (not restless), interested in dating, good sense of humor, initiative, and talkative. The socially neglected students were usually overlooked rather than disliked. They scored neither high nor low on the tested traits. The socially rejected, on the other hand, were rated low on the mentioned traits, but were aggressive enough to draw attention to themselves and thus to be rejected.

Most investigations of social acceptability have been conducted in a school setting with the subjects being drawn from selected classes and given some type of sociometric test to determine their status among their schoolmates. Gronlund and Whitney (C.17), investigating 340 junior high school students in a city in Illinois, expanded their investigation to cover the adolescent's acceptance in the classroom, the school, and the neighborhood. Their contention that scores on sociometric tests conducted in the classroom may be a reliable index of the individual's general social acceptability among his peers is supported by the finding that those individuals who were favorably accepted in the classroom were also favorably accepted in the school as a whole and in their neighborhoods, while those who were unpopular with their classmates were also generally unaccepted by their peers in the neighborhood situation. An earlier study by different authors (C.40) had also noted that the measure of peer status they utilized was a stable measure of adolescent peer acceptance.

To state that a given adolescent is accepted by his peers is not to imply that this adolescent is accorded any great prestige in the peer group. An individual may be accepted by a great many of his peers and yet fail to exert any significant influence or attain any significant status in his group. In a study done in 1953, Keislar (C.31) indicates a distinction between social acceptance and prestige among adolescents. His findings indicate that social acceptance in the group studied was closely associated with popularity in the peer group, while prestige was linked with scholastic success and effort and other similar variables. In a later study, Keislar (C.32) also investigates the peer group ratings of students with above average intelligence, some of whom get high grades and others low grades. In this study he records that the students who got the higher marks were rated higher on such items as liking school work, putting studies first, and persistence. Girls with high marks were regarded as being less popular but more influential with boys, while the boys who received high marks were rated as being more considerate than those of equal intelligence who received low marks.

One area of adolescent prestige influence was investigated in 1959 by Keislar (C.33). He was interested in determining whether an adolescent boy's prestige, established in an area of importance to adolescents in general, would generalize far enough to influence the personal preferences of his peers. A group of 60 adolescent boys with Otis I.Q. scores over 100 were given a preference test following a test of information in which some of the boys had done exceptionally well and thereby gained prestige. Analysis revealed that the prestige of the boys who scored well on the information test generalized enough to influence their peers' responses to the preference test. This was determined by the number of times answers on the preference test were changed to correspond to controlled wrong answers on the papers of the high prestige boys.

In the development of friendship ties, the adolescent who is judged by his peers to manifest socially acceptable personality traits is in an excellent position to form acquaintances with a variety of other adolescents. The number of acquaintances, then, influences the potential number of friends obtainable by him (C.51). In some cases, it has been shown that an experience in social living, such as a camp experience, can positively affect the number of friendship choices obtained by a given adolescent on a sociometric test (C.15).

The investigation of peer relations has also covered the description of friendship characteristics, including the influence of age, sex, I.Q., and various physical characteristics. As early as 1926, Wellman (C.57) investigated friendship pairs with respect to their similarity or dissimilarity in such characteristics as chronological age, mental age, I.Q., scholarship success, extroversion, height, and physical maturation. Among her findings she notes that pairs of girls were most similar in scholarship and least similar in height, while the boys were most similar in height, I.Q., and chronological age and least similar in extroversion, scholarship, and mental age. In a more recent study concerning the friendship choices of adolescents of differing intelligence levels (C.5), it has been shown that children of above average intelligence were preferred as friends over the slow learners by the average and some of the below average students.

Another early study (C.47) conducted at a summer camp

for boys offers support for the notion that children most often choose as friends peers of similar mental and moral development.

Results of a study investigating the influence of social class position on choice of friends was reported by Neugarten (C.45). Her investigation of two groups of children, one with a median age of 11 years 3 months and the other with a median age of 16 years 3 months, utilized a modified Moreno Sociometric Test and an adaptation of Hartshorne and May's Guess-Who Test. The results of this study indicate that there is a definite relationship between social class and choice of friends. The younger group revealed that social class position influenced both reputation and friendship status, the lower status children having fewer friend choices and lower reputations. In this age group, the children's judgments about each other followed extremely stereotyped lines. The older group also reflected the influence of class position in their selection of friends, but their rejection of individuals as friends did not follow any definite class pattern. The lower-class child in the high-school situation was found to be less conspicuous than he was in the grade school, thereby losing many of his distinguishing lower-class features, which had been apparent in the younger child's stereotyped behavior.

Quite frequently, in both the speculative and empirical research, one sees reference to the operation and existence of an adolescent subculture or subcultures (see especially B.20, B.30, C.24, C.54) with distinct attitudes, norms, status systems, and behavior patterns which arise within the adolescent group and which serve to distinguish the adolescent period from the period of childhood and adulthood. While there has been much talk of adolescent subcultures, it is difficult to find research directed to the specific investigation of the existence and content of these subcultures outside of the work done by Coleman (B.20), Elkin (B.30), Cohen (General Bibliography), Gordon (B.35), and Tyron (C.54). The implications of the existence of an empirically demonstrable adolescent subculture(s) in the investigation of adolescent behavior in urban areas have prompted us to devote a separate section to a discussion of professional attitudes toward the existence and validity of an adolescent subculture in the United States.

D / ADOLESCENT IN PREPARATION FOR ADULTHOOD

Among the steps which are to be taken in the period of adolescence, few are more important to the individual's future than occupational and educational decisions. These decisions are not made in isolation, but instead are the product of a complex of interacting variables. Such factors as the adolescent's self-concept, his experience in the school situation, his home environment, his socio-economic background, and his interpersonal relationships all contribute to his educational and vocational attitudes, interests, aspirations, and expectations.

In the studies reported in this section, the emphasis falls on three areas of investigation: the role of self-concept in the development of the adolescent, the adolescent's attitudes and interests in educational and vocational matters, and analysis of the factors involved in varying levels of aspiration.

In the previous section, reference was made to the role of variations in maturity and the development of interpersonal relations and prestige ratings. The work by Jones reported in this section (D.18, D.19, D.20, D.21) deals with relative maturity and behavior, motivations, and self-conceptions. All of the studies involved adolescents who were either physically advanced or physically retarded for their age. In an earlier investigation (D.18), Jones and Bayley found that the physically advanced (early maturers) boys were more acceptable as leaders, were accepted as more mature by adults, and had little need to strive for prestige among their peers. The physically retarded boys (late maturers), on the other hand, revealed more status striving behavior and behavior classified as immature. The late maturers often sought prestige in areas where they would not be in competition with the early maturers.

Later investigations involving the motivations and self-conceptions of early and late maturers (D.19, D.20, D.21) have established that the late maturers were motivated by aggression and desire for social acceptance to a much greater degree than were the early maturers. In the investigation of self-conception in relation to physical maturity, it was found that those boys who were late maturers were characterized by feelings of insecurity, inadequacy, rejection, negative attitudes toward their families, and negative self-conceptions. The early maturing boys, on the other hand, had more positive self-concepts and were found to be more independent, self-confident, and capable of playing an adult role in interpersonal relationships. Among the girls, it has been felt that the late maturer would have an adjustment advantage over the early maturer since she had had a longer period to adjust to the new feelings and physical changes involved in the female development. Investigation of the self-conceptions of this group, then, anticipated that the late maturers among the girls would exhibit better over-all adjustment and fewer negative self-concepts than the early maturers. A 1958 study (D.21) revealed, however, that the early maturing girls were somewhat better adjusted and tended to score more favorably than the late maturing girls on total adjustment. The late maturing girls were also found to have more negative self-concepts than their early maturing peers.

The development of the individual's self-image is perhaps best understood in terms of the Interactionist Hypothesis of Self-Conception. In this hypothesis the development of the self-image arises from the interaction between the individual's concept of his behavior, the response of others to his behavior, and the individual's perception of the response of others to a given behavior. In 1956, a testing of 195 subjects (D.25) led Miyamoto and Dornbusch to the conclusion that, while the response or attitude of others is related to self-conception, the individual's perception of the response of others is a more important factor. It was also concluded that an individual's self-conception was more closely related to his estimate of the generalized attitude toward him than to the perceived response of any particular group.

We have noted in the previous section that one of the functions of the adolescent peer group is to support the adolescent and offer him a source of status and security which he may find lacking in the adult world. Some investigations (D.34) find that this lack of status for the adolescent in the United States is reflected in the lack of a well defined self-concept among adolescents. Moreover, the resultant variety of diverse statuses offered the adolescent by his peer group may account for the great insecurity found in adolescence. The adolescent does not know exactly who he is or who he wants to become.

In addition to the lack of a pervasive self-concept, the development of the adolescent is often characterized in terms of the conflict between generations. This conflict with the emerging maturity of the adolescent when the adult generation seems to resist the development of a distinct personal identity and the assumption of adult roles on the part of the adolescent. In spite of the conflict between the adult and the adolescent worlds, the adolescent often patterns, or attempts to pattern, his personality and behavior after a model he constructs from contact with the adult world. This "ideal self" seems to originate in a childhood identification with a parent figure and by the period of late adolescence to develop into a composite of the parental figure and attractive, successful young adults (D.14). Havighurst and Rieger (D.13) indicate that outside the family there are a very small number of adults who are unusually visible to the adolescent. These adults may be a strong influence in the development of the adolescent's "ideal self" and, directly or indirectly, may influence his educational and occupational aspirations.

It is one thing to say that the adolescent constructs a composite "ideal-self" model, but it is quite a different thing to state that this "ideal self" is consistent and stable over a period of time. As the adolescent develops and broadens his experiential base, his self-concept and his "ideal-self" pattern are subject to some variation. In a study of the stability of the self-concept in adolescence, Engel (D.11) investigated a group of 172 eighth- and tenth-grade students over a period of two years using the same instruments in a test-retest program. In general, she found that the self-concepts remained relatively stable regardless of whether they were positive or negative at the first testing. She also found that those subjects who revealed negative self-concepts at the first testing were less stable than the subjects whose self-concept was positive. Those students whose negative self-concepts were consistent over the two-year period were also characterized by significantly more maladjustment than those who were consistently positive in their self-concept.

Self-concept has also been investigated in its relationship with creativity and achievement. In 1959, Rivlin (D.29), investigating the self-attitudes and sociability of adolescents, applied 14 criteria of creativity to a group of 126 tenth and eleventh graders in the New York City high schools. After establishing a creative and noncreative group, he compared the two groups with regard to their self-attitudes and sociability. This comparison revealed that the creative group was more sociable and had more confidence in interpersonal relationships than the noncreative group. The factors of sociability and higher level of parents' education were found to be associated with creativity, but the over-all self-attitudes of the creative and the noncreative students did not differ significantly.

The results of a study of the relationship between self-concept and achievement (D.31) in a number of reading improvement classes in Texas lend support to the idea that achievement, or lack of achievement, is a function of the needs of the individual's self-concept.

In a study done by Bordin in 1943 (D.3), self-concept is directly related to vocational interests. Bordin assumed that an individual's response to the Strong Vocational Interest Test reflects an acceptance of a particular self-image in terms of occupational stereotypes. The finding of his study support Bordin's hypothesis that the degree of interest revealed by the test will vary positively with the individual's acceptance of the stereotype as self-descriptive. In addition, the results led the investigator to predict that the relationship between the expressed interest and the specific occupation will vary with the status of the occupation, the relationship between father and son, and the length of time the occupation has been in the family.

During the high-school years, the presence of a few adolescents who "know where they are going" vocationally is often contrasted with the much larger number who appear unable to stabilize and direct their vocational interests. While it may well be that the adult ideal is most closely reflected in the stable, directed adolescent, a study by Schmidt and Rothney (D.32) has indicated that, during the high-school years, consistency in vocational choice is the exception while variability is the rule. If the general pattern of adolescent development is considered, it is not difficult to accept the variability of vocational interests as a natural manifestation of the developmental process.

This variability in occupational choice is somewhat challenged by the finding of Ezell and Tate (D.12) who report that, in a sample of 1572 high-school boys and girls, only 10 per cent of the boys and 1 per cent of the girls were doubtful about their future occupation. They also find that most of the questioned students had plans to attend college and that 20 per cent of the boys and 5 per cent of the girls chose occupations similar to those of their parents. As with the creative students mentioned earlier, there was a direct relationship between the educational level of the parents and the vocational choices of the students. Among gifted children (D.37), Strang finds much less indecision in vocational choice than she does among average children. In this case, the gifted child is defined by an I.Q. over 120. (Contrary to possible expectation, she also finds that the gifted child is not much less concerned with scholastic success than the average student.)

Among girls, the conflict between marriage and career that has engendered a great deal of speculation in past years is apparently being resolved by a growing desire among young women to continue their education and to work for a period before getting married (D.38). In interpreting the findings of a national study of adolescent girls, Stratton finds that 94 per cent of the 2000 girls questioned expected to marry eventually, but only 3 per cent expressed a desire to become housewives. The girls anticipate employment in steady, interesting jobs and prefer such occupations as secretary, nurse, teacher and social worker, occupational roles which are traditionally filled by women.

Among the factors that have been investigated in relation to educational and occupational interests and aspirations, none has received more attention than the factor of social class. This emphasis is not too surprising when we recognize that ''social class'' has been a payoff variable for several decades of sociological investigation.

An investigation of the job attitudes of adolescents from families in two occupational strata, white collar and blue collar, revealed to Dyer (D.7) that the white-collar families were more satisfied with the father's occupation than were the blue-collar families. Regardless of this, neither the parents nor the children from either group showed any great desire for the children to follow the father's occupation. Since both of the occupational levels investigated held rather low prestige value, the influence of the father's job on the children's choice of occupation must be tempered by the prestige status of the occupation.

The relationship between adolescent interest behavior and socio-economic status was investigated by Pierce in 1959 (D.28). Using the Home Index Test and the Kuder Preference Test in a random sample of 370 adolescents in a city of 40,000, Pierce finds a definite relationship between interest behavior and socio-economic status. The low status group preferred mechanical, domestic, service, and clerical tasks, while the high status students preferred complex social activities and jobs with high prestige and responsibility. Each group showed a tendency to reject the choice of the other group.

One interesting aspect of the influence of parents on their children is found in the ability of many parents to accurately predict the interest patterns revealed by their children on the Kuder Preference Test (D.15). Parental influence is also revealed in the attitudes of the adolescent toward labor and collectivism. In these areas, the adolescent's attitudes have been found to conform to observed adult patterns (D.5).

A study reported in 1954 (D.40) found evidence to support the following hypotheses involving social factors in the work attitudes and interests of a group of Michigan boys.

1. Social stratification is significantly related to the differential socialization of youth in the home, the school, and the community.

2. The value orientations of the social strata are more important in forming work attitudes than the school, work experience, or type of community.

3. Actual work experience produces changes in behavior, and these changes are then reflected in work attitudes.

4. The school is not successful in removing class-centered attitude differences concerning work which can be seen in adolescents from different strata.

43

The problem of social class and aspirations has been approached in a number of other studies. Notable among these is the study conducted by Sewell, Haller, and Straus (D.33). Establishing a general hypothesis that, with the factor of intelligence controlled, the levels of aspiration of adolescents of both sexes are associated with the social status of their families, the authors surveyed a one-sixth random sample of all nonfarm seniors in public and private high schools in Wisconsin in 1947—1948. The data from this survey was applied to the testing of four null hypotheses which derived from the general hypotheses. These null hypotheses were:

1 and 2. Among females (males), there is no significant association between level of occupational aspiration and social status when measured intelligence is controlled.

3 and 4. Among females (males), there is no significant association between level of educational aspiration and social status when measured intelligence is controlled.

With the rejection of all four of the null hypotheses, the authors find support for the notion that the values associated with varying class positions are an important influence on the development of educational and occupational aspirations.

Exploring this relationship further, Rosen (D.30) hypothesized that achievement motivation (psychological) and value orientation (cultural) vary between the social classes. This hypothesis is based on the proposition that social mobility can be explained in terms of the differing motives and values of the social classes. A testing of 120 male adolescents revealed that achievement motivation, but not value orientations, were related to scholastic graders; and also, that value orientations, but not achievement motivation, were related to educational aspirations. Considering the motives and values of the various classes, it is quite possible that the middle-class children are more likely to be taught both the motives and the values that lead to achievement.

Stephenson, on the other hand, found that the students he examined exhibited a relatively high common agreement in the area of aspirations. Regardless of the social class position, most of the students seemed to hold certain goals in common. These aspirations may be understood as culturally determined. Expectations, however, are strongly influenced by the opportunities and life chances available in the social class position (D.35). In connection with the disparities between aspirations and expectations, it is quite possible to see how the inability to fulfill his aspirations because of social and economic conditions can increase the adolescent's anxiety in establishing realistic educational and vocational goals (D.36).

Wilson (D.39) raised another point in his discussion of the residential segregation of social classes and the aspirations of adolescent boys. The author showed that the values of the membership group (peer group) influence the development of aspirations. He notes that the concentration of social classes in specific areas of a city means that the values of the particular class are also concentrated in that area. This configuration of values affects the value structure of the school and thereby influences the values of the peer group and the individual adolescent. For Wilson, the values reflected by the school influence not only educational aspirations, but also occupational aspirations, academic achievement, and political preferences.

Many investigations of social class differences in levels of aspiration concentrate solely on the absolute differences between the classes and ignore the differences within the classes. In a study reported in 1956, Empey (D.10) investigates both the inter- and intraclass differences. He hypothesizes that: (1) the absolute occupational status aspirations of male high-school seniors from the middle and upper classes are significantly higher than those of seniors from the lower classes; (2) the relative occupational status aspirations of lower-class seniors will indicate that they prefer and anticipate significantly higher occupational status than their fathers; (3) lower-class seniors will be more inclined than middle or upper to reduce their occupational aspirations significantly when faced with the necessity of choosing between their preferred and anticipated occupations. The results of the analysis supported the first two hypotheses, but rejected the third; and in so doing, they raise the possibility that lower-class adolescents may not limit their occupational aspirations to those activities typically associated with the lower class. It was also implied, as mentioned earlier, that lower-class adolescents may have aspirations as high as adolescents from the middle classes.

Within the lower classes some adolescents attempt to "better" themselves while some do not. Some plan to attend college and seek occupations of higher status while others are content to fill some niche within their social class. In an investigation of 24 boys of the upper-lower class including 12 who were and 12 who were not planning to attend college, Kahl (D.22) concludes that those who were aspiring to higher educational and occupational status came from families who were unsatisfied with their position and who encouraged their sons to seek higher educational and vocational opportunities. In other words, the aspiring boys came from families reflecting middle-class values to a greater degree than the families of the boys who were not interested in improving their occupational status. This is also reflected in a study conducted in England (D.16) where it was found that the upwardly mobile lower-class boys had stronger middle-class values than many of the middle-class boys themselves. In addition and similarly, the English middle-class boys had higher aspirations than did the lower-class boys.

In addition to the descriptive and exploratory studies concerned with expectations and aspirations, there have been a number of experimental studies on the psychological factors in aspiration. Only one of these studies is illustrated here. Chapman and Volkmann (D.6), investigating the effect of knowledge on level of aspiration, experimented with two groups, one of which was given practical knowledge of the task to be performed, while the other was only told how various other groups had performed. They note that the group which only had knowledge of the performance of other groups had a significant rise in level of aspiration while the group with the practical knowledge revealed no similar change in aspiration.

A warning note concerning laboratory experiments in aspiration levels was sounded by Ausubel, Schiff, and Zeleny (D.2) in their study of the usefulness of laboratory measures of aspiration as compared to "real life" (subjective individual response) measures. Their examination of academic grade reports and of a series of tests and scales available for 50 adolescents revealed little or no significant relationship between the "real life" and the laboratory measures of vocational and academic aspirations. They attribute this finding to the greater degree of ego-involvement of the adolescent in the "real life" situation as opposed to the typical experimental situation.

E / ADOLESCENT AND THE WORLD IN WHICH HE LIVES

Generally speaking, all studies which concern adolescents are involved, in one way or another, with describing the world of the adolescent. Investigations of the leisure-time activities and interests offer us information in one area of the world of adolescence while studies of the peer relations and the maintenance of teen-age status reveal other important aspects. In the previous sections of this review, many of the values and attitudes which are part of the world of the adolescent have been explicitly or implicitly noted and will not be recapitulated in the present section. Offered in this section is a sampling of various types of attitudinal studies which range from reports of general attitudes to investigations into specific areas of interest. Included are studies dealing with general aspects of attitudes and values (E.1, E.12, E.17), moral attitudes (E.4, E.7, E.28, E.30), adolescent problems and values (E.12, E.16, E.24, E.27), minority group attitudes (E.3, E.8, E.19, E.25), and other areas (E.2, E.5, E.10, E.14, E.20, E.21, E.22, E.23, E.31). The methodology of these studies ranges from the large samples and involved techniques of the survey research team to the more restricted size and problem of the individual researcher.

Within our society, characterized as a whole by certain value orientations, there are numerous groups which operate within the social system and are characterized by value systems which may differ in some respects from that of society as a whole. Aberle (E.1) has noted that each individual participates in a number of these subsystems and that these various subsystems must be integrated with each other to facilitate interaction between the systems. In studying the value systems of the adult and the adolescent world the emphasis should be more on the content of the shared values involved in the interaction of the two systems than on the number and content of the value discrepancies between the two, assuming that it is possible to establish differences between the values endorsed by adolescents and adults. This particular problem will be discussed in the section devoted to the existence of the adolescent subculture.

The existence of variant values in our society is understandable in terms of the diversity and complexity of our social structure. We have seen that values differ between social classes, age groups, ethnic groups, and occupational groups, but variance in the value orientations and problem-solving behavior in these groups may be little more than the expression of the variety of possible solutions for a group to a given problem (E.12).

The role of the community in the formation of individual attitudes was investigated by Newcomb and reported in 1942. In a study of the political and economic attitudes of the girls of Bennington College, he found that the trend of attitude change ran from freshman conservatism to senior nonconservatism. In this connection, it was noted that full assimilation into the college community demanded the assumption of liberal attitudes. Thus, the community reflected rather strong characteristic attitudes toward certain issues. Within the college community were those who assumed the appropriate attitudes and those who manifested what would appear to be "deviant" behavior by associating with groups which did not hold attitudes similar to those of the larger community. The explanation offered for the exceptions to the typical adjustment pattern lies in the interaction between the response of the individual to the total community and the effect of membership in one or more reference groups which may or may be found in the immediate community (E.17).

The relationship between socio-economic status and the value systems of lower- and middle-class adolescents has been investigated by Rothman (E.24). In this study, involving a relatively small sample of 56 ninth-grade students, Rothman was generally unable to establish significant differences between social class membership and operative

48

value systems. Among the seven areas investigated, differentiation could be found only in purposes, actions, and aspirations, but not in attitudes, interests, beliefs, and thinking.

As early as 1936, Symonds described differences between the problems and interests of 784 boys and 857 girls (in Tulsa, Oklahoma, and New York City). At this time, boys showed great interest in safety, health, money, civic affairs, recreations, and study; girls were more interested in personal attractiveness, etiquette, and getting along with other people. Boys ranked money as more of a problem than did the girls, who emphasized personal attractiveness and etiquette as problem areas. The results of this study may reveal more about research orientation of the time than they do about the attitudes of the adolescents involved (E.27).

In 1942, Mooney (E.16) constructed a check list of problem items designed to facilitate the enumeration and description of the problems which adolescents felt to be important. From applying this check list to 603 high-school students in North Carolina, it was found that adolescents' problems could in many of the cases be divided by grade level (age) and/or sex. Freshmen were more concerned with problems of health, while sophomores were more involved in problems of social and recreational activities. The juniors emphasized problems concerning school work, while the seniors were concerned with vocational and higher educational problems. The girls revealed more problems involving home, family and interpersonal relations, while the boys stressed problems involving school work and plans for the future.

A later study incorporating the Mooney Problems Check List attempted to describe the problems of adolescents who were accepted by their peers as compared to those who were unaccepted (E.13). It was found that the unaccepted adolescents had more problems than the accepted. The problems faced by the accepted group centered around social activities, and educational and occupational future; the unaccepted group checked problems relating to concern over social skills, dislike of school, family problems, unhappiness, and lack of status.

Another early study (E.31) discussed the attitudes and behavior of 603 adolescents representing six different class grades. The results of this study led the author to conclude that the school played little part in the formation or alteration of attitudes and behavior related to nonacademic activities. The author notes that moral sentiments (i.e., attitudes toward lying, stealing, swearing, etc.) appear to develop outside of the school situation and that the school does little to bring about changes in these sentiments. While the ability of the school successfully to teach ethics and control conduct may still be debated, little argument will be found concerning the role of the school as an institution within which the adolescent peer group must function.

In view of the attitudes reflected in the mass media in recent years that adolescents are becoming more aware of the realities of the world about them, the results of a study by Boyer (E.2) may be surprising. In an investigation of 569 adolescents in the Milwaukee area, he remarks on the surprising lack of awareness of the adolescent about the critical problems facing the world. Excluding the danger of war, most of the adolescents were willing to adjust to the world as they found it. In addition to their unawareness of the realities of the world, these students found it difficult to appreciate the values of an education except as a possible means of vocational preparation.

The relationship between teen-agers' and adults' attitudes toward adolescents has been shown to contain some interesting discontinuities. The question of status in the adolescent world has been partially answered by the role of the peer group in supplying the adolescent with the status which the adult world has failed to deliver. It may well be that the attitudes held by adults toward adolescents prevent them from recognizing attitudes in adolescents which might lead to a favorable modification in adult attitudes. Such attitudes as the satisfaction adolescents find in the successful completion of developmental tasks, the recognition that freedom should be accompanied by responsibility, and the willingness to assume responsibility (E.26) deserve further attention. Awareness of such attitudes could possibly lead to a shift in the adult attitude, noted by Hess and Goldblatt (E.10), that adolescents overvalue themselves and undervalue adults. In turn, such a shift in the adult attitude might also alter the adolescent attitude that adults tend to undervalue teen-agers.

The following four studies leave the area of general attitudes and values to illustrate the results of concentration on a specific area of interest.

Rose (E.23) investigated the attitudes of adolescents toward problems of mental health. From an original sample of 1400 students in three Minneapolis high schools, he drew a random sample of 100 girls and boys who received questionnaires concerning various problems of mental health. An analysis of the results led him to the conclusion that the girls in the sample had, both quantitatively and qualitatively, more knowledge and revealed better attitudes toward problems of mental health than did the boys. While no evidence was offered to support it, this finding was explained in terms of the more studious attitudes and better academic performance of the girls.

In an investigation of the attitudes of 160 adolescents toward the police and other legal authorities, Chapman (E.5) found that delinquents were more hostile toward the police and other legal authorities than were nondelinquents. In spite of these differences, he was unable to establish statistically significant differences between the two groups.

Ramsey and Nelson (E.20) anticipated a change in adolescents' attitudes toward the family, based on the increase in the divorce rate and the changing role of the family between the years of 1939 and 1952. Their 1952 replication of a study originally done in 1939 used the same questionnaire and controlled for the same variables, but outside of the finding that the girls in 1952 felt less obligation to their family, the authors were unable to establish any significant change in the adolescent's attitude toward his, or her, family.

Utilizing survey research methods, Remmers and Drucker (E.21) examined a sample of 1132 high-school students to establish teen-agers' attitudes and behavior in the area of child management. The results of their survey indicated that the attitudes and knowledge improved as age, maturation, and educational influences increased. At all levels, however, the girls revealed more accurate knowledge than the boys.

Concerning the moral beliefs of sixteen-year-old adolescents, Taba (E.28) characterized them as lacking a well developed ability to apply moral beliefs to their everyday experiences and conflicts. She notes a tendency among adolescents to respond to conflict or choice situations by the use of familiar stereotypes and attempts at compromise solutions. Frequently reported as a moral belief is the concept of friendliness which involves being popular, having many friends, and being amiable and accommodating to all people. The concept of honesty is best understood in terms of property rights and telling the truth, but loyalty beliefs appear confused especially in situations where several loyalties conflict. While adolescents' standards of responsibility are well developed and taken seriously, much doubt and fear is revealed concerning moral courage, especially where a given opinion or action may incur the displeasure of adults or threaten one's popularity with his peers.

A distinct but related subject is the way adolescents react to each other in a situation where a moral norm has been violated. Utilizing a projective questionnaire on a sample of 120 college students and approaching this problem through the role-playing typology, Turner (E.20) has shown that in a situation in which a close friend has violated a norm (in this case, a hypothetical violation of a sex and an honesty norm), the subject's response will vary with his evaluation of the friendship relation and his view of the violated norm. Three personality types are reflected in the observed combinations of response behavior: (1) individuals who feel themselves personally involved in the errors of their friends; (2) individuals who feel a high sense of social responsibility; and (3) moralistic individuals who feel a great personal loyalty to their friends.

In the middle class, one finds a great concern over the expression of aggression between children. Contrary to the attitude of the lower classes, physical aggression between children is not considered as appropriate behavior. It has been shown in an examination of 119 boys and girls in grades 2, 5, 8, and 11 that in a situation where one child is physically aggressive toward another, most children at all ages will tend to turn to an authority figure (parent or other adult) for a judgment on the justice of the aggression. The rest of the children, however, tend to show more concern over possible extenuating and mitigating factors in the particular situation (E.7).

The moral beliefs and "ideal self" of Negro adoles-

cents have been shown to be generally comparable to those
of white adolescents (E.4). Middle-class Negroes tend to
choose "successful" adults for their ideal, while lower-
class Negroes tend toward the more glamorous adults. In
the "ideal self," the middle-class Negro is characterized
by emphasis on moral and intellectual qualities, while the
lower class emphasizes personal glory. Judging from a
white middle-class point of view, the middle-class Negro
has a higher degree of moral development than the lower-
class Negro adolescent.

The views of minority group youth toward themselves
seem to reflect the common stereotypes of the groups.
Cahnman (E.3) has noted that Jewish adolescents view
themselves as clannish, competitive, defensive, inhibited,
and insecure, while the Negro adolescents view their weak
points as drinking, fighting, carelessness, lacking of foresight, community spirit and political organization.

A further view of the racial and ethnic group differences
in social attitudes and adjustment is offered by Pierce,
Ried, and King (E.19). Their investigation of three groups
of adolescents (Negroes, Latin Americans and Anglo-
Americans) revealed only one significant difference between these racial groups, that being the Negroes' greater
negative orientation to society as a whole. While the Latin
Americans showed more feelings of social inadequacy, no
significant difference could be established between Negro
and Anglo-American in this area. It has also been shown
that the differential attitudes (on social distance) held by
adolescent groups are more dependent on the age and race
of the adolescents than they are on the particular residential configuration in which the adolescents live (E.25).

The development of ethnic and racial prejudice among
children and adolescents has long been of interest to sociologists and psychologists. As an illustration of one type
of social psychological approach, the study by Frenkel-
Brunswick (1948) relates home environment to the formation of prejudicial attitudes (E.8). From an original sample of 1500 boys and girls, 120 subjects were selected who
were either extremely prejudiced or unprejudiced. Examination of the family background revealed that the prejudiced adolescents came from families which were extremely status conscious and harsh in disciplinary meas-

ures. The less prejudiced adolescents, on the other hand, had families that were less status conscious, more loving, and less strict in their discipline.

In this section, little attention has been given to the numerous opinion poll attitude surveys which have become popular in recent years. Because it is a particularly valuable source of information on adolescent attitudes, the reader is referred to The American Teenager by H. H. Remmers and D. H. Radler (New York: Bobbs-Merrill Co., 1958), which contains the results of the first 45 polls of the Purdue Opinion Panel. The reader is also referred to subsequent polls conducted by this group, especially Poll #55 entitled Teenagers' Attitudes Toward Teenage Culture, published in May, 1959, since this survey is based on a national sample and deals with the adolescent's perception of his own activities.

F / ADOLESCENT AND DEVIANT BEHAVIOR

The mention of adolescent deviant behavior immediately brings to mind the question of adolescent delinquency. After all, what could be more deviant, in terms of society as a whole, than behavior patterns which violate the values and laws of the society? Delinquency is a major problem in our culture, and extensive research has been conducted by psychologists and sociologists in an effort to understand and control the factors involved in the development and perpetuation of delinquent behavior. We note again what we stated in the Introduction that this review excludes materials on this subject which have already been given extensive coverage elsewhere. The studies cited here (F.6, F.8, F.13, F.15, F.16, F.18, F.21, F.22, F.24), attempt little more than to illustrate some of the areas of interest within which research has been conducted.

Deviant behavior may be defined by other expressions than the most direct one of delinquency. The behavior of the child who has failed to adjust to his surroundings may accurately be described as deviant behavior. Likewise, the development of neurotic and psychotic symptoms may be labeled as deviant behavior. In fact, depending on one's frame of reference, there are relatively few behaviors which, in one way or another, cannot be referred to as deviant. For example, the behavior of the delinquent seems normal enough to him while the socially approved behavior of the "average" adolescent appears "square" or deviant from his values.

Writing in the 1930's, Benedict (F.1) and Levy (F.9) both recognize the role played by the culture in the development of personality problems and maladjustments. Benedict, on a more general level, commented that personality upheavals and maladjustment may develop as the result of the failure of the society in general to provide the youth with direct, tangible support and a well defined status during his transition from childhood to adulthood. Many primitive societies which provide their youth with such support manifest little of the behavior problems which seem to prevail in our society. In our society, with no well defined and supported period of transition, the adolescent may easily develop anxiety which may be expressed in personality maladjustment and fixation at an earlier stage.

For Levy, the sources of conflict in childhood arise from the conscious training of the child by the social group in the form of discipline; and the unconscious emotional stresses in family relations, sexual adjustments, and religious development transmitted to the child by the culture. Because the form of these stresses is culturally determined, Levy concludes that problem children are in part a product of our social organization.

In 1940, Furfey (F.5) commented on the shift in the study of the adolescent from an individual approach to a group approach and from a psychological to a sociological approach. The adolescent is studied more and more as a member of a group, a culture group, and the explanation for the behavior of the group is found less in terms of individual behavior than in terms of behavior patterns transmitted by a subculture.

As early as 1937, the influence of the parent-child relationship on the future development of the child was recognized (F.23). The well adjusted child is much more

55

likely to have had a good relationship with his parents than the delinquent, the problem child, the prepsychotic, and the schizophrenic. In the treatment of the problem child, success is seldom attained without a shift in the attitudes of the parents. In an analysis of the case histories of 25 male and female adolescents who were hospitalized for two years at the Menninger Memorial Clinic, Miller (F.12) noted that many of the patients were in the hospital as a direct result of the conflict-ridden interaction with their parents. With these patients it was necessary to strictly control contact with the family until such time as the adolescent could cope with it.

If the attitudes of the parents are a strong influence on the development of the child, one would expect the attitudes of the parents of problem children toward their children to differ from the attitudes of the parents of well adjusted children toward these children. Contrary to this expectation, Lexton (F.10) found after examination of twenty pairs of parents that there is no significant difference between the attitude scores of parents whose children had excellent adjustment ratings and parents whose children had poor adjustment ratings. There was, however, a greater variety of attitudes among parents of poorly adjusted children than among the parents of well adjusted children.

In previous sections, mention has been made of the role of physical development in the peer relations of adolescents. The degree to which such physical factors as differences in body size, sexually inappropriate physique, facial appearance, body odors, and deformity contribute to the development of deviant behavior and adjustment problems can only be assessed in their relation to the particular psychological configuration of the individual (F.20). In some cases, the particular physical condition may not even be related to the adjustment problem faced by the individual.

In at least one study (F.17), the problem of maladjustment in the area of peer relationships has been associated with discrepancies between the individual's definition of his social class level (an internal measure) and his peers' definition of his social class level (an external measure. The well adjusted adolescent revealed close agreement between the internal and external measures of social class position.

The later effects of behavior problems in childhood are apparent in the marital behavior of former problem children (F.19). In a comparison of a group of average individuals and a group of people who had received psychiatric treatment, it was found that the treated group had significantly more divorces and was composed of more individuals who had been problem children than did the average group.

Among disturbed children, the pattern of sociometric choice is comparable to patterns observed among normal children. In a comparison of groups of normal and disturbed children, Davids and Parenti (F.2) noted that social popularity is associated with good emotional adjustment, presence of positive and absence of negative personality traits. Among the disturbed children who exhibited varying degrees of maladjustment, those who were disliked by their peers were more emotionally disturbed than were those who were ignored by their peers. The most acceptable of the disturbed children reflected the least amount of emotional disturbance.

An interesting study supporting the hypothesis that successful adjustments to the demands of the adult world is dependent upon the successful adjustment of the individual to the informal group life of the adolescent was reported by Demerath (F.3). In this study, the case histories of 10 male and 10 female college-age patients who had been hospitalized for schizophrenia were examined and related to the typical experience of the average, normal adolescent. It was found that, among the 20 patients, none had engaged in the intimate, informal group life of their peers to any significant extent. While the experiences of the patients prior to their breakdown did not seem to differ greatly from the experiences of average students, it was found that in many ways they were overanxious to conform to adult standards of academic excellence and moral perfection. These tendencies undoubtedly contributed to their alienation from the peer group activities and made it increasingly difficult for them to adjust to the status demands of the adolescent group.

Turning to studies illustrating research in the area of delinquency, we see first a re-emphasis on the psychological rather than the cultural approach in Kobrin's research (F.8). To Kobrin, the available statistics on delinquency indicate the presence of a duality of conduct norms rather than a dominant conventional or delinquent culture operating in urban areas of high delinquency. In this view, the determining factor in the assumption of delinquent behavior lies in the personality processes of the individual in the context of conflicting value systems rather than in the cultural transmission of one dominant value system. The critical point in this view, as recognized by Vold (F.21), is determining why an individual identifies with one of the conflicting systems rather than with the other.

The reasons why some adolescents become delinquents, while others do not, undoubtedly involves many complex factors. The possibility that a favorable self-image may act as an insulator against delinquency is proposed by Reckless, Dinitz, and Murray (F.16). In a high delinquency area in Columbus, Ohio, they investigated this possibility and discovered that the adolescents who were not involved in delinquent behavior and who were evaluated by their teachers as "good" boys were characterized by consistently favorable self-images. All of these "good" boys also revealed a family relationship which was stable, well controlled, and supporting. Since these boys came from a high delinquency area, it is all the more significant that they were able to withstand the social pressures which lead to deviant behavior. The self-image concept proposed by these authors suggests that given a change in self-perception, it would be possible to bring about changes in overt behavior.

In a social area analysis of delinquency in the San Diego area done by Polk (F.15), the basis for comparison of group behavior was economic status, family status, and ethnic status within the various census tracts. Analysis revealed that the highest rates of delinquency were to be found in areas which combined low family status, low economic status and high ethnic status. The implication here is that it is the combination of these three factors rather than the presence of any one of them that influences the rate of delinquency in a given area.

A major area of investigation of delinquent behavior has involved an analysis of the available statistics on delinquency to establish sex differentials in delinquent behavior. One illustration of this type of research is the study done on the sex differentials among adolescents who have been referred to the courts (F.6). An analysis of over 18,000 juvenile court cases revealed that, in comparison with the boys, female cases were more likely to be non-white, to come from broken homes, to involve running away from home, and, when not dismissed, to result in commitment than in the case of males.

Much of the research on delinquent behavior has stressed the prevalence of delinquency in the lower classes. Until recently, however, little attention has been paid to the possibility that the class differentials in delinquent behavior may be due more to differentials in arrest and conviction than to any absolute differences in the amount of delinquent behavior expressed among the social classes. Olson, Nye, and Short (F.13) offered evidence that, when official delinquency reports are compared to subjective reports of actual delinquent behavior committed, there was no difference between the delinquent behavior of boys and girls at any given class level. The results also indicated that there was no significant relationship between status and delinquency when status was held constant by two independent measures.

The importance of the home and socio-economic environment in the understanding of delinquent behavior was further noted in the findings of Wattenberg and Balistrieri as they relate gang membership to delinquent behavior (F.22). Among a group of 5878 boys, all of whom had police records, they found that the offenders who were gang members tended to come from lower economic strata and overly permissive families. Those offenders who were not gang members came from more restrictive family environments. It was also found that socio-economic factors were the best predictors of repeating offenses on the part of gang members, while repeating offenses among the nongang boys were best predicted by indices of family relationships.

II. Some Comments on Adolescent Subcultures

Perhaps the most vital task faced by any society, once it has established an efficient system of social control, is the training of the young for responsible adulthood. The reason seems quite apparent; if a society is to flourish and maintain itself over time, it must continuously supply the human resources which are essential to the functioning of that society.

Training of the young is a task faced by every nation, be it large or small in geographical area, developed or in an emergent stage of development as is currently the case with a number of nations. While the goal of child socialization is a universal one, the means by which this training is accomplished varies from one society to the next. The nation whose social structure incorporates the caste system and leaves little room for occupational mobility will in most cases restrict its educational program to an elite group of young people. For the nation which seeks by open competition what occupational roles are to be filled and who will fill them, a different type of educational program will be employed. In a small primitive culture whose economy is based on the cultivation of a few agricultural products, training will be limited and decidedly nontechnical in content. In a society such as ours, however, the problem is multiplied and assumes a variety of unique dimensions. First, ours is a highly industrialized society with a complex division of labor. Second, we pride ourselves on the fact that ours is historically an open class system with each individual having the potential for rising above the occupational position of his father. Third, we have a public school system which is not only open to all youth, but which makes attendance up to a certain age compulsory, regardless of either child and parental preferences or whether the society will ultimately benefit from this attendance. Finally, we allow the individual to make his own occupational decisions. If he chooses to be a doctor, a lawyer, an executive, or a private eye, he can attain his occupational goal by fulfilling certain requirements, none of which are directly related to our current labor supply, or the needs of our society. In other words, even though our nation is in serious need of physicists, we do not "draft" or force our youth into this occupational category. Each of these factors is related to the emergence, development, and impact of the adolescent culture in our society.

The industrial complexity of the United States and the fact that we require a multitude of occupational specialists has brought about a dramatic shift in the nature, location, and agents of child training. Prior to the industrial revolution, training for adulthood was primarily the responsibility of the family, as is still the case in less complex societies. A father could teach his son a trade, and this training could take place within the boundaries of the family. Not only would the immediate family supply occupational training but it would also play the paramount role in determining the kinds of values, norms, and attitudes which would be transmitted to the child. In addition, growing up in a community where people were in relatively close personal interaction reinforced the attachment to both family and community. Next, the homogeneity of population kept at a minimum the potential conflicts that might have arisen between youth and adult members of the community. Finally, and here speculation goes beyond empirical evidence, the less one needed to know for economic survival the more time one had for greater involvement in and identification with other phases of community life.

Whether or not this was the ideal time for raising children, this period of American life came to an abrupt end with industrialization and the founding of the factory system. With industrialization came the mass influx of migrants, great population shifts, the rapid growth of urban centers, the development of mass production machinery, and a growing demand for highly specialized workers. It was the latter factor, the need for skilled and carefully

61

trained persons, which led to the eventual importance of the family as a primary source of child socialization.

No longer could parents give their children the occupational skills required by a highly technical society. Rapid changes and innovations in science, commerce, medicine, agriculture, and other fields led to the centralization of training. New machines were being developed in almost every occupational area, machines which were too great and complex to be owned by private citizens, machines which were to be housed in educational training centers. The youngster who sought to be a doctor had to attend a medical school where specialists would train him in the use of this equipment. The same held true for those who applied to other professions. The many changes taking place in our society put an end to the traditional practice of the father's handing down occupational skills to an apprentice son.

With every decade more and more of the occupational roles in our society require a higher level of training. In the days to come, fewer and fewer laborers and semi-skilled workers will be needed; and the demand for specialists and supervisors will be greater. Thus we will not only have shifted the training center to an agency outside of the family, but we will be keeping the child in the educational program for a longer period of time. Already there are indications that the home is becoming little more than a dormitory for the adolescent and young adult, a place to change clothes, eat meals, and make contacts for the next day's activities.

This setting apart of the young in schools for extended periods of time has had a dramatic effect on the child of high-school age.

We should recognize that school activity is not restricted to formalized teaching but includes an ever mounting involvement in any one of a number of extracurricular programs and events. Not unlike other social institutions in our society, the school no longer serves a single function. On the contrary, we find that the high school does much more than "transmit knowledge and prepare for responsible adulthood." The school provides a number of other functions: It keeps young people out of the labor market; it provides entertainment for the community through athletic events, dances, and plays; it aids in the formation and maintenance of cliques; it acts as a communication center where the adolescent can gain cues as to current fads in music, clothing, and hot-rod components; it is therefore also an ideal market place for manufacturers and merchants.

Within the social system of the high school, the adolescent is forced into a peer group of his own age and is, in a sense, isolated from the total societal complex. It is with the members of his peer group that the adolescent maintains his closest and most personal relationships. Over time and through continued interaction, this peer group begins to take on the characteristics of a small private society. It becomes a society with its own subculture. It is a subculture not lacking in ritual, symbols, fashions, languages, and a rather unique value system.

While there is general agreement among most students of adolescent behavior that adolescent subcultures do in fact exist, there are some who are less inclined to accept this proposition. Several years ago Elkin and Westley, reporting on their study in a suburban Canadian community, stated that the notion of "adolescent culture has a somewhat mythical character." The authors take exception with those social scientists and laymen who characterize the adolescent period as one of "storm and stress" and participation in a "youth culture." Denial of the youth culture hypothesis is based on evidence collected in "Suburban Town," which, according to the authors, indicated that "adolescents in their peer groups are not compulsively independent and rejecting of adult values; they are not concerned solely with immediate pleasurable gratifications."[1]

In what appears to be a direct contradiction to the Elkin and Westley thesis are the findings presented by James S. Coleman in his large scale study of adolescent society.[2] Coleman makes the following statement: "With his fellows, he [the adolescent] comes to constitute a small society, one that has most of its important interactions within itself, and maintains only a few threads of connection with the outside adult society."

[1]See Frederick Elkin and William Westley, "The Myth of Adolescent Culture," American Sociological Review, Vol. 20 (1955); also by the same authors, "The Protection Environment and Adolescent Socialization," Social Forces, Vol. 35, (1957).
[2]James S. Coleman, The Adolescent Society (New York: The Free Press of Glencoe, 1961).

Although differences in interpretation are not new to the behavioral sciences, it is interesting to note that both authors use the same criteria for either accepting or rejecting "youth culture." Elkin and Westley find new significant differences between the actions of youth and the expectations of adults and on these grounds fail to accept the subculture notion. Coleman, on the other hand, observes distinct differences in the expressed values of adolescents and their parents and on the basis of this observation supports the youth culture idea.

Because of our interest in adolescent behavior and a desire to better understand the social structural framework within which adolescents operate, the authors of this volume decided to "poll" a number of social scientists who have studied adolescent behavior in order to tap their thinking on the question of adolescent culture. A nonrandom group of some twenty social scientists received the following letter:

Dear

We are presently engaged in compiling an extensive review of empirical research pertaining to the adolescent culture in urban areas of the United States. This study is being conducted under government contract. In connection with this project, we are very interested in your views on the questions outlined below.

References are made in the literature both affirming and denying the existence of an adolescent culture. Coleman, in his article "The Adolescent Subculture and Academic Achievement" (AJS, LXV, Jan, 1960: 337–347), says in affirmation:

"Industrial society has spawned a peculiar phenomenon, most evident in America but emerging also in other Western societies: adolescent subcultures, with values and activities quite distinct from those of the adult society— subcultures whose members have most of their important associations within and few with adult society. Industrialization, and the rapidity of change itself, has taken out of the hands of the parent the task of training his child, made the parent's skills obsolescent, and put him out of touch with the times—unable to understand, much less inculcate, the standards of a social order which has changed since he was young.

"By extending the period of training necessary for a child and by encompassing nearly the whole population, industrial society has made of high school a social system of adolescents. It includes, in the United States, almost all adolescents and more and more of the activities of the adolescent himself.''

On the other hand, Elkin and Westley, in reporting the results of a study done of 40 adolescent subjects in Montreal, state:

"... youth culture is distinguished in both the sociological literature and the mass media by its affirmation of independence, its rejection of adult standards of judgment, its compulsive conformity to peer group patterns, its romanticism, and a participation in (irresponsible) pleasurable activities. The data from Suburban Town and other empirical studies suggests that the characterization of adolescent culture advanced in the sociological literature needs to be questioned. The empirical data do not deny that there are psychological tensions and distinctive interests among these middle-class groups studied— that the current model of adolescent culture represents an erroneous conception. And, if so, the theories which employ such a culture to analyze the social structure, are without adequate foundation.'' ("The Myth of Adolescent Culture,'' ASR, XX, Dec. 1955: 680—684).

Considering the foregoing remarks, we would like your opinion in respect to the following:

  A. Do you accept the proposition of an adolescent culture?
  B. What criteria do you, or would you, use to establish the validity of an adolescent culture?

We would greatly appreciate hearing from you at your earliest convenience. Thank you for your cooperation.

Although it was not our original intention to make public the responses received, we feel that some of these comments deserve greater visibility and therefore requested permission for publication from a number of writers. Needless to say, we are indebted to our professional colleagues for their cooperation.

While there were some differences in opinion as to the operational or research value of the term "culture" (one respondent pointed out that Kroeber and Kluckhohn had uncovered over 164 definitions of culture and that another one would only add to the confusion), there was consensus as to the existence of an adolescent subculture. With few exceptions, most of our respondents were willing to accept the proposition that there is indeed an adolescent subculture in our society. A number went on to point out that in all probability there is more than one subculture and that others can be identified once we look for variations in socio-economic, ethnic, and religious background as well as differences in age, residence, and perhaps school attended.

Next, there seems to be general agreement as to the operational criteria which should be used in identifying or establishing the existence of the subculture. For the most part, the writers felt that observed differences in values or behavior between adolescents and adults or for that matter adolescents and younger children would be sufficient for acceptance of the subculture dimension.

While the above statement indicates a real agreement in view, the matter is not so simply handled. It would appear that a number of the authors held some reservations as to just how far out on the limb they were willing to go in this question of adolescent subculture and validating procedures. Part of the hesitancy can certainly be attributed to questions of terminology or semantics, that is "exactly what do we mean by culture or subculture?"

The comments of Robert Hess of the University of Chicago reflect this view:

> The difficulty is really one of terminology. If you use the term "adolescent culture" to mean a set of values that are independent of the values of adult society, and to imply that these values are transmitted from one generation to another (i.e., are socialized) it would obviously be difficult to defend the proposition that there is an adolescent culture in the United States. If, however, you used the term to indicate patterns of behavior which characterize certain segments of our teen-age population—patterns that are different and sometimes in conflict with adult values, and also to connote a psychosocial phase that is distinct from both childhood and adulthood, then the argument for adolescent culture or subculture becomes very strong indeed. There is certainly evidence to support the notion that on many basic points, values of the adolescent culture are highly similar to adults. There is also evidence that certain values of adolescents diverge from those of adult society.

A second factor which stimulates some comment is whether there really are great or significant differences between the attitudes and values endorsed by adolescents and those held by adults. In this case, as was noted earlier, there is the feeling that adolescents, or at least some adolescents, do differ from adults in how they feel and in how they behave. The question seems to be just how great are these differences. Bernice Neugarten of Chicago takes the view that "... the issue turns largely upon a matter of semantics, but the concept of an adolescent subculture that operates separately from, or in defiance of, the adult's subculture has been much exaggerated." She goes on to note that, while she has referred to the childs' or adolescent's peer group as having a subculture of its own (see, for example, "The Peer Group," Society and Education, edited by Havighurst and Neugarten), she has also stressed the fact that "...the peer group teaches the adult culture."

And I am of the same opinion today—that adolescents may put their own imprint upon the culture and may produce a somewhat different version; but essentially, theirs is the same set of values, customs, and mores that operates in the adult world.

With respect to the Elkin-Westley position as opposed to the position of Coleman she notes,

In Coleman's own research findings, for instance, the fact that adolescents put athletic prowess ahead of scholarship is itself no evidence that adolescent values differ from adult values. I wonder how a comparable group of adults would have answered the same questionnaire; and if "compulsive conformity to peer group patterns" (Coleman's terms) is not equally characteristic of adult society, but simply displayed somewhat differently.

H. H. Remmers, director of the Purdue Opinion Panel, holds a similar opinion:

The problem of whether there is a "teen-age culture" is, I think, a matter of semantics and operational definition. In terms of the latter there is no question. Teen-agers' behavior differs in many measurable ways from that of the rest of the population. In these terms, I am certain there is also an old people's culture. There are, in other words differential social behavioral norms.
Having said this, I hasten to add that such evidence as I have indicates much greater overlap than differences among these subcultures. My impression is that teen-agers are try ing very hard to "learn the rules of the game" of the adult world.

R. J. Havighurst, considering the same question, concludes that there is probably less of a gap between generations today than there was at the turn of the century.

Actually, one could make a pretty good case for the existence of more of an adolescent culture in 1900 than in 1960 in middle-class America. In 1900 I think there was more of a gulf between the two generations than there is now in the middle class, because the parental generation was more authoritarian and less indoctrinated with the idea of meeting the adolescent generation half way. If you were to interview a group of middle-class men and women who are now about 60 years old, and to ask them to compare their relations with their own parents with their relations with their children as adolescents, I think you would find a good many of them feeling that they had closer relations with their adolescent children than they had with their parents when they, themselves were adolescents.

If you read Alma Mater by Henry Seidel Canby, you will find a description of Yale University students as of about 1910 which indicates a very strong adolescent subculture at that time.

Then there is the literature of the 19th century, showing conflict between the generations which seems to have existed with considerable intensity in the European middle class and is described in such books as Turgenev's Fathers and Sons, Thomas Mann's Buddenbrooks, and Edmund Gosse's Father and Son.

I would be inclined to distinguish between the gulf between the generations on the one hand and the social system of adolescence on the other hand. The gulf between generations has existed especially in the middle class for a long time; and perhaps there is less of a psychological gulf just now than there has been in the past. This is due to greater psychological sophistication and understanding of human motivation on the part of middle-class adults. On the other hand, I think that there is a well defined social system of adolescence in the high school which is more strongly defined now than it was fifty years ago, and also more widespread. Fifty years ago the high school was not a universal institution in America and the social system of adolescence was more visible in the colleges than in the high schools. Now, with the high school almost universal, and with high-school age youngsters having more freedom than they had fifty years ago, I think the social system of the high school has more of a hold on them.

Muzafer Sherif of the University of Oklahoma examines the content of "culture" and then suggests where he would place the research emphasis:

Considering that there exists a controversy over the existence of adolescent culture, however, I am glad to reply to your specific inquiries:

A. The proposition of an adolescent culture is an empirical question whose answer depends upon the definition of "culture." In terms of the criteria by which I understand "culture" (see below), I have spoken of adolescent cultures. However, it might be more precise to deal with the phenomena in question through concepts specified in the criteria themselves.

B. Any culture, adolescent or otherwise, presupposes at least the formation of (a) some system of status or role relations, as measured by differential behaviors in one or several social dimensions (e.g., prestige, respect, and notably effective initiative in the interaction process); (b) some distinctive values or norms (viz. any criterion for defining the relative acceptability of specific modes of behavior or social objects).

Such properties are likely to develop in time, during the course of any interaction among individuals who share common concerns, face common problems, or, the use Elkin and Westley's phrase, experience similar "psychological tensions and distinctive interests." The normative system can be measured in specific instances by (a) "uniformities" of behavior within a definite range or "latitude of acceptance," (b) reactions to deviation outside of that range, (c) sanctions for acceptable and deviant behavior, in the sense of agreed modes of rewarding or punishing (see Sherif and Sherif, 1956, An Outline of Social Psychology, chapter 8).

Being within a society where adult status and norm systems are dominant, adolescent "culture" will inevitably reflect various of its aspects, depending in part upon the adolescents' location within the social scheme. Thus, in many respects, the more distinctive adolescent norms are to be found in areas of social and cultural transition, such as we are currently studying in our project on natural groups in differentiated urban areas. However, even in middle class high schools and neighborhoods, I believe there is evidence of (a) rather distinctive criteria for status stratification and (b) norms distinctive from those of adults, including the use of worlds and phrases quite incomprehensible to most adults.

In any specific situation, I would favor intensive study of the distinctiveness of the status and norm systems and also the extent of its linkage of pre-existing adult values or norms. Probably the degree to which any writer on this topic wishes to generalize for all adolescents depends upon the empirical information at his command, his purpose, and his boldness.

Several writers point out that there are certain methodological problems which must be re-solved prior to any definitive statement as to differences between age groups. Ruth Shonle Cavan of Rockford College touches most of the methodological bases in her response.

What is the standard against which one should measure adolescent deviating cultural forms? The parents' culture? The culture of the specific ethnic group to which the parents belong? Or the general American culture? If the last, what is this culture? Sociologists sometimes speak of a middle-class Protestant ethos as the standard, but a rather large proportion of the population is neither middle class nor Protestant and in fact may be opposed to this particular ethos.

The term subculture is too loose and has come to have too many meanings. It means apparently, basic conformity to the main culture but deviations in some respects. In mild forms, there is no conflict, merely differences. In extreme cases, the subculture is in conflict with the main culture, perhaps to the extent of actively opposing the main culture in a destructive fashion. Milton Yinger has suggested the term contraculture for the destructive type of subculture (e.g., for the delinquent subculture). (See his article, American Soc. Rev., vol. 25, 1960, pp. 625ff.)

Adolescents may have a subculture identical with or congruent with that of their parents, ethnic group, etc. This is probably true of many middle-class suburbs where youth are not upwardly mobile and where there are not a variety of different influences.

Adolescents may have a subculture that differs from that of the parents without necessarily being in conflict with it. One hears now of the middle-class subculture centered around alcohol, sex, automobile. If there is such a subculture it seems to be a variation of the adult pattern, carried to extremes, but later modified to meet the adult pattern as the adolescents become adult.

Adolescents may have a subculture in conflict with the general culture or the parental culture, but not actively destructive of it. This situation would probably exist in ethnic groups in which adolescents were in the process of becoming Americanized; or in upper lower-class groups with upwardly mobile youth. Any major shift creates some deviations of culture.

Other adolescents are members of a delinquent or criminal contraculture.

I accept a variety of subcultures, each related to a specific social situation of stability or change. Why? On the basis of studies published and observation.

Albert K. Cohen adds yet another dimension when he looks at "what we mean by a subculture." In this instance, Cohen points out that differences in behavior between age groups are not sufficient to validate the proposition of a distinct subculture if the observed behavior conforms to age-specific expectations.

The key question is: What do we mean by a subculture? It cannot mean that there are distinct adolescent patterns of behaving, no matter how different they are from those of adults, if those differences are merely ways of conforming to age-specific role expectations. I like to put it in terms of game model. If people are playing different positions, their behavior may differ greatly but the differences derive from the same set of rules or cultural understandings. Even if people are playing different games, their cultures are not necessarily different. Each culture provides rules for different sorts of games, including rules about who may play them and under what conditions, and also rules defining the relative prestige of different games. So, if I play basketball today and hockey tomorrow, my culture has not changed. I am merely engaged in different activities, which run off, to be sure, according to different "rules of the game," but the rules that define both games are part of the repertoire of the same culture.

A culture is a set of norms, beliefs, etc. that are shared by some set of people and that one comes to share by taking them over in a process of interacting with them. Your culture and mine are different, if and to the extent that, they define the "same" games differently (i.e., conceive of the positions or roles differently, or differently define the expectations that go with them), or differently conceive the occasions when these games are appropriate, or attach different valuation or prestige to this game or that or to particular positions or styles of play, etc.

Negatively, this does not mean that the culture of two sets of people are different if they are organized in relatively distinct social systems. This could be equivalent to being involved in different games; the cultures would be different if the participants in the two systems had different notions about the rules under which such systems should operate or whether systems that operate this way are legitimate, etc.

Now to the instant case. The fact that there are "adolescent social systems" does not, of itself, mean that there is a distinct adolescent culture. Adults may avoid involvement in such systems or eschew the activities because they are "childish," "kid stuff," etc., and yet both they and the kids may see the involvement of kids in systems of this sort as quite appropriate. I am quite sure that a great deal of what is interpreted as a distinct "youth culture" is implicit in the common culture in this way, and is not "subcultural." It seems to me equally clear, however, that there are distinct adolescent subcultures. The distinctions may be distinctions of emphasis, of relative valuation, etc., but that does not make them the less distinct. Most cultural differences—e.g., the differences between American and German culture—are like this. I would say, then, that the culture of young people is largely the common culture they share with their parents, but marked, here and there, with differences in subcultural emphasis. These differences may be trifling or they may be of very great consequence.

A sufficient test for me that the cultures of young people are significantly different from my culture is that I don't understand much of what goes on amongst them, and much of what I see I am upset by. I don't understand because I simply don't know what rules they play by, where this or that "fits in," although they obviously know. And equally obviously I and most other adults place very different value upon certain games, or certain ways of playing them, than do the kids.

It is, however, very difficult, it seems to me, to set up workable operational criteria on subcultural distinctiveness, whether we are concerned with possible cultural differences between adults and children, or possible differences among youth cultures. The reason, as indicated, is that differences in the sorts of activities in which people engage, the goals to which they are oriented, the criteria by which they evaluate themselves, etc., need not indicate that they are responding to different cultures. For example, the behavior of a group of boys might change significantly over a period of time (e.g., from relatively peaceable "club-type" behavior to relatively disorderly and combative "gang-type" behavior or vice versa). This might mean an important shift in the shared value scheme of the group. It could also mean, however, that there has been a change in the situation so that a different sort of activity or "game" (with its own role system, ways of keeping score, etc.) now seems more feasible or rewarding or appropriate; but this may be a shift to another activity and set of roles within the same cultural repertoire.

Conclusions

This portion of the review began with a discussion of the structural changes in our society leading to the emergence of adolescent social systems. Briefly, it was proposed that the shift of child socialization and training from the home to the school has given young people a center for the initiating and diffusion of their own relatively closed normative order. We then moved to the responses of a number of social scientists and looked at how they viewed the proposition of adolescent culture. We noted that most of our respondents—with some methodological hedging— agreed that there were specific age-grade behavior patterns to be observed among adolescents and that these patterns could be identified as being part of a distinct subculture. In addition, most of the writers felt that although there was much overlapping, it seemed fair to say that adolescents did behave and hold values that set them apart from other age groups.

In summary then it would seem that while we are willing to accept the notion of adolescent subculture, we are not really clear as to just how and where it departs from the total or more universal culture. The difficulty, it seems, stems from the fact that many investigators allow the subculture hypothesis to stand or fall on the degree of differences observed between adolescents and some other age-grade group. This approach, as several of our respondents indicate, creates a number of methodological and analytical hazards: First, what do we mean by differences? Second, differences in what? Third, how do we isolate values or behavior which are solely the product of the adolescent peer group contact from those which are learned from adults? (It would not be difficult to go on in this way, eventually including other offsetting factors such as background characteristics and certain demographic variables.) Finally, what is accomplished if we do finally note areas of differences between adolescents and adults? Will this prove that the adolescent peer group has more influence on educational aspirations than does parental influence? Will this allow us to predict in what direction an adolescent might go when faced with the pressures of his peers and the desires of his parents? On the contrary, a presentation of differences will do little more than show where young people are in agreement or disagreement with their elders.

To our mind, there is yet another—and from a research angle—more productive way to view and measure adolescent subcultures. The question of whether an adolescent subculture does or does not exist should not be dependent on degrees or types of differences found between adolescents and adults. Differences may be sufficient but they are hardly a necessity for establishing the significance of a particular phenomena. In the case of the adolescent the question is not deviation from some universal norm but rather how involvement in and commitment to the adolescent group influences the behavior and beliefs of the participant. Once we can pinpoint areas of influence and how they operate, we will be in a better position to evaluate the meaning of adolescent subcultures. This approach would get us beyond the descriptive accounts of adolescent behavior which although highly dramatic at times tells us little about how the adolescent perceives himself and his world.

More specifically, we would propose research which took the following lines:

A. In terms of a continuum, what are the dividing points between different degrees of involvement in adolescent social systems? In other words, can we establish different levels of commitment to this system?

B. What are the differences in characteristics between those young people who desire and become part of the system as opposed to those who remain marginal or reject the system?

C. How will the adolescent behave "when the chips are down"? When he is placed in a situation where he must choose between peer pressures and parental or adult expectations, which way will he go? To what extent will his choice be influenced by involvement in or commitment to an adolescent social system?

D. To what extent will membership in some social-civic-religious-educational youth program alter participation in or influence by the adolescent social system found in our high schools? For example, will a member of the 4-H Clubs, Sea Scouts, or Church of God Youth be as vulnerable to the norms of the system as the individual who has no such affiliation?

E. What areas of adolescent life are influenced by the adolescent social system? Is the impact of this normative order and value system limited to current high-school life or is there some carry-over to adulthood? To what extent are educational and vocational plans determined, altered, or reinforced by membership in the adolescent social system? How salient is the system to political attitudes, mass media preferences, clothing styles, etc.

74

F. What variations can be found among and between institutions in respect to the organization of these adolescent social systems? Will we find the same organization in a middle class suburban school as we will in urban lower class schools? To what extent are variations a product of the adults in the community and in the school? What types of schools and communities are most likely to encourage these social systems?

G. What differences occur in the nature of adolescent social systems when the population composition of community and school changes?

The reader will note that the proposed research emphasized the importance of concentrating on both individual and institutional variables. Since the adolescent social system does have its base in our high schools—and no doubt many of our colleges—it is important that we deal with variations between institutions as well as individuals.

III. Annotated Bibliography

A / ADOLESCENT AS CONSUMER

A.1 Anderson, Esther M. "A Study of Leisure-Time Reading of Pupils in Junior High School," Elementary School, XLVIII (1948), 258—267.
PROBLEM: To discover the reading interests of students in the 7th and 8th grades.
METHOD: Questionnaires were administered to a sample of 336 boys and 350 girls attending the Eau Clair Junior High School. Ages ranged from 12—16.
CONCLUSIONS: Analysis of the data revealed: (1) At every age level more girls than boys liked to read. (2) At every age level a greater percentage of girls than boys had a favorite book. (3) Boys read more magazines than girls. (4) Considering boys and girls as a group, the preference ranking ran: comic books, fiction, animal stories, biography, and western.

A.2 Angelino, H., L. A. Barnes, and C. L. Shedd. "Attitudes of Mothers and Adolescent Daughters Concerning Clothing and Grooming," Journal of Home Economics, XLVIII (December, 1956), 779—782.
PROBLEM: A discussion of the existence, intensity, and type of disagreements between mothers and daughters concerning clothing, habits, and manners.
METHOD: Analysis of the data from interviews and questionnaires.
CONCLUSIONS: Within the same social class it was found that there was no difference between daughters or between the mothers. However, a difference between mothers and daughters by social class was found.

A.3 Balogh, K. J. "Television Viewing Habits of High-School Boys," Educational Research Bulletin, XXXVIII (1959), 66—71.
PROBLEM: To examine the effect of T.V. viewing on study time and recreation and to examine the influence of parents in this area.

METHOD: Questionnaires were given to 103 sophomore, junior, and senior male high-school students from all socio-economic levels.

CONCLUSIONS: It was found that, since parents usually insisted that homework be completed before watching T.V., viewing did not affect homework. All of the students spent more time watching T.V. on the weekends than on weekdays. It was also noted that the sophomores spent twice as much time on T.V. as the seniors.

A.4 Baisley, Gene. "The Hot Rod Culture," American Quarterly, II (1950), 353—359.

PROBLEM: Discussion of the hot-rod culture.

METHOD: Nonempirical discussion.

CONCLUSIONS: The author discusses the widely-held image of the hot-rodder as opposed to those considered by hot-rodders themselves the "real" hot-rodders. The typical image depicts a lawless, spoiled delinquent while the true "rodder" is a serious driver and interested in safety and mechanical functioning.

A.5 Burma, John H. "Self-Tattooing Among Delinquents," Sociology and Social Research, XLIII (May, 1959), 341—345.

PROBLEM: An investigation of the phenomenon of self-tattooing.

METHOD: Data gathered from 883 adolescents who were attending training schools.

CONCLUSIONS: It was found that more delinquents than nondelinquents tattoo themselves. Tattooing often serves as a status symbol and offers partial evidence that the individual is a member of a gang.

A.6 Coffin, Thomas E. "Television's Effect on Leisure-Time Activities," Journal of Applied Psychology, XXXII (1949), 550—558.

PROBLEM: To investigate the effect of T.V. on family leisure-time activities.

METHOD: 274 interviews were taken from 137 T.V. and 137 non-T.V. families on Long Island. The television families had a slightly higher socio-economic level.

CONCLUSIONS: The study found that T.V. generally brings about a change in the leisure-time activities of the family. This is reflected in the smaller amounts of time spent in other activities, both in the home and outside. In spite of the smallness of the sample, the author feels that the middle-class family is more affected by T.V. than the upper class.

A.7 "Teen-Age Consumer," Consumer Reports, XXII (March, 1957), 139—142.

PROBLEM: To discuss why advertising is more and more directed to teen-agers.

METHOD: Nonempirical discussion.

CONCLUSIONS: The greater emphasis being placed on the teenage consumer is due to the realization that they control a great deal of money as a group, they are marrying earlier, and they are a great emotional lever with which to influence the spending habits of the family. The author feels that teenagers are not price conscious and have a greater urge to spend than to get high quality. He feels that informed adult consumer guidance is needed for adolescents.

A.8 Croft, Joyce E. " Prediction of Clothing Construction Achievement of High School Girls," Educational and Psychological Measurement, XIX (Winter, 1959), 653—655.

PROBLEM: To develop an instrument to measure the ability of high-school pupils in clothing construction.

METHOD: Questionnaires were given to 188 girls in homemaking classes in Ames, Iowa.

CONCLUSIONS: The results indicated that three tests would satisfactorily predict achievement in clothing construction: (1) Clothing Construction Test, (2) The Miller Survey of Object Visualization Test, and (3) The Finger Dexterity Test.

A.9 Forer, Raymond. " The Impact of a Radio Program on Adolescents," Public Opinion Quarterly, XIX (Summer, 1955), 184—194.

PROBLEM: To study the effects of a radio program designed for adolescents. The author wanted to see if the advice from such a program was acceptable to adolescents, if the program was effective as a socializing agent, and if such a program could supplement the authority and prestige of a primary group.

METHOD: Statistical analysis was made of the data from interviews and questionnaires taken from 2700 Connecticut high-school students.

CONCLUSIONS: It was found that a program that focused on subjects that are felt to be important by the audience would create its own audience regardless of its media rating. The program did act as a socializing device and seemed to have a higher " advice status" than other primary groups, books, and teen magazines. The advice offered for solving problems in the life situation was important to the adolescent audience.

A.10 Freidson, Eliot. " Adult Discount: An Aspect of Children's Changing Taste," Child Development, XXIV (March, 1953), 39—49.

PROBLEM: To see if children's changing tastes in dra-

matic material can be explained in terms of "adult discount," a condition where a stimulus elicits less and less emotional excitement as age increases.
METHOD: Nonstatistical analysis of interviews with 79 lower-class public school boys.
CONCLUSIONS: The results of the study support the idea that children's changing tastes can be explained in terms of "adult discount."

A.11 Ireland, Ralph R. "The Significance of Recreational Maturation," Journal of Educational Sociology, XXXII (February, 1959), 356—364.
PROBLEM: To describe steps in recreational maturation.
METHOD: Descriptive analysis based on work with handicapped people.
CONCLUSIONS: The recreational pattern of the adolescent is characterized by great interest in group activities.
Young adults follow this pattern, but they are better able to afford such nongroup activities as golf, water skiing, and sailing.

A.12 Jennings, Joe. "Leisure Reading of Junior High School Boys and Girls," Peabody Journal of Education, VI (1929), 343—347.
PROBLEM: To see what high-school students read during their leisure hours.
METHOD: Statistical analysis of data from a questionnaire administered to 890 high-school students in Knoxville, Tennessee.
CONCLUSIONS: The article describes the reading habits of this group in terms of frequency of and preference for newspapers, magazines, books, and serials.

A.13 Johnstone, John, and Elihu Katz. "Youth and Popular Music: A Study in the Sociology of Taste," American Journal of Sociology, LXII (May, 1957), 563—568.
PROBLEM: To investigate the role of dating behavior and peer group relationships in the formation of preferences in popular music.
METHOD: Self-administered questionnaires were completed by 133 teen-age girls who were members of eight Hi-Y clubs in two neighborhoods of South Side Chicago. 53 of the girls were from clubs in the Hyde Park area and 80 were from clubs in the South Shore area.
CONCLUSIONS: It was found that preferences in popular music varied according to the neighborhood in which a girl lived and her popularity among her peers. While the study design did not permit the conclusion that peer groups influence musical preferences, it did establish that the peer group influenced the listening habits to the extent that a

given disc jockey was consistently preferred, thus limiting
the music to which members of the group listened.

A.14 Keislar, Evan R. "Differences Among Adolescent Social
Clubs in Terms of Members Characteristics," Journal of
Educational Research, XLVIII (December, 1954), 297—303.
PROBLEM: To describe the adolescent social clubs in
terms of members' characteristics.
METHOD: The study was made of teen-age social groups
to which membership was gained by invitation of the members.
CONCLUSIONS: Of the three variables studied (intelligence, grade-point average, and the father's occupation),
grade point average proved to differentiate the groups most
consistently. There was less differentiation by intelligence
and none by the father's occupation.

A.15 Kiell, Norman. "Behavior of Five Adolescent Poker Players," Journal of Human Relations, V (1957), 79—89.
PROBLEM: To observe, in an adolescent poker game, the
participants' interactions and the establishment of leadership in the game.
METHOD: Analysis is made on the basis of observation
and examination of a recording of five adolescents (ages 15
and 16) engaged in a poker game. The majority of the boys
were upper-middle class.
CONCLUSIONS: As the game progressed, the amount of interaction increased. Each player strove to establish a
"man-to-man" relationship with the other players and as-
sert his maturity in the game.

A.16 Lynd, Robert S., and Helen M. Lynd. Middletown (New
York: Harcourt, Brace and Co., 1929).
PROBLEM: To study the contemporary life of an American
community. This notation considers only the comments on
leisure activities. Other areas will be noted in the appropriate sections.
METHOD: The study was done in an industrial community
of approximately 35000 inhabitants. Interviews were held
with 164 housewives and questionnaires were administered
to three-fourths of the high school population (between 700
and 800 sophomores, juniors, and seniors). All families
were native-born and white.
CONCLUSIONS: (Leisure time) It was found that during
the last 35 years there had been an increase in the formal
organization of leisure time activities and their standardization; differences in the ways in which members of the
working class and the business class spent their leisure
time were found to be widening.

In the area of traditional pursuits, the trend was away from spontaneous interest in art and music; there was a greater variety shown in reading and listening than was true a generation earlier, but there was also probably less time spent reading. There was a pronounced change in habits and a creation of new problems resulting from the acceptance of new inventions (e.g., cars and radios).

A.17 Lyness, Paul I. "Patterns in the Mass Communication Tastes of the Young Audience," Journal of Educational Psychology, XLII (December, 1951), 449—467.
PROBLEM: To describe the interest patterns of five different age groups of boys and girls with respect to the content of the mass media.
METHOD: The sample, stratified by father's occupation, was drawn at random from grades 3, 5, 7, 9, and 11 of the Des Moines public school system. 691 boys and 727 girls comprised the sample. In addition to the questionnaires, the third-grade students (115) were interviewed.
CONCLUSIONS: (limited to the upper grades) The ratings for "educational content" in all media were low for all the girls. They were low for all boys except for the magazines, where Popular Mechanics and science magazines were rated high. Male interest in adventure and violence movies and books was high in all grades, but adventure and violence in radio and magazines was more popular among fifth-grade boys than among eleventh-grade boys. The girls' rating of the love, private life, and glamor categories revealed a tendency for magazine stories and features and movies to become more popular relative to the other media in grades 5—11.

A.18 McCluggage, Marston, M., and Jackson L. Baur. "Drinking Patterns of Kansas High School Youth," Social Problems, V (Spring, 1958), 317—326.
PROBLEM: To obtain factual information on drinking among high-school students.
METHOD: Questionnaires were given to 2000 high school students. These questionnaires concerned their drinking behavior. The sample was drawn from the Kansas public high schools.
CONCLUSIONS: (1) A positive relationship was found between the size of the community and the number of students who drank; (2) drinking by students was positively correlated with drinking by parents; (3) student drinking increased with age and also with weakening of parental control; (4) hard liquor was usually first tasted with peer groups rather than with the families.

81

A.19 McKellar, Peter, and Ralph Harris. "Radio Preferences of Adolescents and Children," British Journal of Educational Psychology, XXII (1952), 101—113.
PROBLEM: To determine the radio preferences of a group of British adolescents and children.
METHOD: Questionnaires were administered to 1400 boys and girls between the ages of 8 and 14.
CONCLUSIONS: In a simple choice situation between radio and movies, radio was preferred by a ratio of almost three to one. Favored were the entertainment type rather than the serious type of program. The author feels that the influence of radio on young people has not been fully examined, and that there has consequently been an overstatement of radio's undesirable effects and an understatement of its constructive values.

A.20 MacDonald, M., C. McGuire, and R. J. Havighurst. "Leisure Activities and the Socio-Economic Status of Children," American Journal of Sociology, LIV (May, 1949), 505—519.
PROBLEM: To test the hypothesis that children in different socio-economic groups have different leisure activities and to examine children's leisure activities which are typical of their socio-economic groups.
METHOD: The sample consisted of 241 fifth, sixth, and seventh graders (ages 10—12) in a public school located in a heterogenous urban community. Socio-economic status was determined by father's occupation and type of housing.
CONCLUSIONS: Systematic differences were found in the leisure-time activities of members of the four social strata. Significant differences were also found between the social strata with regard to the number of activities within the family, the highest stratum having the most family activity. The number of respondents who read books increased as one moved from the lowest to the highest stratum. Those in the lower strata attended significantly more movies than did those in the upper strata. The authors also found that a significant number of lower-class children were participating in predominantly middle-class activities.

A.21 Patel, A. S. "Newspaper Reading Interests of Secondary School Children," Journal of Education and Psychology, XI (1953), 34—43.
PROBLEM: To investigate the reading interests of adolescents.
METHOD: The study was conducted on a group of tenth- and eleventh-grade boys and girls ranging from 15 to 18 years old.

CONCLUSIONS: Boys ranked foreign news, scientific news, and comics as the most important, while girls ranked comics, social events and the women's section as most important. With the groups combined, comics were most frequently selected as the preferred topic.

A.22 "Recreational Interests and Needs of High School Youth" (A resumé of study conducted in New York), Recreation, XLVII (January, 1954), 43—46.
PROBLEM: To determine availability, quality, degree of use, and desired additions to the recreational facilities in Schenectady, New York.
METHOD: Questionnaires were administered to a sample of 1252 students (725 boys and 527 girls) ranging in age from 11 to 20 years. The students were distributed in four junior and three senior high schools in Schenectady.
CONCLUSIONS: The needs of these adolescents seemed to be: (1) a centrally located, well-supervised roller skating rink; (2) adequate indoor and outdoor swimming facilities; (3) additional parks and playgrounds with facilities for organized activities; (4) youth centers or canteens where adolescents could dance and congregate in an organized atmosphere; (5) a desire for leadership was expressed in various ways by a large number of the subjects.

A.23 Riley, Matilda W., and Samuel H. Flowerman. "Group Relations as a Variable in Communications Research," American Sociological Review, XVI (April, 1951), 174—180.
PROBLEM: To investigate the notion that individuals respond to mass media not only as isolated individuals but also as members of the various groups to which they belong and with which they communicate.
METHOD: A pilot sample consisting of 50 children in a New York City progressive school. The second sample consisted of 400 students in a New Jersey public school. These students were questioned on their group attachments, behavior, and reactions to a communication.
CONCLUSIONS: In the pilot sample it was found that those adolescents whose verbal communications were mainly with their peers differed considerably from adolescents who discussed things mainly with adults. Differences were noted in mass media relations, general activities, and interests. In the second sample the group was divided into "high" and "low" communicators on the basis of verbal interaction with their peers. In this sample it was found that the high communicators experience the content of the media in terms of its significance for group life. It was found that the "high" group was more active in clubs, more popular with peers and less adult-oriented than the low group.

A.24 Silverman, Sylvia S. Clothing and Appearance: Their Psychological Implications for Teen-Age Girls (New York: Bureau of Publications, Teachers College, Columbia University, 1945).

PROBLEM: The purpose of this study was to gain insight into the clothing and grooming behavior of adolescent girls with reference to four main areas: (1) girls' actual clothing and grooming behavior; (2) motivating factors influencing girls' choices of clothing and their attention to appearance; (3) influence of the economic factor in relation to clothing and grooming behavior; (4) relationship between care of appearance and aspects of personality.

METHOD: Responses to a questionnaire were received from 373 female students in grades seven to twelve in a suburban New Jersey high school. The age range was 12 to 18 years old. For area 4, a group of 170 girls in the eleventh and twelfth grades were evaluated by their teachers for high and low ratings on appearance.

CONCLUSIONS: The following findings were selected and abbreviated from the study. Area 1: (1) All age groups were found to conform closely in the style of dress for daily wear, with sweaters and skirt, socks and flat-heeled shoes being the predominant style. Weekend apparel showed differences between age groups, with older girls dressing more maturely. (2) the use of make-up increased with age, but lipstick and powder were used even at age twelve. (3) the use of beauty parlor facilities was, in nearly all cases, restricted to special occasions.

Area 2: With slight variations in age groups, the motives in clothing and grooming revolved around the desire for approval, the desire for sexual attractiveness, and the internal feelings of poise, self-confidence and happiness.

Area 3: Economic differences were reflected only in the area of luxury items. The subjects seemed to be more affected by their desire to conform to accepted modes of behavior.

Area 4: The group rated as high in appearance tended to be brighter, to have a slightly higher economic background, to participate in more school activities, to place a higher value on activities involving their own sex, and to be sought more as leaders than the group rated as low.

A.25 Sterner, Alice P. "Radio, Motion Picture, and Reading Interests: A Study of High School Pupils," Teachers College Contributions to Education, No. 932, Teachers College, Columbia University (1947).

PROBLEM: The purpose of this study was to investigate the habits of high-school students in seven different language media, to study three major interests (adventure, humor, and love) offered in these media, to see if the media rather than the interest attracts the adolescent, and to note the relationship of sex, school grade, intelligence and socio-economic status to adolescent choices of media and interests.

METHOD: 372 students at Barringer High School, Newark, N. J., were used to obtain records of radio listening, book reading, and involvement in other media.

CONCLUSIONS: It was found that, while the interests of adventure, humor, and love attracted adolescents to the media, no two media were used to the same extent to satisfy these interests. Also, from knowledge of sex, age, intelligence, and socio-economic status, it was impossible to predict the interests, media, or type of radio programs the individual would choose. It was also found that the students selected generally the same specific titles in each medium with the exceptions that boys and girls did not read the same types of books or magazines and that juniors and seniors differed as to type of books read.

A.26 Sullenger, T. E. " Leadership and Leisure-Time Interest of Grade School Boys," Sociology and Social Research, XXV (March—April, 1941), 351—355.

PROBLEM: To investigate the leisure-time activities and leadership traits important to boys.

METHOD: The study was conducted on 2750 grade school boys of scout age (9—16) in Omaha, Nebraska.

CONCLUSIONS: In the students' eyes, the most important leadership qualities were the ability to understand boys and the attitude of being interested in them and liking them. The most common free-time activities were sports and creative activities. Boys' magazines and classic boys' books were popular reading material along with the local newspaper. While many of the boys studied would like to belong to the Boy Scouts, it was found that only about 30 per cent were members.

A.27 Swensen, J., and J. Rhulman. " Leisure Activities of a University Sophomore Class," Educational and Psychological Measurement, XII (1952), 452—466.

PROBLEM: An investigation of the leisure interests of undergraduate students.

METHOD: The results are based on polls and questionnaires given to 1217 male and female undergraduate students.

CONCLUSIONS: It was found that relaxation, working with people, opportunities for service, and professional interests were the chief reasons for participation in leisure activities. It was also found that girls were more interested and participated more in activities than men. While the highest percentage of participation was found in social living units, the amount of participation within the fraternities and sororities was less than in other living units.

A.28 Wax, Murray. "Themes in Cosmetics and Grooming," American Journal of Sociology, LXII (May, 1957), 588—593.
PROBLEM: This paper is a discussion of themes in grooming and is based upon personal experiences in motivational research in this area.
COMMENTS: "The clearest expression of the (casual) plastic motif is afforded by the ideal of a girl in late adolescence. Continually experimenting with new styles of dress and grooming, she is, in effect, trying on this or that role or personality to see what response it will bring her. She is most aware of new products and new styles, and she uses them to manipulate her appearance this way and that" (591).
"To some social observers, however, the teen-ager appears as the slave to fad and fashion and not as the experimenter. A more accurate formulation would be that the teen-ager follows fad and fashion to the extent that she does, and not all do, because she is experimenting with herself and has not yet developed a self-image with which she can be comfortable. An older, more stable woman, who knows herself and her roles and how she wishes, can ignore fad and follow fashion at a distance" (591).

A.29 Weiland, I. H. "The Psychological Significance of Hot Rods and Automobile Driving to Adolescent Males," Psychiatric Quarterly Supplement, XXXI (1957), 261—275.
COMMENTS: In this discussion the author regards the automobile as a substitute for the mother in the Oedipal triangle. The automobile is a focus for father-son conflict and by lending itself to modification permits exhibitionism as an outlet for reaction formations against anal smearing impulses.

A.30 Witty, P. A., and P. Kinsella. "Children and TV—A Ninth Report," Elementary Training, XXXV (1958), 450—456.
PROBLEM: This is the ninth in a series of studies which began in 1950. The purpose of this study is to determine the relationship of T.V. to school grades and reading habits, and the extent to which teachers associate behavior and adjustment problems with T.V.
METHOD: Interviews and questionnaires were used to gather data from 2800 students in Evanston and Skokie, Illinois. The inquiries were directed to the children, their parents, and teachers.
CONCLUSIONS: The study found: (1) there is little relationship between television and school grades; (2) children

seem to be reading more since the advent of television; (3) teachers seem to feel that adjustment and behavior problems are related more to other factors than to television viewing and are hesitant to regard T.V. as the primary source of undesirable behavior.

A.31 Survey Research Center. A Study of Adolescent Boys. A report of a national survey of boys in the fourteen to sixteen age range. Conducted by Survey Research Center, Institute for Social Research, University of Michigan, Ann Arbor, Michigan, for the National Council, Boy Scouts of America, New Brunswick, N. J., 1955.

PROBLEM: As part of a larger study concerning the Explorer Scout program, this study investigates the broad problem of adolescent group membership. Information is offered on the following six questions: (1) What are the dominant needs, problems, and concerns of boys 14—16 years old? (2) How much leisure time do boys have? What nonleisure demands do they have on their time? (3) What are boys' principal leisure activities: What do they most like to do? (4) How important a part do voluntary group memberships play in boys' lives? (5) What are the sources of motivation for joining groups? Who are the boys who do not join? (6) What kinds of groups are most attractive to boys?

METHOD: Interviews were taken from a representative cross-section of 14—16-year-olds who are attending school and who are in the seventh—twelfth grades. The sample size was 1045.

CONCLUSIONS: The following conclusions are taken from chapter summaries in the report. Extensive specific findings are given in the body of the report. (1) The most important needs and concerns of boys center on achievement—in the present and future, and attainment of maturity in personal controls and relations to others. Occupational strivings and the need to make a job choice also concern the boys. Leisure activities and organizational membership are infrequently raised as sources of either satisfaction or concern. Desire for peer acceptance is not a concern verbalized by many boys. (2) With regard to leisure activities, half of the sample works part time, dating is a popular and common pattern at this age, and most of the boys have had experience with a good variety of leisure activities. Specific activities that are most popular are swimming, hunting, working on cars, and team sports. (3) In the area of group membership, the following findings are reported: (a) Three boys in ten do not belong to clubs or organizations. An equal number belong to a single group, and the remaining forty per cent have two or more group affiliations; (b) most boys who do not belong to organizations explain their nonmembership to some external pressure as lack of time; (c) the largest proportion of boys' memberships are in national activity organizations; (d) boys suggest sports and games, outdoor activities, and social activities most frequently as activities they would like a club to offer. (4) Following a discussion of the heterogeneity of the population of boys 14—16 years old the study notes, ''. . . no single organization, however broad its program, can expect to appeal to all (or even a majority) of adolescent boys'' (111). (5) In the discussion of the boys who do not belong to clubs, the report notes: (a) Boys who belong to clubs are from families with higher social status and greater social stability than boys who have no organizational affiliations; (b) the leisure interests of group members are broader than those of nonmembers. Group members are particularly more active in hobbies, outdoor activities, and social activities. They date more often than nonmembers; (c) in addition to the needs for particular activities which are served by group membership, there are a number of more general psychological needs expressed in joining clubs. These are the need to adopt an adult role and develop independence in the direction of one's behavior, and also the need for social mobility (140).

B / ADOLESCENT AND SOCIAL INSTITUTIONS: SCHOOL AND FAMILY

B.1 Abrahamson, Stephen. ''Our Status System and Scholastic Rewards,'' Journal of Educational Sociology, XXV (April, 1952), 441—450.
PROBLEM: To investigate the relationship between social class status and the scholastic rewards and punishments received by students in high school.
METHOD: Questionnaires were administered to groups of children in two urban, two suburban, and three semirural areas.
CONCLUSIONS: Findings showed that: (1) middle-class students received a disproportionate share of the high grades; (2) most class and school offices were filled by middle-class students; (3) middle-class students engaged in

more extracurricular activities; (4) no lower-class students ever received the American Legion Award. On the basis of the above findings, the author concludes that, within our status system, more rewards and fewer punishments go to the higher classes.

B.2 Arsenian, Seth. "Change in Evaluative Attitudes During Four Years of College," Journal of Applied Psychology, XXVII (1943), 338—349.
PROBLEM: To investigate the amount and direction of change of attitudes in four years of college. Economic, social, political, and religious areas are investigated.
METHOD: The Allport-Vernon Study of Values test was applied to an original sample of three successive freshman classes at a men's college in New England. Of this group, 76 who graduated were retested.
CONCLUSIONS: It was found that there was a great deal of change in the value patterns of the students during their college years. The direction of change, which was not always in line with the accepted pattern of contemporary society, appeared to depend on the content of the curriculum and extracurricular activities in the given school environment. Serious attitudinal changes were found in religious attitudes.

B.3 Baker, H. L. "High-School Teachers' Knowledge of Their Pupils," School Review, XLVI (1938), 175—190.
PROBLEM: To determine the extent of teachers' knowledge of the individual differences in behavior and background of their students. The author also desired to learn why some teachers, more than others, had adequate knowledge of their pupils.
METHOD: Questionnaires were applied to 27 teachers and 250 students selected from high schools of varying size in different types of communities.
CONCLUSIONS: It was found that there was great variation in the amount of knowledge of pupils held by various teachers. Most of the teachers knew less than one-quarter of the facts held necessary by guidance counselors for the educational treatment of individual children. The amount of knowledge was felt to be related to such factors as: (1) the size of the class of which the student was a member, (2) the amount of student-teacher association in extracurricular activities, (3) the amount of time the teacher spent in conferences with the students.

B.4 Bartlett, Claude J., and John E. Horrocks. "A Study of the Needs Status of Adolescents from Broken Homes," Journal of Genetic Psychology, XCIII (September, 1958), 153—159.
PROBLEM: Two hypotheses were tested to determine the

needs of adolescents from homes where one parent was deceased in comparison with the needs of adolescents from homes where both parents were living. (1) Adolescents from broken homes will reflect a greater need for affection; and (2) adolescents from broken homes will tend to form dependent relationships more often than adolescents from unbroken families.

METHOD: An experimental form of the Horrocks-Lucas Needs Questionnaire was administered to a total of 88 subjects. Half of the adolescents were from broken homes, the remaining 44 were from families where both parents were living.

CONCLUSIONS: The first hypothesis was supported by the finding that adolescents from broken homes tended to seek affection in attention from the opposite sex. The second hypothesis was neither supported nor rejected.

B.5 Becker, Howard S. "Social-Class Variations in the Teacher-Pupil Relationship," Journal of Educational Sociology, XXV (April, 1952), 451—465.
PROBLEM: To describe the reactions of public school teachers to socio-cultural differences in the student body.
METHOD: The study is a descriptive analysis of 60 interviews with teachers in the Chicago public school system.
CONCLUSIONS: Class differences in teachers reactions were most noticeable in the areas of teaching procedures, discipline, and moral acceptability. The lower-class students fail to live up to the teachers' concept of the ideal pupil and thereby do not compare favorably with the upper classes. The lower-class pupils are also more difficult to control and discipline and often display behavior that is morally unacceptable to the teacher.

B.6 Benedict, Ruth. "Transmitting Our Democratic Heritage in the Schools," American Journal of Sociology, XLVIII (May, 1943), 722—727.
COMMENTS: In this article, the author is concerned with the place of education in teaching values and in transmitting the democratic heritage to students. It is the author's contention that educational policies and programs by themselves cannot increase the stability of a society. She feels that the democratic heritage must be reflected in the fundamental philosophy and method of education. The transmission of our democratic heritage, then, involves preparing the child to act with initiative and independence as an adult rather than merely subjecting him to formalized instruction in the school.

B.7 Berg, Irwin A. "Expressed Standards of High-School Stu-

dents, Teachers, and Parents," Personnel and Guidance
Journal, XXXIV (1956), 261—267.
PROBLEM: The purpose of this study was to determine the
extent of agreement among pupils, parents, and teachers on
how students should and should not act in a variety of typical
school situations.
METHOD: A questionnaire comprised of open-end questions
was administered to three groups related to the Ohio State
University schools. The first group consisted of 225 students in the seventh through the twelfth grades in the school.
The second group consisted of 19 of the teachers in this
school, and the third group was made up of 18 parents of
children attending the O.S.U. school. Seven situations including behavior in the classroom, school team, class trips,
between classes, and public bus were examined.
CONCLUSIONS: There was substantial agreement between
the three groups on appropriate behavior in the specific situations. There was disagreement, however, between parents
and students on how to attain these standards.

B.8 Bernard, Jessie. " The Neighborhood Behavior of School
Children in Relation to Age and Socioeconomic Status,"
American Sociological Review, IV (October, 1939), 652—662.
PROBLEM: To determine the point at which a child's development becomes emancipated from the neighborhood in
which he lives, and to see if socio-economic class effects
this emancipation.
METHOD: The sample of 420 adolescents consisted of four
groups, one each from a grade school, a public high school,
a private high school, and a college sophomore class.
Analysis was based on the questionnaire response of these
groups.
CONCLUSIONS: The findings revealed: (1) a definite trend
for neighborhood attachment to decline with age, with the
greatest relative decline noted in the middle-class children
at age 17 and in the lower-class at age 15; (2) the children
in the lower socio-economic groups tended to show more
neighborhood attachment than children in the upper groups.
It was tentatively concluded that age was more important
than socio-economic status in influencing neighborhood activity whereas socio-economic status was more important
than age in affecting neighborhood attitudes.

B.9 Biddulph, Lowell G. " Athletic Achievement and the Personal and Social Adjustment of High School Boys," Research
Quarterly of the American Association for Health, Physical
Education, and Recreation, XXV (1954), 1—7.
PROBLEM: To study the personal and social adjustment of
sophomore and junior high-school boys, as compared in
terms of high and low athletic achievement.

METHOD: Data were gathered from 461 high-school boys. CONCLUSIONS: It was found that students who ranked high in athletic achievement displayed greater personal and social adjustment than did those who ranked low in athletics. On the basis of this finding, the author recommended greater emphasis on intramural athletics as opposed to interscholastic athletics.

B.10 Bledsoe, Joseph C. "An Investigation of Six Correlates of Student Withdrawal from High School," Journal of Educational Research, LIII (September, 1959), 3—6.
PROBLEM: To investigate six factors related to school drop-outs.
METHOD: Case histories were secured from 247 students in a Georgia town of 20,000. These students had dropped out of school in the eighth, ninth, and tenth grades.
CONCLUSIONS: There are three main factors behind school withdrawal: low intelligence, dissatisfaction with the school program, and economic reasons. The findings suggest that boys may be more likely than girls to drop out of school and that the level of parent education and the occupation of the parent are closely related to the student's level of aspiration.

B.11 Boehm, Leonore. "The Development of Independence: A Comparative Study," Child Development, XXXVIII (1957), 85—92.
PROBLEM: To study in a sample of Swiss and American children, the differences in social development.
METHOD: 29 Swiss and 40 American children between the ages of 6 and 16 were studied by means of Piaget's méthode clinique.
CONCLUSIONS: It was found that the American sample: (1) was more emancipated from their parents at an earlier age, (2) was less subjugated to adults, (3) developed freedom of thought and independence of judgment earlier, and (4) developed a more autonomous, but less complex, conscience than the Swiss boys.

B.12 Bonney, Merle E. "Sociometric Study of Agreement Between Teacher Judgments and Student Choices, in Regard to the Number of Friends Possessed by High School Students," Sociometry, X (May, 1947), 133—146.
PROBLEM: (1) To determine how well high-school teachers can distinguish students with the most friends from those with the least friends; (2) to determine the reasons for the differences between teacher ratings and student choices.
METHOD: On the basis of the results of a rating scale given to the students of Demonstration High School, North

Texas State College, a sample of 110 students was divided into three groups: high, middle, and low in number of friends. Thirteen teachers were asked to rate the 110 students.

CONCLUSIONS: In general, it was found that teachers were not very accurate in their evaluations, even when they were rating students they knew fairly well. The differences between the student and teacher ratings may have been due to the use of different criteria in the judgments.

B.13 Bowman, P. H., and M. Pellman. "Socially Underprivileged Youth and the Schools," High School Journal, XLI (May, 1958), 331—335.

COMMENTS: In this article the authors discuss the treatment and lack of understanding that meets the socially underprivileged student. The proposal of a curriculum to satisfy the needs and abilities of these students follows from a discussion of the problems of adjustment, achievement, and conflict with middle-class teachers. The point is made that a good program for the socially underprivileged will benefit the average and the gifted student as well as helping to develop the capabilities of the underprivileged.

B.14 Burchinal, Lee G. "Adolescent Role Deprivation and High-School Age Marriage," Marriage and Family Living, XXI (November, 1959), 378—384.

PROBLEM: Taking marriage as an index of role change among adolescent girls, the author investigates the proposition that role change is directly related to role deprivation. Three hypotheses are investigated: (1) Marriage is directly related to dissatisfaction with parental relations. (2) Marriage is directly related to the amount of heterosexual involvement of the girls. (3) Marriage is a result of role deprivation and is desired for expected satisfactions in a change of roles.

METHOD: The sample of 60 girls in each of two groups (total = 120), one group married, the other unmarried, was matched for grade, age, father's occupation, parents' educational level, religion, size of family, and other items. Questionnaires were administered to the two groups.

CONCLUSIONS: Little support was found for hypothesis 1. Regarding hypothesis 2, it was generally found that the girls who married before graduation had had more heterosexual involvement than the other girls. Hypothesis 3 was tested by a comparison of the personality needs of girls in both groups. Little variation was found in the needs scores of the two groups.

B.15 Butler, Ruth M. "Mothers' Attitudes Toward the Social

Development of Their Adolescents," Part I, Social Case-work, XXXVII (1956), 219—226.

PROBLEM: This study is an examination of mothers' evaluations of adolescent behavior and development and its effects on family and social relationships. Part I covers the period of early adolescence.

METHOD: Interviews were conducted with the mothers of 135 children between the ages of 12 and 20.

CONCLUSIONS: Among the mothers of early adolescents (12 to 14 years), the following attitudes and responses to social development were common: (1) Mothers were generally emotionally unprepared for their children's need for greater freedom and were disturbed by the children's attitudes toward the home, the neighborhood, and the community; (2) mothers had little comprehension of the significance of their children's rebellious behavior; (3) most mothers were confused and disturbed by the lack of cultural standards regarding the appropriate role for themselves in this period.

B.16 Butler, Ruth M. "Mothers' Attitudes Toward the Social Development of their Adolescents," Part II, Social Case-work, XXXVII (1956), 280—288.

PROBLEM AND METHOD: See B.15. This article covers the periods of middle and late adolescence.

CONCLUSIONS: In the middle period of adolescence, the child attempts to displace the parent within the family while assuming more mature roles outside the family. Demands for the car, later hours, changes in the school program, and increased heterosexual relations characterize this stage. Late adolescence is characterized by the adolescent's greater identification with the family, larger financial contribution to it, and ability to be accepted as an adult within it.

In response to the third stage of adolescence, mothers' attitudes and responses usually reflect: (1) greater pleasure in the mother-child relationship and an increased awareness of self on the part of the mother; (2) a move toward acceptance of the child's role as an adult and increased consideration of the child's preferences; (3) greater comfort and satisfaction in the marital relationship.

B.17 Calvin, A. D., et. al. "A Further Investigation of the Relationship Between Manifest Anxiety and Intelligence," Journal of Consulting Psychology, XIX (1955), 280—282.

PROBLEM: To determine the relationship between intelligence and anxiety in an undergraduate group. It was hoped that a negative correlation could be established between the two factors.

METHOD: The Taylor Manifest Anxiety Scale and the Wechsler-Bellevue Intelligence Test were administered to two groups of undergraduates at Michigan State University. Group A was composed of 36 students in an undergraduate psychology class. Group B was made up of 15 students with a lower I.Q. score who were having academic difficulty.
CONCLUSIONS: Evidence was found to support the notion that there is some negative correlation between intelligence and performance on the anxiety scale.

B.18 Cava, Esther, L., and H. L. Raush. "Identification and the Adolescent Boy's Perception of His Father," Journal of Abnormal and Social Psychology, XLVII (1952), 855—856.
PROBLEM: The hypothesis of this study is as follows: "Those individuals who show greater conflict in areas of personality related to the identification process will indirectly perceive themselves as less similar to their like-sex parent than will those who show less conflict in these areas" (855).
METHOD: The sample consisted of 37 twelfth-grade high-school boys in attendance at Ypsilanti High School, Ypsilanti, Michigan. These boys were given the Strong Vocational Interest Blank as an indirect measure of perceived similarities and the Blacky Pictures (Nos. 1 and 2) as an indication of identification disturbance.
CONCLUSIONS: The findings generally supported the notion that the boys who revealed less conflict in the area of identification would tend to perceive their fathers as more similar to themselves than the boys who showed more conflict.

B.19 Cavan, Ruth S. "The Relation of Home Background and Social Relations to Personality Adjustment," American Journal of Sociology, XL (September, 1934), 143—154.
PROBLEM: "The emotional and social adjustment of the young adolescent is not fixed at birth, but it is, in part at least, determined by the experiences which he has had in his various social groups. This study is an attempt to measure objectively the home background and the social relationships in terms of their tendency to produce well-adjusted children" (143).
METHOD: A questionnaire containing 36 questions on family relationships and 40 questions on social relationships was administered to a group of "problem" and a group of "nonproblem" children.
CONCLUSIONS: The results indicated that, with only a few exceptions, the effect of a good home environment is the production of socially well-adjusted adolescents.

B.20 Coleman, James S. "The Adolescent Subculture and
      Academic Achievement," American Journal of Sociology,
      LXV (January, 1960), 337—347.
      PROBLEM: This study is an examination of the status sys-
      tems in several high schools. It examines the status sys-
      tems, the effects of these status systems, and the possible
      source of these systems.
      METHOD: The sample consists of 10 Midwest high schools,
      5 in small towns, 1 in a working-class suburb, 1 in a well-
      to-do suburb, and 3 in cities of varying sizes. All but one,
      a Catholic boys' school, are coeducational and public. In
      addition to this group, two upper-middle class schools were
      included to answer certain questions rising from the analy-
      sis of the original group. Data were gathered from school
      grade records, I.Q. test results, and questionnaires
      on how the student would most like to be remembered in
      his school and what was required for entrance into the
      "leading crowd."
      CONCLUSIONS: In all the schools, students wanted to be
      remembered not as a brilliant student, but rather as a star
      athlete, leader in activities, or most popular. The explana-
      tion of this lies in the values of the adolescents. In this
      case, the prestige and status were awarded in nonacademic
      areas. In the explanation of the grade records and I.Q.
      scores, the author supports the notion that in a high-school
      social system which does not reward scholastic achieve-
      ment, those who are considered as "intellectuals" will, in
      fact, not be the students who have the most ability. The
      most able students will seek status in other, more profit-
      able, areas. The author suggests that the lack of status as-
      sociated with scholastic achievement may be related to the
      emphasis on interscholastic athletics and suggests that in-
      terscholastic competition in scholastic areas will affect the
      status systems.

B.21 Cook, Edward S., Jr. "An Analysis of Factors Related to
      Withdrawal from High School Prior to Graduation," Journal
      of Educational Research, L (November, 1956), 191—196.
      PROBLEM: The reasons offered at the time of withdrawal
      are not reliable indices of the real reasons. This study at-
      tempts to describe the differences between those who with-
      draw and those who finish their high-school education.
      METHOD: Case histories, I.Q. scores, and a series of ad-
      justment and interest scales were examined for a group of
      95 withdrawals and 200 randomly chosen nonwithdrawals
      from a metropolitan high school.
      CONCLUSIONS: Analysis revealed that the withdrawals
      were older than their classmates, retarded educationally,
      and were the middle of three or more children in the fam-
      ily. It was also found that they had more poor marks, bad

attendance records, and low scores on I.Q. tests. Poor personal orientation and adjustment to the family and the school was found to characterize the withdrawal group.

B.22 Cook, Lloyd A. " An Experimental Sociographic Study of a Stratified Tenth Grade Class," American Sociological Review, X (April, 1945), 250—261.
PROBLEM: This two-year study attempts to describe the friendship structure of a tenth-grade class in terms of changes and the effect of social status. The second phase involved the improvement of the learning situation by means of individual guidance and group management.
METHOD: The sample consisted of 44 male and female tenth-graders in a high-school social studies class in a Midwestern community of about 4500 persons. The technique of the sociogram was employed in this study.
CONCLUSIONS: The data revealed that (1) during the two-year period the average number of "best friend" choices increased from 2.40 to 4.51 per student, indicating an increase in the amount of social interaction; (2) 75 per cent of all the positive choices were made within the tenth grade, and a majority of the positive choices were same-sex and same-status choices; (3) upper-class children tended to be overchosen, and lower-class children tended to be underchosen throughout the two-year period; (4) the period of individual guidance showed both success and failure, but the period of group management resulted in the class becoming factionalized.

B.23 Coster, John K. "Some Characteristics of High School Pupils from Three Income Levels," Journal of Educational Psychology, L (April, 1959), 55—62.
PROBLEM: This is a comparison of certain characteristics of students who have been divided into three income groups.
METHOD: 878 students from nine Indiana high schools were chosen from a sample of 3000 students. This group was divided into three income levels and compared on such items as sex, schooling of parents, and participation in school and community activities.
CONCLUSIONS: Students in the high income group were found to be more likely than the students in the middle and lower groups to participate in school and community activities, to get high marks and honors in school, to attend church regularly, and to continue their education. It was also found that attitudes toward school and community experiences varied considerably between the groups. To a certain extent this contradicted the results of an earlier study by the author.

B.24 Dales, Ruth J. "A Method for Measuring Developmental Tasks: Scales for Selected Tasks at the Beginning of Adolescence," Child Development, XXVI (June, 1955), 111—122.

COMMENTS: In this study, the author discusses developmental tasks and reports on the development of scales to measure progress in achievement of developmental tasks. The three tasks selected for inclusion in the scales dealt with interpersonal relations with the emphasis on affection, social group, and sex role. The scales were administered to 510 children in grades six through nine in three schools in New York State. The results of this application established the value of the scales.

B.25 Davis, Allison, "Socialization and the Adolescent Personality," Forty-Third Yearbook of the National Society for the Study of Education, Part I (1944) (University of Chicago Press), 198—216.

COMMENTS: This author contends that the successful socialization of the adolescent depends on the amount of socialized anxiety that his society has been able to place in him. Considering the different social classes in the United States, he points out that the differences in the expected end-products of socialization within the lower and middle classes help maintain divergent cultures. Since the social reality of individuals differs between classes, the reactions of these individuals from different classes will be reactions to different situations, and a socialized lower-class boy may be regarded as totally unsocialized by the middle class.

B.26 Davis, Kingsley. "The Sociology of Parent-Youth Conflict," American Sociological Review, V (August, 1940), 523—535.

COMMENTS: In this paper, the author discusses the problem of the amount of parent-adolescent conflict found in contemporary Western society. It is his contention that the parent-youth conflict arises from the interaction of relational universals and certain variables found in modern culture. The universals include: (1) the age differential between parent and child; (2) the deceleration of socialization with age, and (3) the physiological, psychological, and sociological differences between the age groups. The variables which interact with the above mentioned universals to produce conflict include: (1) the rate of social change, (2) the complexity of the social structure, (3) the degree of integration in the culture, and (4) the force of vertical mobility. In explaining the presence of conflict in Western society, the author stresses the incompatibility of the rural-stable and the urban-industrial-mobile societies.

B.27 Davis, Kingsley. "The Child and the Social Structure," Journal of Educational Sociology, XIV (December, 1940), 217—229.
COMMENTS: In this discussion, the author examines the ascription of status and the place of socialization and solidarity in relation to the handling of children in our society. The ascription of status is seen as basic to the process of socialization and the maintenance of structural solidarity. Thus, the needs of society are served in the ascription of status in socialization of children. The author expresses concern over the possibility that educational philosophy will be more concerned over the needs of the child than the needs of society, thereby endangering the value of the socialization process and the solidarity of society.

B.28 Davis, Kingsley. "Adolescence and the Social Structure," Annals of the American Academy of Political and Social Sciences, CCXXXV (November, 1944), 8—16.
COMMENTS: In this discussion of the place of adolescents in the social structure, the author makes the point that adolescence in our society, as opposed to many other societies, is a period apparently not functionally tied to the social structure. It is interstitial between the period of childhood and adulthood and is accorded little meaningful status by the society at large.

B.29 Edwards, T. Bently, and Allen B. Wilson. "The Association Between Interest and Achievement in High School Chemistry," Educational and Psychological Measurement XIX (Winter, 1959), 601—610.
PROBLEM: To test the proposition that interest in the subject matter of a course is closely related to the achievement in the course.
METHOD: The Anderson Chemistry Test was administered to students enrolled in a basic chemistry course at an urban high school in the San Francisco area.
CONCLUSIONS: By controlling variables in achievement other than interest, the analysis established that interest in science was correlated with achievement in the chemistry course.

B.30 Elkin, Frederick, and William A. Westley. "The Myth of Adolescent Culture," American Sociological Review, XX (December, 1955), 680—684.
PROBLEM: The purpose of this paper is to discuss the characterization of adolescence as a period of "storm and stress" and "youth culture" and whether there is empirical evidence to support this characterization.
METHOD: Empirical evidence is based on (a) interviews with 20 high-school adolescents and their parents, the chil-

dren being 14 or 15 years old, Protestant, Anglo-Saxon and from business and professional families, and (b) case histories of 20 college students who lived in the community. The study was conducted in a suburban community of Montreal.

CONCLUSIONS: Acceptance of the characterization of adolescence as a period of "storm and stress" and "youth culture" assumes that the storm and stress is peculiar to the period and the youth culture is a dominant and widespread phenomenon linked to the storm and stress. However, in the middle-class group investigated, the authors found few sharp conflicts between parents and adolescents, little discontinuity in the socialization processes, and no youth culture pattern which prevailed over the family guidance pattern. These findings lead them to question the validity of the present concept of an adolescent culture.

B.31 Ellis, Albert. "Love and Family Relationships of American College Girls," American Journal of Sociology, LV (May, 1950), 550—556.

PROBLEM: The purpose of this study was to gather data on attitudes and behavior with relation to love and family relationships.

METHOD: Questionnaires were administered to a sample of 500 girls with different backgrounds who were enrolled in 19 colleges in a number of geographical regions.

CONCLUSIONS: These girls revealed a greater love for their mothers and sisters than for their fathers and brothers. They also indicated that "being in love" was a serious matter for them and directly affected their happiness.

B.32 Franzblau, Abraham N. "Religious Belief and Character Among Jewish Adolescents," Teachers College Contributions to Education, Teachers College, Columbia University (1934).

PROBLEM: To examine the proposition that acceptance of traditional religious dogma is conducive to the development of superior character. This principle is felt to be fundamental in most religions.

METHOD: This proposition was tested by the analysis of the results of 13 standard character tests administered to 701 Jewish adolescents. 392 of the subjects attended Reform Institutions and 309 attended Orthodox Institutions. The sample included 305 boys and 396 girls.

CONCLUSIONS: The findings gave no support to the proposition. The author suggests that other denominations and age groups be investigated along similar lines.

B.33 Frick, Willard. "The Adolescent Dilemma: An Interpretation," Peabody Journal of Education, XXXII (1955), 206—210.

COMMENTS: This interpretation of the adolescent period of development in our society stresses the situation of adolescents who have no reliable frame of reference for analysis of their behavior and who are faced with inconsistent expectations on the part of adults. The reaction of adults is often one which demands maturity while insisting on the immaturity of the adolescent. The author feels that urbanization and industrialization have been prime factors in the development of this situation. To those who feel a long period of adolescence is necessary for the preparation of the adolescent for the adult world, the author suggests that we have not utilized this period to the best of our ability.

B.34 Friedenberg, Edgar Z. The Vanishing Adolescent (Boston: Beacon Press, 1959).
COMMENTS: The prime task of adolescence is the development of clear and stable self-definition. This self-definition can only take place in a context of prolonged conflict between the individual and society—adolescence is conflict. The "real adolescent," struggling through inner conflict to define his self-image is being replaced by the conformist adolescent whose identity reflects the homogeneity of the institutional approach, particularly that of the school. The school is a prime agent in the clarification of experience for the adolescent, a clarification necessary in the development of self-definition. The school also plays a prime role in the establishment of self-esteem, but the author feels that the schools fail to meet their responsibilities, or, in some cases, succeed too well. In the words of the author, "What is needed [in the schools] is no program of technical training-cum-indoctrination, but the patient development of the kind of character and mind that conceives itself too clearly to consent to its own betrayal" (144).

B.35 Gordon, Wayne. The Social System of the High School (New York: The Free Press of Glencoe, 1957).
PROBLEM: To investigate the hypothesis that the behavior of the adolescent is related to the general social position he holds in the social structure of the school.
METHOD: Experimenter-administered questionnaires and high-school records were utilized to gather material on 576 high-school students from a school in a Midwestern suburban community.
CONCLUSIONS: The findings support the hypothesis that behavior is associated with generalized status position in the school's social structure. The author found a definite tendency to seek roles which would gain, for the individual, positions of prestige in the informal structure. It was also found that achievement in student activities was more sig-

nificantly related to general status than was grade achievement.

B.36 Grambs, Jean D. "The Community and the Self-Governing Adolescent Group," Journal of Educational Sociology, XXX (October, 1956), 94—105.
PROBLEM: This report is one of a series in a volume concerning the Youth Community Participation Project at New York University. This particular paper is concerned with the conditions under which the community supports and encourages the development of self-governing, civically-oriented youth groups.
METHOD: The analysis is based on the weekly project reports of five youth groups engaged in the larger study.
CONCLUSIONS: The group experience of the adolescents seemed to be influenced by three variables: (1) the way in which the adult community was organized to help adolescents through its various institutions; (2) what adolescents felt about the community; (3) the mores, norms, and values that are a part of the democratic community (p. 94). All of the groups were affected in some way by the ethnic and racial experience of the group members and the adult community, the experience of the adult community with adolescents, the socio-economic level of the adult community, and the age and sex of group members (p. 94).

Three general postulates emerged from the analysis: (1) civically-oriented self-governing youth groups probably cannot develop or survive without active community help and localized institutional support (p. 96); (2) the broader American culture predisposes a group toward prescribed organizational forms, group procedures, and group goals (p. 99); and (3) many adolescents perceive adolescents to be judged by the community as being bad until proven good (p. 102).

B.37 Hallworth, H. J. "Sociometric Relationships Among Grammar School Boys and Girls Between the Ages of 11 and 16 Years," Sociometry, XVI (February, 1953), 37—70.
PROBLEM: Examination of a series of hypotheses relating to group structure and development. Group formation, stability, and value formation are examined.
METHOD: The subjects for this study were 150 boys and girls from a coeducational grammar school outside of London. Interviews and questionnaires contributed to the sociometric analysis.
CONCLUSIONS: Analysis revealed that various groups organized around different value systems and leaders for different purposes. As the groups developed, the values became embodied in a few central figures with some students

unable to integrate in the larger group. The development of groups follows a definite pattern, but relatively stable groups are found on all levels of development.

B.38 Havighurst, Robert J. "Research on the Developmental-Task Concept," School Review, LXIV (May, 1956), 215—223.
COMMENTS: In this discussion of the literature on the developmental-task concept, the author points out the value of the concept in helping the educator maintain the proper perspective between the motives of the students and the ideals of society in the area of educational objectives. He also notes three problem areas in which research has been conducted. These areas include the definition and discovery of the tasks, their variation with age and cultural background, and the measurement of developmental tasks.

B.39 Havighurst, Robert J., and Dorothy Neubauer. "Community Factors in Relation to Character Formation," in R. J. Havighurst and H. Taba (eds.), Adolescent Character and Personality (New York: John Wiley and Sons, Inc., 1949), pp. 27—46.
PROBLEM: This chapter "describes the moral setting in which Prairie City boys and girls live" (27). While the entire volume is concerned with the development and measurement of character and personality, each chapter is presented as a separate study. The subjects of all these studies, investigated by different means, are a group of 144 adolescents who became 16 years old in the calendar year of 1942. This chapter deals with the general moral environment in the community.
CONCLUSIONS: "Through the home, school, church, youth organizations, recreational agencies, and the informal 'peer culture' of the children's own world, values and moral standards are taught to boys and girls by their parents, teachers, and other adults in positions of prestige, and by leaders of their own age groups.
"Boys and girls tend to learn the values and standards of their own homes, churches, and social classes, but the adolescent peer culture of the high school is a pervasive middle-class influence, affecting all boys and girls who go to high school. In general, the school teaches middle-class values.
"The 'character-building' youth organizations teach middle-class values and appeal mainly to middle-class youth, though they also succeed in serving a minority of lower-class youth.
"The commercial recreation places vary in their moral influence" (46).

B.40 Heaton, Margaret. "Sororities and the School Culture." Journal of Educational Sociology, XXI (1948), 527—535.
PROBLEM: This article investigates the problem of high-school sororities, what they mean, what factors foster them, and how they affect the lives of the girls involved in them.
METHOD: Questionnaires were administered to all the tenth-grade students in a high school located in a residential section of a Midwestern city.
CONCLUSIONS: It was generally felt that the problem of high-school sororities grew out of the larger problem of inadequate school planning for the needs of adolescents. The development of cliques and sororities was seen as the result of unsatisfactory group life in the school.

B.41 Hollingshead, August B. Elmtown's Youth (New York: John Wiley and Sons, Inc., 1949).
PROBLEM: This is an investigation of the hypothesis that the social behavior of an adolescent is related functionally to the position of his family in the social structure of the community. This study is part of a long-range field study conducted in a typical Midwestern community under the Committee on Human Development of the University of Chicago.
METHOD: Various methods of investigation were employed on an accidental sample of 735 male and female adolescents who had graduated from the eighth grade between the years 1938 and 1941. All the subjects were native white and three-fourths lived in a community of about 10,000. One-fourth were rural.
CONCLUSIONS: It was discovered that Elmtown was stratified into five social classes. The complex of traits within each class was regarded as the class culture. The investigation of the behavior of the adolescents within each class indicated that class lines were apparent to the individual and that the social class position of the adolescent's parents directly and extensively influences his behavior in relation to the school, the church, the job, recreation, peers, and family. The influence of social class position seems of primary importance.

B.42 Hurlock, Elizabeth B. Adolescent Development (New York: McGraw-Hill Book Co., 1955).
COMMENTS: In this discussion of the development of the individual in the years of adolescence, the author cites many studies that have been done on various aspects of development. The chapter on "Family Relations" is particularly applicable in this context.

B.43 Johannis, Theodore B., Jr. "Participation by Fathers, Mothers and Teenage Sons and Daughters in Selected Social Activity," The Coordinator, VII (December, 1958), 24—25.

PROBLEM: To measure the degree of family participation in 10 selected social activities.

METHOD: Questionnaires were administered to 1027 high-school sophomores from nonbroken, white homes in Tampa, Florida. Questions were asked relating to family participation in such activities as belonging to clubs, visiting friends of the family and of the children, outings, and entertaining.

CONCLUSIONS: It was found that eight of the ten activities investigated were shared by 78 per cent or more of the families. The remaining two activities, visiting the child's friends and family participation in clubs, were shared by more than 50 per cent of the families.

B.44 Johannis, Theodore B., Jr., and James Rollins. "Attitudes of Teen-Agers Toward Family Relationships and Characteristics of Their Parents," Sociology and Social Research, XLIII (July—August, 1959), 415—420.

PROBLEM: This investigation was undertaken to determine the extent to which male and female adolescents differed in reporting their parents' backgrounds, and the degree of marital happiness in the family. It was also desired to determine adolescents' attitudes toward their parents.

METHOD: Questionnaires were administered to a total sample of 1584 students in the eight high schools in Tampa, Florida. From this group, only the responses of the white students were utilized. This brought the final sample to 1400 tenth-grade students.

CONCLUSIONS: Results revealed: (1) 80 per cent of the respondents rated their parents' marriages as happy; (2) 82 per cent of the respondents were satisfied with their home life; (3) there was no difference between the males and the females with regard to the way they rated their parents' marriages; and (4) the responses indicated that the students had more positive attitudes toward their mothers than toward their fathers.

B.45 Johnson, Thomas F. "Conceptions of Parents Held by Adolescents," Journal of Abnormal and Social Psychology, XLVII (1952), 783—789.

PROBLEM: To compare two adolescent groups with regard to their attitudes toward their parents. It was felt that adolescents living away from their parents would hold different and more positive attitudes toward parents than adolescents living with their parents.

METHOD: A projective type (Sentence Completion) test was administered to a group of 113 adolescents at a school for delinquent boys and girls. The same instrument was applied to a group of 111 public school students. From this sample, 42 matched pairs were selected. The ages ranged from 13 to 17 years old.

CONCLUSIONS: The results indicated that the adolescents who were not living with their parents expressed more positive feelings toward parents and family more often than did those subjects who were living with their parents. No significant differences were found between the two groups in the expression of negative feelings.

B.46 Jones, Mary Cover. "A Study of Socialization Patterns at the High School Level," Journal of Genetic Psychology, XCIII (September, 1958), 87—111.

PROBLEM: This study was an attempt to isolate factors influencing the individual's participation in the social life of the school and thereby influencing his contact with the socializing forces in the school.

METHOD: The subjects were selected on the basis of a three-year study of a high-school newspaper. Selection was made according to whether the individual contributed or did not contribute to the group life of the school. This examination yielded a "high mention" group of 12 boys and 12 girls and a "low mention" group of 9 boys and 9 girls. The two groups were then compared on ten points including: skeletal age, behavioral ratings, drive ratings, intelligence, reputation, physical abilities, socio-economic status, attitudes, self-concepts, and role patterns.

CONCLUSIONS: Of the ten points compared, only four revealed significant differences and these were not conclusive in determining those who would be outstanding in the activities of the school. The behavior ratings (by adults) for the "high mention" group were more favorable than for the "low mention" group. The high mention group had higher reputational scores. A small difference in socio-economic status was observed but was of minimal influence. No significant differences were found in attitudes, self-concepts, intelligence, and physical abilities.

B.47 Kasdon, Lawrence M. "Early Reading Background of Some Superior Readers Among College Freshmen," Journal of Educational Research, LII (December, 1953), 151—154.

PROBLEM: To gather information on the background of superior readers: When did they start reading? What aroused their interest in reading?

METHOD: 50 students entering college in the Los Angeles area were selected on the basis of reading scores. Open-ended questions were used in interviewing the subjects.

CONCLUSIONS: Of the 50 students interviewed, 27 (54 per cent) were able to read before the first grade. Of these, 18 had been taught by some member of the family. 20 (40 per cent) attributed comprehension to the fact that they read a lot. 25 (50 per cent) felt they became interested in reading because of an interest in book content. Only five mentioned school or teacher as reason for becoming fast compre-henders, and only three mentioned teacher as source of in-terest in reading.

B.48 Kay, Barbara, S. Dinitz, and W. C. Reckless. ''Delin-quency Proneness and School Achievement,'' Educational Research Bulletin, XXXVI (December, 1957), 131—136.
PROBLEM: To see if there is a relationship between de-linquency proneness and achievement in reading and arith-metic.
METHOD: This study, an outgrowth of the study reported in F.15, compares a group of 125 white boys in the sixth grade who were classed as ''delinquency insulated'' by their teachers and a group of 101 boys classed as ''delin-quency prone.'' The schools were located in areas of high delinquency in Columbus, Ohio.
CONCLUSIONS: It was found that the delinquency prone boys had more trouble in reading and arithmetic than did the insulated group. The insulated group had a mean I.Q. 11 points higher than the delinquency-prone boys.

B.49 Kinch, John W., and C. E. Bowerman. ''Changes in Family and Peer Orientation of Children Between Fourth and Tenth Grades,'' Social Forces, XXXVII (March, 1951), 206—211.
PROBLEM: To investigate the assumed change or orienta-tion from family to peers as the child progresses from childhood to adolescence.
METHOD: Questionnaires were administered to a group of 686 students from the fourth through the tenth grades in a white middle-class school district north of Seattle, Wash-ington.
CONCLUSIONS: The study found that increasing age leads to increasing activity with peers and thus to greater orien-tation to the peer group than to the family. This result varied with the degree of adjustment to the family in the period of expanding peer orientations. If the family was able to adjust to this change in the adolescent during this period, the adolescent was not likely to completely change his orientation.

B.50 Kuhlen, Raymond G., and Martha Arnold. ''Age Differ-ences in Religious Beliefs and Problems During Adoles-cence,'' Journal of Genetic Psychology, LXV (1944), 291—300.
PROBLEM: An examination of the hypothesis that adoles-cence is a period of increasing religious problems.

METHOD: The sample consisted of 547 students from the sixth, ninth, and twelfth grades (12, 15, and 18 years of age). Protestants constituted the majority of the sample with Catholics second and Jewish students third. Questionnaires including 52 items on religious interest were applied to this sample.
CONCLUSIONS: A comparison between the groups revealed many significant differences in the area of religious beliefs. An increase was noted in the statements concerned with the subject's "wondering about" certain beliefs. But, analysis of these statements did not support the idea that adolescence is a period of generally increased religious doubts and problems. It was also found that adolescents were dissatisfied with the conventional church services and the availability of help for religious problems.

B.51 Landis, Paul H. "The Ordering and Forbidding Technique and Teen-Age Adjustment," School and Society, LXXX (October, 1954), 105—106.
PROBLEM: To investigate the effect on teen-age adjustment of democratic and authoritarian family relationships.
METHOD: Questionnaires were administered to 1900 boys and 2410 girls. All the subjects were high-school seniors.
CONCLUSIONS: With regard to personal and social adjustment, it was found that the child from the democratic family had a distinct advantage over the child from the authoritarian family. More parent-child disagreements arise in the authoritarian family than in the democratic.

B.52 Landis, Paul H. "The Families That Produce Adjusted Adolescents," Clearing House, XXIX (May, 1955), 537—540.
PROBLEM: This study deals with teen-age adjustment in relation (1) to authoritarian or democratic family background, (2) large and small families, and (3) broken and unbroken families.
METHOD: Data were gathered from questionnaires administered to a sample of 5500 high-school seniors.
CONCLUSIONS: (1) The child from the democratic family was generally better adjusted and had fewer teen-age problems. (2) The only child had slightly more problems than the child in a larger family. The only child also showed fewer friends than the boys in larger families (who had the most friends). Only children were found to be the most active outside the home and were also the most introspective. (3) While the adolescents from broken homes had a few more problems than those from whole families, the differences were not great. There seemed to be more strain in children from broken homes and they appeared to be more mature and ready to accept responsibilities.

B.53 Langworthy, Russell L. "Community Status and Influence in a High School," American Sociological Review, XXIV (August, 1959), 537—539.
PROBLEM: Noting that studies of communities suggest the reflection of the status structure on the operation of local institutions, the author examines the high school to see if it reflects community status systems. He also examines grade and sex stratification in the high school.
METHOD: A paper and pencil test was applied to a sample of freshman and junior boys and girls in a high school in a New England town.
CONCLUSIONS: Analysis showed that the status system of the community was definitely reflected in the high school. Preferences and ethnic choices definitely followed the pattern of the community. Within the school, influence was mainly held by the juniors over the freshmen. It was also found that the individual's life was more influenced by members of his own sex than by members of the other sex.

B.54 Latham, Albert J. "The Relationship Between Pubertal Status and Leadership in Junior-High-School Boys," Journal of Genetic Psychology, LXXVIII (June, 1951), 185—194.
PROBLEM: To determine the effect of physical maturity on the selection of leaders in different age groups.
METHOD: 447 boys, 13 and 14 years of age, were divided into two groups. One group was physically mature and the other was physically immature. Questionnaires were applied to these two groups.
CONCLUSIONS: Three types of leadership were distinguished in the study: elective, appointive, and athletic. Of these three only the athletic leadership consistently preferred physically mature boys. No significant relationships could be established between physical maturity and the elective and appointive positions. It was found that mature thirteen-year-old boys participated in athletics more than did the immature fourteen-year-olds.

B.55 Levinson, Boris M. "The Problems of Jewish Religious Youth," Genetic Psychology Monographs, LX (1959), 311—347.
PROBLEM: To see how religiously raised college freshmen view themselves and to see the effect of the impact of the college culture on the expressed problems of these students.
METHOD: The Mooney Check List on college adjustment was applied to a sample of 220 Yeshiva College freshmen. Almost 90 per cent of these students came from Yeshiva high schools.
CONCLUSIONS: Out of 380 items on the check list, 139 were underlined by 10 per cent or more of the students.

The average number underlined was 42. The subjects had particular difficulty with problems in the areas of social and recreational activities, health and physical development, and adjustment to school work. The author attributed these problems to scholastic overloading resulting from overemphasis on academic areas.

B.56 Lewis, W. D. "A Comparative Study of the Personalities, Interests, and Home Backgrounds of Gifted Children of Superior and Inferior Educational Achievement," Journal of Genetic Psychology LIX (1941), 207—218.
PROBLEM: To examine two groups of gifted children with respect to personality traits, home background, and interests in order to establish the causes for the differences in educational achievement between the groups.
METHOD: The subjects in this study were selected from 455 schools in 310 communities in 36 states. The advanced group, educational age a year or more over mental age, contained 1078 students. The retarded group, 756 subjects, had an educational age a year or more lower than mental age. Personality inventories and ratings were used in conjunction with questionnaires.
CONCLUSIONS: It was found that the educationally advanced group was rated significantly higher in desirable personality traits and generally came from superior home backgrounds. These advanced students were rated high on such traits as dependability, originality, self-reliance, and investigativeness. The retarded group was found to come from relatively inferior homes and to possess less desirable personality traits.

B.57 Liccione, John V. "The Changing Family Relationships of Adolescent Girls," Journal of Abnormal and Social Psychology, LI (November, 1955), 421—426.
PROBLEM: It was hypothesized that the relationship between mother and daughter during the pubertal period would be characterized by more conflict than the relationship between the father and daughter in the same period.
METHOD: Conflict and relational change was measured by use of the Thematic Apperception Test applied to 200 girls ranging in age from 9 to 17.
CONCLUSIONS: At all age levels there was a greater amount of both conflicting and nonconflicting interaction between mother and daughter than between father and daughter. The greater amount of conflict between mother and daughter is explained on the basis of greater general interaction between the two during this period.

B.58 Lippitt, Ronald, and Ralph White. "An Experimental Study of Leadership and Group Life," in E. E. Maccoby, T. M.

Newcomb, and E. L. Hartley (eds.), Readings in Social Psychology (New York: Henry Holt and Company, 1958), pp. 496—511.

PROBLEM: An attempt to study, comparatively and experimentally, the effect of three types of adult leadership (authoritarian, democratic, and laissez-faire) on the behavior of four clubs of eleven-year-old children. They also investigated the effects of varying the leadership type within the groups.

METHOD: Data were collected on each group by the use of eight types of club records covering such items as continuous group structure analysis, record of social interactions, and accounts of all conversation. Utilizing five instruments, including interviews with the subject and the parents, and talks with the subjects' teachers, data were also collected on the lives of the club members.

CONCLUSIONS: Among the findings we see: (1) The pattern of interaction and emotional development of the groups was directly and strongly influenced by the leadership type imposed on the group; (2) the differences in club behavior were established as due to the effect of the difference in leadership types rather than to the characteristics of the clubs; (3) in general, the democratic type leadership proved more productive and beneficial to the group than either the authoritarian or the unstructured, passive laissez-faire types of leadership. The study also establishes the validity of experimental research in the area of small-group life.

B.59 Lundberg, George A., and Lenore Dickson. "Selective Association Among Ethnic Groups in a High School Population," American Sociological Review, XVII (February, 1952), 23—24.

PROBLEM: The purpose of this study was to examine the social interaction of various ethnic groups in a large American high school. Examined were the choices of associates from the students' own or other ethnic group, the relative popularity of different ethnic groups, and the relevance of certain background factors in choice of associates.

METHOD: Questionnaires constructed by the researchers were administered by teachers to a random sample of 1544 students of different ethnic groups in Seattle, Washington. The ethnic breakdown in terms of per cent was: 59.6 white Gentile; 15.9 Jewish; 9.6 Japanese; 8.5 Negro; 4.8 Chinese; and 1.6 other.

CONCLUSIONS: (1) All the minority groups became progressively ethnocentric as their choices ranged from "leaders" (least) through "work partners" and "dates" to "friends" (most ethnocentrism). (2) Every ethnic group showed a preference for its own members on sociometric tests of leadership, work, dating, and friendship relationships. (3) It was found that the Jews were relatively non-ethnocentric as compared to the Negroes who were relatively ethnocentric. (4) The Jewish and the Japanese group rated each other most often as "least liked." (5) The white Gentiles were most often chosen for leadership, work, and dating but were chosen less often for friendship. The authors conclude that prejudice and ethnocentrism is not confined to the majority group but is often more strongly felt in minority groups toward the majority and other minority groups. They seem to feel that prejudice in these groups is more related to specific relationships than to generalized ones.

B.60 Lundberg, George A., and Lenore Dickson. "Inter-Ethnic Relations in a High-School Population," American Journal of Sociology, LVIII (July, 1952), 1—10.
PROBLEM: This is a replication of study described in B.59 using a different sample. The purpose here is to determine the influence of the size of the ethnic group on interethnic relationships and to examine the reciprocity and prediction of reciprocity in the choices made in the sociometric test.
METHOD: A sample of 1732 was drawn from the high-school population of Seattle, Washington. In composition, the sample was predominantly non-Jewish white (91.3 per cent). The remaining 8.7 per cent was divided among Chinese, Japanese, Negro, and Jewish. The same questionnaire was used.
CONCLUSIONS: It was found that: (1) the degree of ethnocentrism between the two schools did not differ markedly; (2) mutual friends were more apt to be of the same sex, class, and ethnic group than were nonmutual friends; (3) prediction of reciprocity of choice was accurate in about two-thirds of the cases; (4) 90 per cent of the subjects were chosen as friends by at least one person, but only 50 per cent were named as enemies; (5) measuring social adjustment by reciprocated choices and predicted reciprocal choices revealed that the girls' social adjustment scores were higher than the boys'. It was also found that this measure of adjustment increased with age.

B.61 Lynn, David B. "A Note on Sex Differences in the Development of Masculine and Feminine Identification," Psychological Review, LXVI (1959), 126—135.
COMMENTS: The paper discusses existing literature and research findings on differences in formation of masculine and feminine sex identification. The author formulates four hypotheses which seem to be supported by the discussed research. The hypotheses proposed are: (1) with increasing age, males become relatively more firmly identified

with the masculine role and females less identified with the feminine role; (2) a larger proportion of females than males will show preferences for the role of the opposite sex; (3) a higher proportion of females than males adopt aspects of the role of the opposite sex; (4) males tend to identify with a cultural stereotype of the masculine role, whereas females tend to identify with aspects of their own mother's role specifically.

B.62 McArthur, Charles. "Subculture and Personality During the College Years," Journal of Educational Sociology, XXXIII (February, 1960), 260—268.
COMMENTS: The discussion in this paper, based on existing research in sociology and education, is concerned with the listing of factors relating success in college to attendance at public or private high schools. No specific samples are described. In discussing the differences between the public and private high-school boys' performance and behavior in college, the following points are made: (1) with I.Q. held constant, the public school boy outperforms the private school boy; (2) greatly differing childhood experiences in the two groups are reflected in their Thematic Apperception Tests; (3) the two groups reflect different social values; (4) the college grades of the public school boy can be predicted more accurately than the performance of the private school boy; (5) occupational aspirations among public school boys usually center in monetary success and science, while the private school student reflects social, aesthetic, and higher status desires.

B.63 McClelland, F. M., and J. A. Ratliff. "Use of Sociometry as an Aid in Promoting Social Adjustment in a Ninth Grade Home Room," Sociometry, X (May, 1947), 147—153.
PROBLEM: The purpose of this study was to determine if it is possible for a teacher to control the social adjustment of his pupils through the application of sociometric techniques.
METHOD: Sociometric techniques were applied to a group of ninth-grade students from low income families. The fathers were semi-skilled or unskilled workers or small business owners.
CONCLUSIONS: It was hoped by the use of sociometric analysis of the class to determine the composition of the group and to offer the teacher information which would enable him to plan the organization and activities of the group in order to increase acceptance and thereby increase adjustment and performance. Favorable results are reported.

B.64 McCord, W., J. McCord, and A. Howard. "Early Familial

Experiences and Bigotry,'' American Sociological Review, XXV (October, 1960), 717—722.
PROBLEM: To examine the familial basis of prejudice.
METHOD: The sample of 45 lower-class white males was originally part of the Cambridge-Somerville Youth Study. This group was examined between 1937 and 1940 and re-examined in 1948 with regard to their attitudes toward Jews and Negroes. At the time of the first interview, the subjects were between 9 and 12 years of age.
CONCLUSIONS: Results of the interviews indicated that prejudices in the lower-class boys was likely to be based on the acceptance of cultured stereotypes and not related to specific personality needs or to specific family environments. This differs from the middle-class pattern, which apparently reflects personality needs and experiences within the family.

B.65 McKeachie, Daniel S. ''Students Ratings of Instructors: A Validity Study,'' Journal of Educational Research, LI (January, 1958), 79—83.
PROBLEM: To establish a relationship between students' ratings of instructors and selection of further courses in their field.
METHOD: Instructor evaluations and students' course backgrounds were collected over a period of three years from students taking courses in psychology.
CONCLUSIONS: It was found, in two of the five semesters examined, that students' ratings of instructors was significantly related to the number of students taking further courses in the field.

B.66 McNeil, John D. ''Changes in Ethnic Reaction Tendencies During High School,'' Journal of Educational Research, LIII (January, 1960), 199—200.
PROBLEM: (1) to compare the prejudicial stereotypes of entering tenth-grade students and graduating students; and (2) to compare the tenth-grade stereotypes with the twelfth-grade stereotypes of the same group.
METHOD: Analysis was based on students' reactions to a list of stereotype words covering such items as occupations, racial groups, and personality types. For the retest two years later, 28 of the original 50 students were available.
CONCLUSIONS: (1) The first comparison revealed that the twelfth-grade students had significantly more negative responses than the tenth-graders. Ethnic and racial stereotypes were more than double those of the tenth-graders; (2) the second comparison revealed that the twelfth-graders had increased in stereotyped reactions over their response

in the tenth grade. Those who were most prejudiced in the
tenth grade were also the most prejudiced in the twelfth.

B.67 McQueen, R., and K. C. Williams. "Predicting Success in
Beginning High School Algebra," Psychological Reports,
IV (September, 1959), 603—606.
PROBLEM AND METHOD: To determine the variables
which could be used to predict how a student will do in first
year algebra, by comparing mental ability, reading ability,
algebraic ability, and eighth-grade arithmetic marks.
CONCLUSIONS: From the results of the tests, it appears
that it would not be valid to use reading ability and intelligence scores in predicting algebraic success; however, the
use of eighth-grade arithmetic scores and scores on tests
of ability in algebra indicates prediction with a considerable degree of accuracy.

B.68 Maas, Henry S. "The Role of Members in Clubs of Lower-
Class and Middle-Class Adolescents," Child Development,
XXV (1954), 241—251 (J. Seidman (ed.), The Adolescent: A
Book of Readings (New York: Holt, Rinehart and Winston,
1960), pp. 294-304).
PROBLEM: To compare the type of relationship existing
between (a) the lower-class adolescent club member and
the adult leader, the president, and other members, and (b)
the middle-class adolescent club member and these figures.
METHOD: Observation, participation, and specially developed tally-sheet records were used to gather data from
(boys and girls) aged 12 to 16, 126 members in lower-class
and middle-class clubs.
CONCLUSIONS: (1) Lower-class and middle-class adolescents have different perceptions and different means of ful-
fillment of the club membership role; (2) the membership
role for lower- and middle-class adolescents appears to
offer equal opportunity, but different channels for release
of aggression in teen-age clubs.

B.69 Mangus, A. R. "Personality Adjustment of Rural and Urban Children," American Sociological Review, XIII (October, 1948), 566—575.
PROBLEM: To determine whether a farm background, as
compared to an urban background, is a help or a detriment
in making desirable personality adjustments.
METHOD: Questionnaire, rating scales, and personality
tests were used to gather data from 1229 children enrolled
in third and sixth grades in Ohio in 1946.
CONCLUSIONS: In general the majority of the children with
farm backgrounds were found to be equally or better able
to make necessary personality adjustments. Farm chil-

dren were especially outstanding in areas of self-reliance, personal worth, sense of belonging, lack of withdrawal tendencies, and possession of social skills.

B.70 Marshall, Helen R. "Factors Relating to the Accuracy of Adult Leaders Judgments of Social Acceptance in Community Youth Groups," Child Development, XXIX (September, 1958), 417—424.

PROBLEM: To ascertain what, if anything, determines the amount of accuracy displayed by adult leaders in judging social acceptance of adolescents.

METHOD: The ratings by 36 adult women volunteers of 263 girl members of 22 4-H clubs were compared to the ratings made by the girls themselves.

CONCLUSIONS: The accuracy of the adult judges increased as the popularity of the girl being rated increased; adult judges were better able to rate the older girls; and the larger the group, the lower the accuracy of the adult raters.

B.71 Meek, Hayden, Harriett Cramer, and Judith Chaffey. The Personal-Social Development of Boys and Girls with Implications for Secondary Education. American Education Fellowship, Committee on Immediate Social Relations of Adolescents, Committee on Workshops Progressive Education Association, (1940).

PROBLEM: To analyze the factors that have a bearing on the personal social growth of boys and girls in the period of adolescence and puberty.

METHOD: Discussion of previously published materials.

CONCLUSIONS: The three most important conclusions appear to be: (1) the importance of the perpetual interaction between every individual and his environment; (2) the truly meaningful things are not capable of being taught, but become a part of the personality through emotional and esthetic experiences; and (3) the most motivating factor in the adolescent's growth is his desire to learn how to act in the varied situations encountered in life.

B.72 Midcentury White House Conference, "The Course of Healthy Personality Development," in J. Seidman (ed.), The Adolescent: A Book of Readings (New York: Holt, Rinehart and Winston, 1960), pp. 218—237.

PROBLEM: To discuss the idea that there is a primary problem in each individual stage of human development which must be solved if the person is going to be able to go on confidently to the following stage.

METHOD: Theoretical discussion; not a report of research.

CONCLUSIONS: Eight stages and central problems were formulated: (1) first year of life—sense of trust; (2) 12—15 months—sense of autonomy; (3) 4—5 years—sense of initiative; (4) 6—11 (approx.)—sense of accomplishment; (5) onset of adolescence—sense of identity; (6) adolescence—sense of intimacy; (7) adulthood—parental sense; (8) stage VIII—sense of integrity.

B.73 Montague, Joel B., Jr. " A Study of Anxiety Among English and American Boys," American Sociological Review, XX (December, 1955), 685—689.
PROBLEM: To discuss the proposition that by determining and comparing the frequency of the occurrence and expression of anxiety by a group of individuals representative of a particular class and culture, conclusions may be drawn on the differences of each group in defining situations.
METHOD: Questionnaires were administered to 600 English boys and 700 American boys in the age group 13—14, representing most of the social classes.
CONCLUSIONS: It was found that greater anxiety was manifested in the United States sample, this being attributed to the greater institutional demands of American culture (the lowest classes in both samples showed the least amount of anxiety, which gives further credence to the idea that excessive demands are responsible for the manifestation of anxiety). It was concluded that the frequency of anxiety in a culture is roughly proportional to amount demanded for adaptation of the individual in that culture.

B.74 Moreno, J. L., Helen H. Jennings, and Richard Stockton, "Sociometry in the Classroom," Sociometry, VI (November, 1943), 425—428.
PROBLEM: The objectives of this study were to add to the knowledge of group structure (425).
METHOD: Students in four fifth-grade classes averaging 25—35 pupils were instructed to choose spontaneously those pupils they would prefer to be associated with in their classroom (425).
CONCLUSIONS: "The self-assigning revealed that if the children had organized themselves of their own accord they would have chosen neighbors in their classrooms different from the ones they have now and would have developed definite groups with leaders and followers, drawing in outsiders from other classes into their midst and cutting off members of their class mates as undesired. Furthermore, teachers' estimates of the most and least desired of their pupils were surprisingly inaccurate" (425, 428).

B.75 Morrison, Mildred M., and Pairlee J. Stinson. "Sex Differences Among High School Seniors," Journal of Educational Research, LIII (November, 1959), 103—108.

PROBLEM: To investigage the hypothesis that the existence of sex differences might account for differences in the results of the Differential Appitude, Cooperative English, Wechsler Adult Intelligence tests and grade point averages among seniors.

METHOD: The above-mentioned tests were administered to 36 boys aged 16—19, and 33 girls aged 16—18 in a senior class in a high school in Missouri.

CONCLUSIONS: The findings showed significant sex differences in six areas: (1) The boys were higher on numerical reasoning, mechanical reasoning, cooperative reading, and vocabulary; (2) the girls were higher on clerical speed and accuracy, spelling, and grade point average.

B.76 Mussen, Paul, and Jerome Kagan. "Group Conformity and Perceptions of Parents," Child Development, XXIX (March, 1958), 57—60.

PROBLEM: To test the hypothesis that adolescents classified as extreme conformists would be more apt to characterize their parents as harsh, restrictive, and punitive in Thematic Apperception Test stories.

METHOD: TAT's and the Asch conformity experiment were given to a group of 27 male college students in order to determine their feelings toward their parents.

CONCLUSIONS: The findings showed that a significantly large enough number of those undergraduates designated as conformists did regard their parents as harsh, punitive, rejecting, and restrictive. This also gives credence to the idea that conformity in adulthood is a generalization of conformity behavior learned early in childhood.

B.77 Neal, Edmund R. "A Study of the Relationship Between Prior Experiences and the Quality of Creative Writing Done by Seventh Grade Pupils," Journal of Educational Research, LI (March, 1958), 481—492.

PROBLEM: To study the effect of intelligence and environment on the quality of creative writing.

METHOD: Manuscripts, observation, and field study techniques were used to gather data from 90 seventh-grade students.

CONCLUSIONS: (1) The students of higher intelligence and more "desirable" environmental backgrounds were noticeably lacking in creative quality, while those from "poor" environments were extremely creative. (2) Derived experiences seemed to furnish material for papers of higher quality that did direct experiences, which most of the subjects used for background reference.

B.78 Nelson, Marjory J., Gertrude Raffel Schmeidler, and Marjorie Bristol. "Freshman Rorschachs and College

Performance," Genetic Psychology Monographs, LVIX (February, 1959), 3—44.

PROBLEM: To determine in what manner Rorschach tests can be used to predict success in college and as an aid in counselling undergraduate college students.

METHOD: To gather data, college records after graduation of 633 students at Barnard College were compared with Rorschach tests given to these students as freshmen.

CONCLUSIONS: It was found that in general the Rorschach tests proved fairly reliable in indicating how a student might perform in particular areas and in predicting the campus careers of those students shown to be potentially creative.

B.79 Norton, Daniel P. "The Relationships of Study Habits and Other Measures to Achievement in Ninth Grade General Science," Journal of Experimental Education, XXVII (June, 1959), 211—218.

PROBLEM: To determine which is the more responsible for achievement in ninth grade general science: study habits or intelligence, reading ability and aptitude.

METHOD: 41 ninth-grade boys and 53 ninth-grade girls picked from general science classes, who had had the same testing programs and teachers in seventh and eighth grades, were observed and studied to gather data.

CONCLUSIONS: Test results and ratings of the instructor showed that study habits are not more closely equated to success than intelligence, aptitudes, and reading ability. Among individual students, the boys' study habits are more closely related to their achievement. For both sexes, aptitudes were the most accurate predictor of the student's achievement.

B.80 Nye, Ivan. "Adolescent-Parent Adjustment: Socio-Economic Level as a Variable," American Sociological Review, XVI (June, 1951), 341—349.

PROBLEM: To ascertain whether the adjustments between adolescents and parents are affected by their socio-economic levels.

METHOD: Questionnaires were given to 1472 students enrolled in the eighth through eleventh grades from public schools in Michigan. The group was drawn from all socio-economic levels and controlled for rural and urban dwellers.

CONCLUSIONS: Although socio-economic placement was not equally significant in all groups, it was shown that generally this index does have a definite influence in adolescent-parent adjustment.

B.81 Parsons, Talcott. "Age and Sex in the Social Structure of

the United States," American Sociological Review, VII
(October, 1942), 604—616.
PROBLEM: To present a tentative statement concerning
certain areas of age and sex roles in this culture and how
they influence a variety of problems.
METHOD: Discussion of the views and past experience of
the author; no research reported.
CONCLUSIONS: Throughout childhood, sex differentiation
is secondary to individual ability and class position; in
adolescence, when sex roles begin to gain importance, the
male role in particular, instead of emphasizing responsibility, deliberately puts emphasis on frivolity and irrespon-
sibility as both cause and effect of some of the tension connected with the transition between adolescence and adulthood. The youth culture then acts to ease the strain and
to satisfy emotional need partly by an unrealistic romanticism.

B.82 Payne, Donald E., and Paul H. Mussen. "Parent-Child
Relations and Father Identification Among Adolescent
Boys," The Journal of Abnormal and Social Psychology,
LII (May, 1956), 358—362.
PROBLEM: To determine the relationship between a boy's
view of and identification with his father.
METHOD: Interviews were administered to a stratified
sample of 72 boys, 40 of the lowest and highest identifiers,
mean age 17 years, and consisting of 16 seniors and 24
juniors. Their parents filled out questionnaires, and teachers rated the subjects on nine characteristics.
CONCLUSIONS: The findings revealed: (1) high identification with the father correlated with perception of him as
warm, affectionate, and rewarding; (2) boys with higher
father identification scores perceived the father as slightly
more rewarding than the mother and more so than the boys
with lower identification; (3) those identifying strongly with
the father viewed their relationships with their parents
collectively as warm and rewarding; (4) in general, strong
father identification seemed to be correlated with calmness
and friendliness.

B.83 Peck, R. F. "Family Patterns Correlated with Adolescent
Personality," Journal of Abnormal and Social Psychology,
LVII (1958), 347—350.
PROBLEM: To attempt to make a comparison of personality traits of adolescents with the quality and type of home
life they lead.
METHOD: Case histories, inverviews, questionnaires, and
field study techniques were used to gather data from 17
girls and 17 boys and their families, all of whom represented a cross section of the population born in 1933.

CONCLUSIONS: Personality traits of adolescents appeared to have significant relationship to parents' disciplinary methods and emotional ties. Adolescents coming from warm, democratic families showed more positive characteristics than those living in autocratic, distrustful, and disapproving atmospheres.

B.84 Peckham, Charles W., and Thomas Ford Howell. "Religion as a Cultural Factor in One Aspect of the Personality of Selected College Students," Journal of Educational Sociology, XXXI (October, 1957), 75—81.
PROBLEM: To determine whether in a college controlled by a given religous denomination those students embracing that denomination will have better grades than those who do not.
METHOD: Case histories were used to gather information on this topic from all the students graduating from an Evangelical United Brethren college between 1945—1950. These groups were matched for race, age, occupation of father, place of residence, rank in high school, and I.Q. scores.
CONCLUSIONS: The grades of the group who were of the same denomination as the college were .129 higher than those who were not of the same denomination, which is not enough difference to substantiate the hypothesis.

B.85 Pierson, Jerome, Herbert Greenburg, and Stanley Sherman. "The Effects of Single Session Education Techniques on Prejudiced Attitudes," Journal of Educational Sociology, XXI (October, 1957), 82—86.
PROBLEM: To determine the effect on prejudice of a number of educational techniques used in a single session.
METHOD: 290 students in introductory psychology classes were tested for prejudice and then given a series of lectures, each one consisting of a different method for combating prejudice. They were retested after the series was complete.
CONCLUSIONS: On the basis of the results of the retests, it appeared that there was no significant change in the attitudes of the students involved after hearing these lectures.

B.86 Prahl, Marie R., Louis A. D'Amico, and Howard J. Bryant. "The Relation Between Miller Analogies Test Scores and Achievement in Junior College Subjects," Educational and Psychological Measurement, XIX (Spring, 1959), 611—616.
PROBLEM: To determine with what degree of accuracy MAT scores can be used to predict grades in junior college.
METHOD: The grades of 450 students at Flint Junior College were compared with the results of MAT tests administered to them during the 1956-1957 school year.

CONLUSIONS: It was concluded that scores on the MAT tests are valid enough to justify their use for prediction of achievement in junior college.

B.87 Psathas, George. "Ethnicity, Social Class, and Adolescent Independence from Parental Control," American Sociological Review, XXII (August, 1957), 415—423.
PROBLEM: To find out how ethnic affiliation and social class membership affect parents' control of adolescent independence.
METHOD: Questionnaires were given to 467 high-school boys, median age 15.10 years, who were of Southern Italian and Eastern European Jewish background.
CONCLUSIONS: Four different areas of independence were isolated: (1) permissiveness in activities outside of the family; (2) regard of parents for judgment of adolescent; (3) those activities associated with status; (4) permissiveness in age-related activities.
These results show that when comparing ethnic behaviors, one must always take into account differences resulting from class affiliation.

B.88 Racky, Donald J. "Predictions of Ninth Grade Woodshop Performance From Aptitude and Interest Measures," Educational and Psychological Measurement, XIX (Spring, 1959), 229—236.
PROBLEM: To develop a formula which can be used to predict success for boys in shop work.
METHOD: A test battery was used to gather data from 215 freshmen high-school boys enrolled in shop classes in Chicago Public Schools.
CONCLUSIONS: It appears that use of the tests for final decisions involving selection or elimination of students is not warranted; however, they could serve a definite purpose in showing which pupils might be expected to have difficulty with shop courses.

B.89 Reals, Willis H. "Leadership in the High School," The School Review, XLVI (1938), 523—531.
PROBLEM: To determine what factors in the home life account for the development of leaders and nonleaders.
METHOD: Interviews were given to a total of 74 high school students designated as leaders and nonleaders and their mothers.
CONCLUSIONS: The findings show that although there were slight differences in the homes of the two groups, they are more of degree than of content.

B.90 Reuter, Edward B. "The Education of the Adolescent," Journal of Educational Sociology, XIV (October, 1940), 67—78.

PROBLEM: To discuss the role and its differences in the past and present of education in the transitional period of adolescence.

METHOD: Analysis and interpretation of original manuscripts.

CONCLUSIONS: High schools, and colleges to some degree, have evolved and are presently carrying on a more elaborate extension of their original functions as places in which to contain and entertain adolescents, that segment of the population as yet unready for work or such other adult activity.

B.91 Roberts, Helen Erskine. "The Reactions of a Group of High School Sophomores to Their Experiences in Special Classes," California Journal of Educational Research, X (November, 1959), 220—228.

PROBLEM: To discover how the majority of students in this study viewed grades, extra assignments, special section placement, longer homework assignments, and other aspects of special classes.

METHOD: Interviews and opinion polls were administered to 94 sophomore students enrolled in special geometry, Spanish, and English sections.

CONCLUSIONS: Although somewhat divided on opinions regarding marks (a small majority feeling that better grades are achieved in regular classes), most of the participants in the special classes felt that participation was a distinctly rewarding experience, that the classes should be extended to future tenth grades and continued in the eleventh grade, and that they should require more work than regular classes.

B.92 Rosen, Bernard C. "Conflicting Group Membership: A Study of Parent-Peer Group Cross Pressures," American Sociological Review, XX (April, 1955), 155—161.

PROBLEM: Using the observance or nonobservance of Kosher meat laws as an index, this study attempted to determine the manifestation of the influence of pressures on the adolescent from his parent and from his peers.

METHOD: Interviews, opinion polls, and observation of 50 Jewish adolescents in a high school in a small city in upper New York State were used to gather data for the study.

CONCLUSIONS: It was found that two situations in particular caused conflicting expectations and pressures: (1) peer observant, parents nonobservant; (2) peer nonobservant, parents observant. On the whole, the data indicate that the peer group exerts greater influence on the choice of the adolescent in this matter than do the parents.

B.93 Ryan, F. J., and James S. Davie. "Social Acceptance, Academic Achievement, and Academic Aptitude Among

High School Students," Journal of Educational Research, LII (November, 1958), 101—106.
PROBLEM: To determine the relationship in the student culture between social acceptance and grades.
METHOD: Questionnaires were given to 326 students in four classes in the senior high school of a suburban town; 232 of these students were college preparatory pupils.
CONCLUSIONS: (1) Although small, there is a significant and positive relationship between grades and acceptance among the high-school students tested: (2) The data tend to refute the theory that rejection by peers will cause a student to turn to higher grades; instead academic success might earn the student a certain amount of prestige.

B.94 Scheidlinger, Saul. "A Comparative Study of the Boy Scout Movement in Different National and Social Groups," American Sociological Review, XIII (December, 1948), 739—750.
PROBLEM: The author is using the Boy Scout Organization to study, comparatively, various cultural impacts used to foster nationalism in youth organizations.
METHOD: Discussion of the problem with reference to published materials and documents. No sample.
CONCLUSIONS: "The institution of scouting has become a tool for inculcating into the young a total system of integrated behavior patterns considered desirable by the particular national or social group which is making use of the scout program. The specific national and cultural interests of the group and given time factors cause variations in the methods and objectives of the International Boy Scout Movement" (750).

B.95 Spaulding, Charles B., and Ruth S. Bolin. "The Clique as a Device for Social Adjustment among Freshmen High School Girls," Journal of Educational Sociology, XXIV (November, 1950), 147—153.
PROBLEM: To test the hypothesis that although the U.S. is a society based predominantly on secondary relationships, it does use primary groups for making certain adjustments.
METHOD: Sociometric tests and interviews were used to gather data from 220 girls in a freshmen class in a high school in Los Angeles.
CONCLUSIONS: (1) Girls used friendship groups already in existence as a means of easing adjustment to a new high-school environment; (2) those girls who had no previous clique memberships established them shortly after entering high school.

B.96 Trow, W. C., A. F. Zander, W. C. Morse, and D. H. Jenkins. "The Class as a Group: Conclusions from Research

in Group Dynamics," Journal of Educational Psychology, LXI (1950), 322—338 (J. Seidman (ed.), The Adolescent: A Book of Readings (New York: Holt, Rinehart and Winston, Inc., 1960), pp. 437—442).
PROBLEM: To discover methods for use by teachers in creating the best possible learning situation in their classrooms, and to answer other related questions.
METHOD: Review of the existing literature with any pertinence to this topic.
CONCLUSIONS: It appears that the learning progress is definitely affected by group phenomena as well as by the kind of teaching that occurs. Three sources of increased motivation were identified: goal determination, supportive atmosphere, and participating members.

B.97 Warnath, Charles F. "The Relation of Family Cohesiveness and Adolescent Independence to Social Effectiveness," Marriage and Family Living, XVII (November, 1955), 346—348.
PROBLEM: To determine the relationship of the type of family environment to the social acceptance of its adolescent members.
METHOD: Data were collected from 142 ninth-grade boys through the use of interviews and questionnaires.
CONCLUSIONS: From this study, it seems that the home environment is a place for the learning and development of social skills and perhaps the desire to participate in group activities; those adolescents coming from affectionate, democratic type families, are better able to fit into the social structure of the adolescent peer groups.

B.98 Weckler, Nora L. "Social Class and School Adjustment in Relation to Character Reputation," in Havighurst and Taba, (eds.), Adolescent Character and Personality (New York: John Wiley & Sons, 1949), Chapter 5.
PROBLEM: To determine the validity of the hypothesis that character reputation of adolescents is a function of their social class status.
METHOD: Case histories and interviews were conducted among sixteen-year-old boys and girls in "Prairie City."
CONCLUSIONS: The findings show that the character reputation of the adolescent (in Prairie City at any rate) is largely dependent on the amount of conformity to the school, which had middle-class values and ideologies. To the degree that Prairie City can be considered representative of other communities, it would seem then that social class does play some part in the formation of character reputations for most schools are middle-class oriented.

B.99 Witryol, S. L. "Age Trends in Children's Evaluations of Teacher-Approved and Teacher-Disapproved Behavior," Genetic Psychology Monographs, XLI (1950), 271—326.
PROBLEM: To identify and compare the behaviors named by children and teachers as most approved or disapproved by teachers.
METHOD: Open-end questionnaires were given to 2240 sixth- to twelfth-grade students, 80 teachers, and 540 education students in order to gather necessary data.
CONCLUSIONS: In general there was substantial agreement between students from grades six to twelve and experienced teachers in naming social values thought to be teacher approved or disapproved. This accuracy increases with the age of the pupils, the experience of the teacher, and is slightly greater for girls than boys.

B.100 Bassett, Raymond E. "Cliques in a Student Body of Stable Membership," Sociometry, VII (1944), 290—302.
PROBLEM: To report on relationships within and between cliques and of relationships between clique membership and place in the student body, based on such factors as class and place of residence (290).
METHOD: Sociometric data were secured from questionnaires administered to 147 of the 148 students attending Gorham Normal School about a month before the close of the college year, 1943 (290).
CONCLUSIONS: The results seem to suggest the following: (1) In a closed community of stable membership, individuals rejected by those they at first choose, tend in time to choose each other (292); (2) some tendency is seen for the popularity of a clique to vary directly with the popularity of its most popular member (297); (3) the leaders, receiving about as many choices from outsiders as from clique mates when the community as a whole is considered, receive only half, as many choices from outsiders as from clique mates in the leadership group alone (298).

B.101 Cameron, Mary Y. "An Enquiry into the Factors Governing Memberships of Youth Clubs and Juvenile Organizations," British Journal of Educational Psychology, XVIII (February, 1948), 48—52.
PROBLEM: To discover why so large a number of young people are not attached to any organization.
METHOD: Questionnaires were administered to a sample of 150 boys and 150 girls between the ages of 14 and 18, who were divided into club and nonclub members.
CONCLUSIONS: The passivity of the nonclub members may be due to lower intelligence, poorer physical stamina, negative social attitudes, lack of intellectual stimulus,

interest in nongroup activities, or simply to lack of opportunity.

B.102 Hurlock, E. B., and L. C. McDonald. "Undesirable Behavior Traits in Junior High School Students," Child Development, V (September, 1934), 278—290.
PROBLEM: To find if there is a relationship between specific behavior traits by chronological age and by sex.
METHOD: Questionnaires were filled out by the teachers of 790 junior high-school students, aged 11 to 14 (predominantly Jewish and from well-to-do homes), relating to their observations of 37 specific undesirable behavior traits.
CONCLUSIONS: The data indicate that there is a relationship between chronological age and behavior traits, depending in a measure upon sex difference. In this sample, the peak for ages showing the greatest number of undesirable traits was 14 years for the girls and 12 years for the boys. The only traits they found for the boys bearing no relation to age, were fearfulness, temper tantrums, and lack of interest. In girls, they were lack of interest, laziness, bullying other children, and rudeness (289).

B.103 Landis, Judson T. (Kenneth C. Kidd collected and tabulated the data under the directorship of J. T. Landis). "Attitudes and Policies Concerning Marriages Among High School Students," Marriage and Family Living, XVIII (May, 1956), 128—136.
PROBLEM: To better understand the nature of the concerns that school administrators have about high school marriages, the policies they pursue concerning such marriages, and the extent of positive programs in family life education in California high Schools (128).
METHOD: Questionnaires were sent to the principals of each of the 469 high schools listed by the California Association of Secondary School Administrators (61 per cent were returned) (129).
CONCLUSIONS: (1) Almost all schools cease to require attendance after marriage. (2) Opinions are divided as to whether or not married students are a problem in the classroom, although very few feel they are an asset. (3) Policies concerning pregnancy vary from immediate expulsion to leaving the choice to the student. (4) Schools are offering courses in marriage preparation more than ever before, but the majority are at the senior level and the marriages are occurring at all levels.

C / ADOLESCENT AND HIS PEERS

C.1 Anastasi, Anne, and Shirley Miller. "Adolescent 'Prestige Factors' in Relation to Scholastic and Socio-Economic Variables," Journal of Social Psychology, XXIX (February, 1949), 43—50.
PROBLEM: By comparing two groups of adolescents matched in sex ratio, approximate age, and grade level, but sharply different in scholastic achievement and socio-economic level, to study the part that additional factors (besides age and sex) may play in the behavior commonly associated with adolescence.
METHOD: Questionnaires were administered to a sample of 100 male and female high-school students in a small suburban community in the New York City area.
CONCLUSIONS: In general, group differences were greater than sex differences. Factors chosen by all the students as important fell into the stereotype of the popular, well-dressed, conformist to the group ideals; although the college-prep group put more emphasis on serious-mindedness, creativity, individuality, and enthusiasm, the noncollege-prep students were more concerned with athletics, appearance, and maturity.

C.2 Ausubel, David Paul, H. M. Schiff, and E. B. Gasser. "A Preliminary Study of Developmental Trends in Socioempathy: Accuracy of Perception of Own and Others' Sociometric Status," Child Development, XXIII (1952), 111—118.
PROBLEM: To devise a method for measuring various developmental aspects of socioempathy (i.e., changes in teachers' socio-metric rating ability with changes in students' age).
METHOD: Rating scales designed to determine the ability of the individual to accurately place himself on a spectrum of sociometric status were administered to elementary and junior high school pupils from the public schools in Bloomington, Illinois, and to the junior and senior classes of the University High School.
CONCLUSIONS: At all grade levels, there were generally high correlations between actual and predicted sociometric status, with a trend toward increased ability with advance in age. Children at all grade levels tended to use the upper parts of the rating and predicting scales disproportionately. There is a possibility that as the age of their pupils increases, the socio-empathic ability of the teachers decreases. From these findings, it seems that a reasonably accurate measure of socioempathy has been developed.

C.3 Ausubel, David P. "Socioempathy as a Function of Sociometric Status in an Adolescent Group," Human Relations,
VIII (Spring, 1955), 75—84.
PROBLEM: To determine the validity of the hypothesis that
persons of "like" sociometric status perceive one another,
more accurately than to those of "unlike" sociometric
status.
METHOD: Data were gathered by having students rate each
other on a five-point scale for acceptability, and, in addition rating themselves as they thought they would be rated
by their classmates.
CONCLUSIONS: While sociometric status did not significantly affect self-perception and perception of others in
one's group, there was a relationship between sociometric
status of the subjects perceived and socioempathy.

C.4 Ausubel, David Paul. The Theory and Problems of Adolescent Development (New York: Grune and Stratton, 1954. A
summary of that part of the book dealing with the adolescent
and his peers).
PROBLEM: To explain the functions of the adolescent peer
group.
METHOD: Discussion of literature and its findings on adolescence.
CONCLUSIONS: The functions of the peer group are: (1)
to provide the adolescent with primary status; (2) to act
as the major source of derived status during adolescence;
(3) to relieve the disorientation and loss of stability during
the change from childhood to an adult frame of reference
by acting as a combined frame of reference; (4) to aid the
adolescent in his strides toward emancipation from parental
control; (5) to act as a solid front in combating authority;
(6) to act as a major training institution for adolescence in
our society; (7) to provide an opportunity and set of norms
for increased heterosexual contacts and adolescent sex behavior; (8) to lighten the load of frustration and to anchor
the whole of the transitional period.

C.5 Barbe, Walter B. "Peer Relationships of Children of Different Intelligence Levels," School and Society, XXC (1954),
60—62.
PROBLEM: In what manner do children of above and below
average intelligence choose their friends?
METHOD: School children were asked to pick out their
friends or those with whom they would like to be friends.
CONCLUSIONS: It appears that above-average students
better liked than the slow learners by the average and be-
low-average students; the bright children were chosen more
often as friends than the slow learners by the average child
in the class.

C.6 Bogardus, Ruth, and Phyllis Otto. "The Social Psychology of Youth," Sociology and Social Research, XX (1936), 260—270.
PROBLEM: To gather data on chumming.
METHOD: The data were gathered from questionnaires submitted to 300 college students in sociology classes.
CONCLUSIONS: The findings show that most chum friendships begin in high school and continue in college averaging at least four years, and that women chums mean more to each other than do men chums. While most chums share similar standards and ideals, personality traits, ages and college classification, many differ significantly in sociability and in their chosen life's work. Also of major importance to all chums was neatness and the quality of sociability.

C.7 Bonney, Merle E. "Popular and Unpopular Children, A Sociometric Study," Sociometry Monographs, No. 9 (Beacon House, 1947).
PROBLEM: To develop a classification of personality-trait syndromes that will cover all traits involved in gaining social acceptance and in acquiring friends.
METHOD: From an original group, numbering 100 white male and female sixth graders, case histories, observation, and sociometric tests were used to limit the sample to 10 subjects from whom the data were acquired.
CONCLUSIONS: The findings clearly showed that it is impossible to classify "popular" and "unpopular" children on the basis of their personality traits, as it was shown that a person is liked or disliked, not for his individual traits, but for his "whole" personality and its total impression.

C.8 Bossard, James H. S. The Sociology of Child Development (New York: Harper and Brothers, 1948. Summary of that part of the book dealing with peer groups).
PROBLEM: To discuss the role of the peer group.
METHOD: Discussion of information presented. No sample.
CONCLUSIONS: The roles of peer groups in child development include: emphasis on the rights of others, controlling agencies for their membership, a place of determination for personality roles, and as cultural entities. Although the nature of the individual child's contact with peer groups depends a great deal on (1) the length of his membership and (2) the amount of his need for peer group activities, this experience in and with peer groups is one of the major experiences in his life, and accounts for at least one of the fundamental influences in shaping the personality he will assume in his adult life.

C.9 Bretsch, Howard S. "Social Skills and Activities of Socially Accepted and Unaccepted Adolescents," Journal of Educational Psychology, XLIII (December, 1952), 449—458.

PROBLEM: To show what relationship exists between classmates' ratings of acceptibility and self-ratings concerning participation in social skills.

METHOD: Out of an original group of 696 ninth-grade students, data were collected from the rating scores which fell into the highest and lowest quartiles, and subsequently compared.

CONCLUSIONS: In the higher group, the boys appeared to give above-average self-ratings, but this trend was significant for the girls only in the area of swimming (and the mean self-rating scores). The pupils who were judged to be more acceptable to their classmates were found to participate in a slightly greater number of social activities.

C.10 Cameron, W. Jaffray. "A Study of Early Adolescent Personality," Progressive Education, XV (November, 1938), 553—563.

PROBLEM: In order to achieve a more harmonious blending of the school's objectives and the needs and motives of students, this study investigated the social needs and interests arising in early adolescence.

METHOD: Case histories, interviews, and participant observation were used to gather data from 200 children in a number of schools.

CONCLUSIONS: The characteristics of the adolescent group as a whole (i.e., the "in" group) were a combination of physical and social maturity, friendliness, good looks, and high popularity. The majority of the subjects were concerned with acceptance by their peers, approval from the opposite sex, and social activities; all of these were accompanied by feelings of acute insecurity.

C.11 Centers, Richard. "Social Class Identification of American Youth," Journal of Personality, XVIII (1950), 290—302.

PROBLEM: To ascertain the substance and scope of the feelings of adolescents on class membership.

METHOD: Data were gathered from questionnaires administered to groups of adolescents.

CONCLUSIONS: (1) Adolescents are class conscious and their patterns closely resemble those of adults in similar occupational stratification, with the major difference being that adolescents place themselves more toward the upper-middle classes than do adults; (2) maturity is significantly related to self-placement on the class scale; (3) girls seem to classify themselves higher on the class scale than do boys of the same strata; (4) adolescents who are children of manual workers are not significantly influenced by their parents' union membership, but the opposite is true of the children of white collar workers.

C.12 Christensen, Harold T. "Dating Behavior as Evaluated by High-School Students," American Journal of Sociology, LVII (May, 1952), 580—586.

PROBLEM: To determine adolescent attitudes toward dating practices.

METHOD: From 8000 teen-agers spread across the United States, a representative sample of 25 was chosen to represent the high-school population of the nation, and the data were gathered from opinion polls submitted to them.

CONCLUSIONS: It was discovered there are definite male and female patterns of dating: the boys are considered more natural, but also more lacking in manners, more inconsiderate, more discourteous, and more aggressive in making a greater play for sexuality familiarity; the girls on the other hand are thought to be more socially and sentimentally disposed and, therefore, are more likely to appear superficial, arrogant, sensitive, possessive, or avaricious. Boys and girls are generally agreed on: (1) what to look for in choosing a mate; (2) conduct characteristic of each of the sexes; (3) self-criticisms as they affect the dating situation. However, they disagree principally in the area of projected blame, each sex identifying with the patterns of his or her respective sex.

C.13 Cottrell, Leonard S., Jr. "The Adjustment of the Individual to His Age and Sex Roles," American Sociological Review, VII (October, 1942), 617—620.

PROBLEM: To discuss the problem of adjusting to culturally assigned age and/or sex roles.

METHOD: A review and summarization of the conclusions of others into a series of propositions concerning the principal determinants of the extent of adjustment an individual is likely to make in a given social role in a given culture.

CONCLUSIONS: Cottrell focuses on role as "... an internally consistent series of conditioned responses..." and emphasizes the cultural role ("... a modal system of responses which constitutes the culturally expected behavior") as opposed to the unique role ("... the particular system of responses with which a specific individual operates") (617). The author presents 12 propositions, which, if applied to any given cultural role, would fairly precisely indicate "... the degree of adjustment which individuals are likely to make to such a role" (619).

C.14 Crist, John R. "High School Dating as a Behavior System," Marriage and Family Living, XV (1953), 23—28.

PROBLEM: To report on the conclusions of a study on high-school dating.

METHOD: Data were collected from adolescent high-school students.

CONCLUSIONS: (1) Dating is generally controlled by the family but approved by peers; (2) early dating is done usually because it is an expectation of the group; (3) many students date solely because they wish to be accepted by their group, not because they are particularly interested in dating.

C.15 Davis, O. L., Jr. "The Effect of a School Camp Experience on Friendship Choices," Journal of Educational Sociology, XXXIII (1960), 305—313.
PROBLEM: To test the validity of the hypothesis that social living experience at a school camp subsequently will increase participants' popularity with schoolmates.
METHOD: 32 male and female eighth-grade students enrolled in a campus laboratory school were interviewed and later tested sociometrically.
CONCLUSIONS: The findings show that friendship of those participating were significantly affected; more were named as friends after the camp than before. Boys and girls were affected differently, however, as the boys were chosen on more items of the sociometric tests than the girls after the camp experience.

C.16 Gronlund, Norman E., and Loren Anderson. "Personality Characteristics of Socially Accepted, Socially Neglected, and Socially Rejected Junior High School Pupils," Educational Administration and Supervision, XLIII (October, 1957), 329—338.
PROBLEM: To compare the various and perhaps explanatory characteristics of the socially neglected and rejected with the traits of the socially accepted.
METHOD: The data were collected from sociometric tests and social analysis forms given to 158 seventh- and eighth-grade pupils in central Illinois.
CONCLUSIONS: The traits of the socially accepted boys and girls were very similar, chief among them being: good-looking, tidy, friendly, likable, enthusiastic, cheerful, interested in dating, quiet (not restless), humor, initiative, talkative. Among the socially neglected, it was a case of being overlooked on these items. The rejected, however, were rated negatively on all the above traits.

C.17 Gronlund, N. E., and A. P. Whitney. "Relation Between Pupils' Social Acceptability in the Classroom, in the School, and in the Neighborhood," School Review, LXIV (September, 1956), 267—271.
PROBLEM: To ascertain the connection between pupils' acceptance by classmates in the school situation and friends in the neighborhood.

METHOD: Sociometric tests were administered to 340 junior high school students in a northern city of Illinois. CONCLUSIONS: The results showed the status of the student in the classroom is a fairly accurate indication of his general acceptance by his peers, for pupils who were highly sought after in school tended to have high general acceptibility in the home, and neighborhood, while those who were "unpopular" with their classmates were also generally unacceptable to their peers in their neighborhood.

C.18 Harper, Robert A. "Is Conformity a General or a Specific Behavior Trait?" American Sociological Review, XII (February, 1947), 81—86.
PROBLEM: To determine if conformity can be considered a general behavior trait or if it is in actuality a specific response to an individual situation.
METHOD: Questionnaires and interviews were administered to a sample consisting of male students living in a dormitory in a large state university, females in a small state school, males studying in a Catholic university, conscientious objectors residing in a civilian public service camp, and a group of incoming inmates of a federal reform school for young men.
CONCLUSIONS: From the data gathered, it appears that conformity is not a general behavior trait, but is associated with specific situations. However, the majority of the scores fell in the median range and the extremes were rare. More women seem to be conformists than men; the tendency to conform increases with age for both sexes. The smaller the town the greater the tendency to conformity; the non-farming occupations have the greatest amount of nonconformity.

C.19 Harris, D. B., and Sing Chu Tseng. "Children's Attitudes Toward Peers and Parents as Revealed by Sentence Completions," Child Development, XXVIII (1957), 401—411.
PROBLEM: To find out how children feel toward their peers and parents.
METHOD: Sentence completion forms were given to 3000 students, third grade to high school, from public and parochial schools in a county seat town in rural Minnesota.
CONCLUSIONS: (1) the majority of boys and girls feel favorably toward their peers particularly those of like sex, at every age; (2) in general boys are more neutral in their feelings, and boy-girl antipathies are caused by girls changing their attitudes toward their peers of opposite sex; (3) boys and girls express more positive than negative attitudes toward their parents with mothers receiving posi-

tive ratings slightly more often than fathers; (4) when there is a difference in attitudes toward mothers and fathers, the mother usually receives more positive ratings.

C.20 Hartley, Ruth Edith. Sociality in Pre-Adolescent Boys, Teachers College, Columbia University, N. Y., Bureau of Publications, 1946.
PROBLEM: To study and analyze the workings of sociality —the amount of acceptance an individual accords to his peers.
METHOD: Through questionnaires and observation, the data were gathered from 140 boys ages 10—12 in an elementary school in N.Y.C.
CONCLUSIONS: (1) For the subjects tested, there was a low correlation between self-judgment of personal sociality and actual performance; (2) although in determining their own sociality, students seemed to be influenced by their success in establishing and keeping social contacts, popularity appears to have no direct relationship to desire for social contact.

C.21 Harvey, O. J., M. Sherif, and B. J. White. ''Status in Experimentally Produced Groups,'' American Journal of Sociology, LX (January, 1955), 370—379.
PROBLEM: To test the hypothesis that when individuals are presented with goals having common appeal and requiring interdependent action for their completion, they will form a definite group structure made up of differentiated status positions and reciprocal roles.
METHOD: Twenty-four twelve-year-old boys at a summer camp were studied in a situation group interaction type study.
CONCLUSIONS: The hypothesis is that given a number of individuals, a definite structured group would form was substantiated. In addition, it was shown that when group members are confronted with an unstructured task, assuming sufficient motivation, their evaluations of each other's performances are influenced by each others statuses in the social hierarchy.

C.22 Hildreth, Gertrude. ''The Social Interests of Young Adolescents,'' Child Development, XVI (1945), 119—121.
PROBLEM: To test the hypothesis that as well as maturing early physically, girls also tend to mature earlier in their heterosexual social interest.
METHOD: The Hildreth Personality and Interest Inventory (High School Form) was given to 87 boys and 105 girls ages 10—14, all of whom had above average socio-economic backgrounds.

CONCLUSIONS: The findings support the hypothesis that girls mature earlier in those social interests that are related to their earlier physiological sex maturation.

C.23 Hill, Thomas J. "Dating Patterns and Family Position," Clearing House, XXIX (May, 1955), 552—554.
PROBLEM: To determine what consequence socio-economic status has on the dating habits of the adolescent within his school.
METHOD: Questionnaires were administered to 229 students in grades 9—12 of a laboratory school in Florida. The students were of several economic levels.
CONCLUSIONS: (1) The majority of the students date within their social and school class, the pupils in the higher social classes having the greatest number of dating partners. (2) The pupils from the lower classes have a tendency to choose dating partners outside the school, and it was also observed that when a student dates outside of his social class, he usually dates outside his school class too. (3) There is a steady increase in grades 9—11 in the amount and number of dates and partners followed by a definite decrease in grade 12.

C.24 Hobart, Charles W. "Some Effects of Romanticism During Courtship on Marriage Role Opinions," Sociology and Social Research, XLII (may—June, 1958), 336—343.
PROBLEM: Is the existence of the unrealistic, romantic attitudes held by adolescents affecting their perceptions of the marital role?
METHOD: A specially constructed Marital Role Inventory was administered to 831 undergraduate students at a co-educational sectarian college on the West Coast.
CONCLUSIONS: (1) At different phases of courtship, opinions on the marital role will differ, with adolescents at the premarital stage having unrealistic opinions; (2) a cyclic movement was observed which caused the opinions of those adolescents who were at the beginning and at the end of their courtships to be the most similar; (3) it was concluded that only the concept of a youth subculture permits an adequate explanation of the finding that in some respects the nondating students were closer to the married students in their attitudes than were the going steady and engaged students.

C.25 Hollingshead, A. B. "The Concept of Social Control," American Sociological Review, VI (April, 1941), 217—224.
PROBLEM: To discuss the hypotheses (1) that social behavior is the conditioned response of an individual to the controls which he has learned and are a concomitant of

his membership in group life and (2) that differences in behavior by class, group, or society are caused by differential associations.
METHOD: Critical analysis of published materials.
CONCLUSIONS: (1) Interrelations among people operating within the limits of rules, practices, and beliefs customary to their culture make up society. (2) Conformity is established through folkways, ideologies and institutions. (3) People are taught and restrained by social systems of behavior control.

C.26 Hussmann, L. A., and Gene Levine. "Social Class and Sociability in Fraternity Pledging," American Journal of Sociology, LXV (January, 1960), 391—399.
PROBLEM: To discover the differences between freshmen who decide to attend Rush Week and those who do not; to determine what happens during Rush Week; to find out the differences between those who pledge and those who do not.
METHOD: Case histories, interviews, and questionnaires were used to gather data from 890 freshmen students at an Eastern male college of engineering and science.
CONCLUSIONS: (1) The greater the income of the rushee's family, the higher the chance that he will pledge; (2) the youth with money, regardless of his personality, and the student with social experience, regardless of his lack of money, will both be picked over the poor and socially inexperienced rushee; (3) those students who "rush" have spent less time studying in high school than those students who do not attend Rush Week.

C.27 Jones, Edward E., and Richard deCharms. "Changes in Social Perception as a Function of the Personal Relevance of Behavior," in E. E. Maccoby, T. M. Newcomb, E. L. Hartley (eds.), Readings in Social Psychology (New York: Henry Holt and Co., 1958), pp. 102—109.
PROBLEM: To test the hypothesis that depending on whether or not a behavior has personal meaning for the perceiver, different inferences will be derived from the same behavior.
METHOD: The data were gathered from volunteers (in groups of five or six) in an introductory psychology course at North Carolina.
CONCLUSIONS: Findings indicate that behavior will be perceived and interpreted differentially depending on the personal relevance of the action to the maintenance of the values of the individual perceiver.

C.28 Jones, Harold E. "Adolescence in Our Society," in Jerome M. Seidman (ed.), The Adolescent: A Book of Readings

(New York: Holt, Rinehart and Winston, Inc., 1960), pp. 50—60.

PROBLEM: To summarize the results of a 25-year study of the relationship between physical growth, acceptance by peers, and self-acceptance.

METHOD: Case histories, systematic observation and peer rating scales were obtained from children at various stages of their development.

CONCLUSIONS: (1) One of the chief findings was that in urban American culture, girls are faced with more serious difficulties in adjusting to changing social expectations than boys; (2) contradictory expectations for girls in the beginning of adolescence include: both being quiet, unassuming and being talkative, and showing aggressive good fellowship; (3) on the other hand, boys appear to have a more uniform set of standards to be met in the process of developing their sex roles in the same period of growth.

C.29 Josselyn, Irene M. ''Social Pressures in Adolescence,'' Social Casework, XXXII (May, 1952), 187—193.

PROBLEM: To study the proposition that our culture presents the adolescent with a set of expectations but does not provide him with a means to meet these expectations.

METHOD: Discussion of published materials and existing literature.

CONCLUSIONS: (1) The social situation as it now exists tends to heighten adolescent apprehension and bewilderment; (2) the presence of half-truths adds to confusion and unpredictable behavior; (3) norms of adult expectations are such that it is extremely difficult for those who do not meet them to establish themselves in their peer group.

C.30 Kanin, Eugene J. ''Male Aggression in Dating-Courtship Relations,'' American Journal of Sociology, LXIII (September, 1957), 197—204.

PROBLEM: To determine which of the following were relevant factors in explaining male aggression in dating: (1) protective influence by the family, (2) alcohol, or (3) place of the occurrence.

METHOD: Questionnaires were administered to the female members of ten university classes in Sociology and English in 1956.

CONCLUSIONS: From the findings, it appears that the factors mentioned above are not to be considered primary causes of male aggression in dating; it seems that seasonal peaks (spring and summer) and length and involvement of the relationship are more important factors in determing the reasons for aggression in male-female dating relationships.

C.31 Keislar, Evan R. "A Distinction Between Social Acceptance and Prestige Among Adolescents," Child Development, XXIV (1953), 275—283.
PROBLEM: To test the hypothesis that there is a distinct difference between social acceptance and prestige and that these two traits will show different patterns of association on sociometric tests.
METHOD: Students were administered tests designed to show if there are distinctions between perception of prestige and social acceptance.
CONCLUSIONS: The findings show that social acceptance was closely associated with popularity with one's peers, while prestige was linked with scholastic success and similar variables.

C.32 Keislar, Evan R. "Peer Group Ratings of High School Pupils with High and Low Grades," Journal of Experimental Education, XXIII (June, 1955), 375—378.
PROBLEM: To discover how grades affect acceptance by one's peers.
METHOD: "Guess Who" rating scales were given to 196 girls and 194 boys in the eleventh grade of a high school in Los Angeles.
CONCLUSIONS: It was concluded that: (1) the group receiving higher marks (both sexes) was rated higher on enjoyment of and persistence in school work and in putting studies before eveything else; (2) girls with high marks were considered to be less popular but more influential with boys; (3) the boys receiving the higher marks were rated as being more considerate.

C.33 Keislar, Evan R. "The Generalization of Prestige Among Adolescent Boys," California Journal of Educational Research, X (September, 1959), 153—156.
PROBLEM: To study the hypothesis that on a preference test, an adolescent boy will try to imitate one of his peers who has been judged to have high achievement in tasks important to adolescent boys, and that he will do the opposite for a peer with low achievement in such tasks.
METHOD: Systematic observation of 60 ninth-grade boys with Otis scores over 100.
CONCLUSIONS: Subjects changed their "right" answers to those of their peers judged to be successful, even when their answers were deliberately made wrong by the testers, in a situation where they had an opportunity to be influenced by the peer's answer. It was concluded that the hypothesis was substantially upheld.

C.34 Kelley, H. H., and Edmund H. Volkart. "The Resistance to Change of Group-Anchored Attitudes," American Sociological Review, XVII (August, 1952), 453—465.

PROBLEM: To discover what effect the presence of different values on membership held by members has on the tendency to resist change of attitudes firmly entrenched in group norms.

METHOD: Interviews and questionnaires were used to gather information from 145 Boy Scouts on their attitudes toward camping before and after listening to a speech denouncing the emphasis on the scouting organization on camping and recommending in its place various city activities. The expressed attitudes were noted both in private, confidential interview sessions and in public, group discussions.

CONCLUSIONS: (1) It was found that public conditions carried more influence than private or confidential did; (2) the extent of the effect of the message is inversely proportional to the amount of value placed on group membership; this relationship was even stronger under private as opposed to public conditions.

C.35 Komarovsky, Mirra. "Cultural Contradictions and Sex Roles," American Journal of Sociology, LII (November, 1946), 184—189.

PROBLEM: To explain the essence of certain irreconcilable sex roles demanded by our society of college women.

METHOD: From interviews and autobiographical essays, information was gathered from 73 senior members of a course on the family and from 80 senior female members of a social psychology class.

CONCLUSIONS: Women college students commonly appear to be confronted with inconsistent and mutually exclusive adult sex role expectations—homemaker on the one hand and career girl on the other. As a result, some girls feel they must vacillate with the pressures of the moment, and all of them suffer from the resulting manifestations of uncertainty and insecurity.

C.36 Komarovsky, Mirra. "Functional Analysis of Sex Roles," American Sociological Review, XV (August, 1950), 508—516.

PROBLEM: Since it is generally accepted that there is in the role of the middle-class urban woman a definite strain, it is here attempted to discover why today's sex roles are so fraught with mental and social conflict, and which of the sexes is best equipped psychologically to shift from parental-family to married living.

METHOD: Case histories and secondary sources were used to gather data from middle-class, urban, married women.

CONCLUSIONS: In the woman's childhood such strong ties to the parental family are established that the woman is severely handicapped in the psychological shift from devotion to her parental family to loyalty to her family of procreation. Men are given more freedom and privacy and they are given it earlier in childhood, enabling them to prepare themselves psychologically for the future shift which marriage demands.

C.37 Kuhlen, R. G., and B. J. Lee. "Personality Characteristics and Social Acceptability in Adolescence," Journal of Educational Psychology, XXXIV (1943), 321—340.
PROBLEM: To ascertain what personality characteristics are seen to favor social acceptability among like-sexed adolescents.
METHOD: Data were obtained from questionnaires administered to 600 sixth-, ninth-, and twelfth-grade students.
CONCLUSIONS: (1) Among characteristics attributed to those who were the most acceptable socially were: popular, happy, enthusiastic, friendly, initiator of activities; (2) changes were noted in progressing from the sixth to the twelfth grade in the characteristic considered necessary to social acceptance. Twelfth-grade boys are more active, aggressive socially, and tend to be extroverts; however, looks are not as important to them as to boys in grade six; (3) for girls, most of these characteristics applied, with the addition of being sociable and enjoying a joke.

C.38 Lessing, Elise Elkins. "Mother-Daughter Similarity on the Kuder Vocational Interest Scales," Educational and Psychological Measurement, XIX (Fall, 1959), 395—400.
PROBLEM: To measure the degree of homogeneity between mothers and their daughters on vocational interests.
METHOD: Interviews, and mailed or personally administered questionnaires were used to gather data from 54 female students and their mothers.
CONCLUSIONS: (1) In relation to persuasive and mechanical interests, mother-daughter pairs were significantly alike in their responses; (2) factors of intelligence or special environment were not found to be significant in these correlations; (3) there was no evidence to suggest that mothers and daughters have the least resemblance on scales designed to test immaturity, unrealistic ideas, and other interests which might be assumed to predominate more among adolescents than adults.

C.39 Lowrie, Samuel H. "Dating Theories and Student Responses," American Sociological Review, XVI (June, 1951), 334—340.
PROBLEM: To discover if suspected discrepancy between sociological usages of the terms courting and dating and

actual usages really do exist, and to find out if any of the old definitions are still in practical usage today.

METHOD: Questionnaires were given to 931 girls and 914 boys in grades 11 and 12 and through the junior year of college.

CONCLUSIONS: (1) It was shown that there is some confusion in the definition and usage of these terms; (2) it was discovered that today the primary reason for dating is love and the necessity of mate selection; this reason was followed by the desire to learn; (3) girls appear to put the most emphasis on learning from dating, while boys are most concerned with having a good time and gaining prestige.

C.40 McGuire, Carson, Monroe Lanmon, and George White. "Adolescent Peer Acceptance and Valuations of Role Behavior," American Psychologist, VIII (August, 1953), 397.

PROBLEM: To denote lucidly and to quantify the ways that adolescents are valued and perceived by one another.

METHOD: Sociometric valuations were given to 674 senior high-school students.

CONCLUSIONS: (1) It was found that, in general, acceptance of individuals by their peers did not vary significantly from year to year; (2) the index of peer status was found to be relatively stable as a measure of peer acceptance among adolescents.

C.41 Marks, J. B. "Interests, Leadership, and Sociometric Status Among Adolescents," Sociometry, XVII (November, 1954), 340—349.

PROBLEM: To attempt to link stated, inventoried interests with social acceptability.

METOD: Interest tests and sociometric questionnaires were administered to 370 students in grades 8—12, and from them those with the most unacceptable and the most acceptable sociometric scores were matched by grade and sex for futher analysis.

CONCLUSIONS: (1) It seems that, in general, adolescents are companionable, show an interest in people, and are impulsive; (2) it appears that, for boys, mechanical interests, and, for girls, intellectual interests may provide compensation for isolation, but at the same time add to isolation; (3) the accepted girls expressed more interests that can be considered sociable, heterosexual, and disapproved by adults, and had considerably fewer intellectual-cultural interests; (4) the accepted boys had scores negatively correlated with nonconformist tendencies and a curvilinear relationship with interest maturity.

C.42 Meyer, William J. "Relations Between Social Need Strivings and the Development of Heterosexual Affiliations,"
Journal of Abnormal and Social Psychology, LIX (1959),
51—57.
PROBLEM: To determine the influence of succorance and
playmirth on the development of heterosexual affiliations.
METHOD: Questionnaires were distributed to 212 girls
and 175 boys in grades 5 through 12 of a rural community
in New York State.
CONCLUSIONS: The findings of this study substantiate the
assumption that a system of social reinforcements is used
during the school years to maintain sex-typed behavior.

C.43 Mohr, George J., and Marian A. Despres. The Stormy
Decade: Adolescence (New York: Random House, 1958.
Summary of those sections dealing with the adolescent
peer group).
PROBLEM: To explain the adolescent peer group.
METHOD: Discussion and interpretation of published
materials.
CONCLUSIONS: The peer group plays an important part
in fulfilling the basic needs of the adolescent, which include at this time association with others his own age and
support in the beginnings of his break with his family. Adolescents may go from one group to another, or they may
join and rejoin the same group, dropping out permanently
with the assuming of adult responsibility and more individual relationships.

C.44 Neiman, Lionel J. "The Influence of Peer Groups Upon
Attitudes Toward the Feminine Role," Social Problems,
II (October, 1954), 104—111.
PROBLEM: To test the hypothesis that peer groups have
an important influence in setting adolescent norms, including those toward feminism.
METHOD: Kirkpatrick's "A Belief Pattern Scale for Measuring Attitudes Toward Feminism" was given to 107 males
and females between the ages of 11 and 13, 108 between 15
and 18, and 107 between 20 and 24, all from the lower
socio-economic class.
CONCLUSIONS: The findings suggest that during adolescence there is a lessening of importance of family norms
as the influence of peer-group norms becomes more significant.

C.45 Neugarten, Bernice L. "Social Class and Friendships
Among School Children," American Journal of Sociology,
LI (January, 1946), 305—313.

143

PROBLEM: To answer the question, Does the social class position of the family play an important part in the child's choice of friends or in his reputation among his peers?

METHOD: Sociometric opinion polls and questionnaires were administered to 174 boys and girls in grades 5 and 6 and to 206 boys and girls in grades 10 and 11, representing all of the social classes of the town.

CONCLUSIONS: (1) A striking relationship between the socio-economic position of the family and the child's sociometric status was found to exist at two levels; (2) although both age groups make distinctions along class lines in the picking of friends, the older children are not using this distinction to determine whom they reject as friends.

C.46 Bardis, Panos D. "Attitudes Toward Dating Among High School Students," Sociology and Social Research, XLII (1958), 274—277.

PROBLEM: To attempt to ascertain the extent to which sex and age influence attitudes toward dating and related practices.

METHOD: 113 high-school juniors ages 16—21 in a Michigan city were interviewed, given opinion polls, and generally observed through the processes of field study.

CONCLUSIONS: (1) Females at all ages were less liberal than males; (2) males and females had begun to date at approximately the same age, 14, but were in agreement that girls should start to date earlier than boys; (3) unchaperoned activities were favored, but intimate physical relationships were somewhat frowned upon.

C.47 Partridge, E. De Alton. "A Study of Friendships Among Adolescent Boys," Journal of Genetic Psychology, LXIII (1933), 472—476.

PROBLEM: To test the hypothesis that children exhibit a tendency to choose their friends from other children of similar mental and moral development.

METHOD: Interviews and questionnaires were used to gather data from 142 boys, between the ages of 12 and 17, attending a summer camp.

CONCLUSIONS: The findings appear to substantiate the hypothesis that children pick for their friends children of like mental and moral development.

C.48 Phelps, Harold, and Horrocks, John E. "Factors Influencing Informal Groups of Adolescents," Child Development, XXIX (March, 1958), 69—86.

PROBLEM: To investigate attitudes and activities leading to the establishment of informal adolescent groups.

METHOD: Interviews and questionnaires were used to obtain data from a random sample of 200 boys and girls in grades 7 through 12.

CONCLUSIONS: (1) The most important over-all reason for the establishment of informal groups among adolescents is to achieve a degree of emancipation from adult control; (2) they are formed by lower-class adolescents to fulfill a need for status and recognition not afforded by the middle-class values of students and faculty of the school; (3) the middle-class adolescents form such groups for a variety of reasons such as pressure toward social conformity, home pressure to assume as semiadult social role, opportunities for unchaperoned activities, pressure to play the masculine role and to escape the moral code of the home and school.

C.49 Pope, Benjamin. "Socio-Economic Contrasts in Children's Peer Culture Prestige Values," Genetic Psychology Monographs, XLVIII (1953), 157—220.

PROBLEM: To get information concerning the possibility of sex and/or socio-economic differences in prestige values within adolescent peer cultures.

METHOD: A "Guess Who" test was given to 400 sixth-grade students.

CONCLUSIONS: The findings show that boys and girls of the higher socio-economic classes place higher value on conforming to adult standards and "Conventional" codes of conduct, while those in the lower socio-economic classes emphasize self-assertion and aggression.

C.50 Reuter, E. B. "The Sociology of Adolescence," American Journal of Sociology, XLIII (November, 1937), 414—427.

PROBLEM: To critically analyze present knowledge in the area of adolescent research and to describe a method for the sociological study of the adolescent world.

METHOD: Author's discussion of adolescent diaries. No sample.

CONCLUSIONS: Most of the individuals in society make the transition to adulthood without suffering noticeable mental strain or social disorder. The age at which this change begins and ends depends entirely on the individual child, and apparently even individual sex maturation sets no limit on the length of this phase.

C.51 Scandrette, Onas C. "Social Distance and Degree of Acquaintance," Journal of Educational Research, LI (January, 1958), 367—372.

PROBLEM: To establish how degree of acquaintanceship affects friendship choices.

145

METHOD: Acquaintanceship scales were given to 77 members of a ninth-grade class who then rated each of the other 244 students in the ninth grade.
CONCLUSIONS: (1) Degree of acquaintanceship is definitely related to the number of times a student was picked as a desired friend; (2) if an individual possesses socially acceptable personality traits, the stronger the degree of acquaintanceship the greater should be his chances of being chosen as a friend; however, this can also work conversely.

C.52   Seidler, Murray B., and Mel Ravitz. "A Jewish Peer Group," American Journal of Sociology, LXI (July, 1955), 11—15.
PROBLEM: To prove that the peer group under study "was so strongly integrated that it became a primary group for its members and took over the role from the respective families."
METHOD: Case histories, personal participation and systematic observation were used to accumulate data from the activities of the 10 members of this group which was started when the members were about 14 and lasted until the time of the review.
CONCLUSIONS: "The authors feel that their hypothesis was proven by the high incidence of out-marriages (3 out of 10), of nonconformist ideas, and of professional [occupations]—physicians, psychiatrists, and social scientists—as opposed to businessmen. In any case the intense solidarity of the group and its long duration fostered a situation which was extremely favorable to the members' internalization of its culture and all the personalities of the group were fundamentally affected by the group culture."

C.53   Stouffer, Samuel A. "An Analysis of Conflicting Social Norms," American Sociological Review, XIV (December, 1949), 707—717.
PROBLEM: "To test the viewpoint that the range of approved or permissable behavior as perceived by the given individual is an important datum for the analysis of what constitutes a social norm in any group, and especially for the analysis of conflicting norms" (708).
METHOD: Open-end type questionnaires were given to 196 Harvard and Radcliffe students enrolled in a course in social relations.
CONCLUSIONS: Three types of reactors were isolated: those who found an identical range of alternatives held by by authorities and students, those who found them completely incompatible, and those who managed to strike an acceptable compromise between the two. The most important discovery is the unreality of using the stable "social norm" as a starting point in drawing conclusions and

formulating hypotheses, for it may be the very existence of some flexibility of social norms which makes behavior in groups possible (717).

C.54 Tyron, Caroline M. "The Adolescent Peer Culture," 43rd Yearbook of the National Society for the Study of Education, Part 1 (February, 1944), University of Chicago Press, pp. 217-239.
PROBLEM: To discuss the adolescent peer culture.
METHOD: Analysis of published materials and case histories. No sample.
CONCLUSIONS: (1) There is a tendency to overlook the significance for education of the experiences of the child in his peer group; (2) many of the developmental tasks boys and girls are faced with during puberty and later adolescence can only be solved through the medium of the adolescent peer group; (3) in our society it appears that the presence of youth unshackled by adult authority will always mean a subculture will be operating; (4) peer groups are used for group solidarity and support in rebelling against adult authority and interference; (5) adolescent peer groups have much the same form and purposes as their adult counterparts, and their general characteristics are extremely similar.

C.55 Waller, Willard. "The Rating and Dating Complex," American Sociological Review, II (October, 1937), 727—734.
PROBLEM: "To discuss the customs of courtship which prevail among college students" (727).
METHOD: A casual survey was made of published material and integrated with the personal experiences and studies of the author.
CONCLUSIONS: (1) In spite of the strength of the old morality, among college students dating is largely dominated by the quest for thrill and amusement; (2) the rating and dating complex varies tremendously from one school to another; (3) there is an established class system or gradient of dating desirability on campus and it is clearly recognized and adjusted to by the students; (4) rating for boys depends on fraternity standing, activities, money, clothes, "smooth line," dancing well, and access to a car; (5) for girls, it is based on clothes, "smooth line," dancing well and popularity as a date.

C.56 Wallin, Paul. "Cultural Contradictions and Sex Roles: A Repeat Study," American Sociological Review, XV (1950), 288—293.
PROBLEM: To report on repetition of a study done in 1946 by Komarovsky on incompatible sex roles confronting the college girl.

147

METHOD: A random sample of 163 female undergraduates
were selected for interviews and questionnaires from which
the data were gathered.
CONCLUSIONS: The results are essentially in agreement
with Komarovsky's findings, but the author feels that the
great majority of college women who face incompatibility
of their sex roles either do not take the situation seriously
or are very readily able to solve the problem.

C.57 Wellman, Beth. "The School Child's Choice of Companions," Journal of Educational Research, XIV (1926),
126—132.
PROBLEM: Do children choose their close friends by
similar or dissimilar characteristics such as chronological
age, mental age, I.Q., scholarship success, extroverted
tendencies, height and physical maturation?
METHOD: 63 boys and 50 girls evenly distributed over the
seventh, eighth, and ninth grades were given a battery of
tests designed to reveal information on the physical and
mental characteristics listed above.
CONCLUSIONS: (1) From the findings it appears that
friendship pairs of girls are most similar in scholarship
and least similar in height; (2) the boys were found to be
more similar in height, I.Q., and chronological age, and
least similar in extroversion, scholarship, and mental age.

C.58 Whyte, William Foote. "A Slum Sex Code," American
Journal of Sociology, XLVIX (1943), 24—31.
PROBLEM: To indicate the presence of an elaborate and
highly developed sex code in an area formerly considered
characterized by lax sex behavior.
METHOD: Through long-term participant observation,
the information was gathered from a number of men in
street corner gangs in an Italian slum district of a large
city.
CONCLUSIONS: The findings indicate the existence of
very complicated and strict sex codes in slum areas. The
women are divided into categories for each of which there
is an acceptable form of sex behavior which is sanctioned
and furthered by the mores of the group.

C.59 Whyte, William Foote. "Corner Boys: A Study of Clique
Behavior," American Journal of Sociology, XLVI (March,
1941), 647—664.
PROBLEM: To delineate the characteristic relationships
of small groups.
METHOD: Case histories, field study, interviews, and
personal participation were all used for the purpose of
gathering data from Boston Italian slum men in the age

range 20–35. This data is part of the larger body of data obtained for the author's Street Corner Society.
CONCLUSIONS: (1) a hierarchial structure is the basis of organization for informal groups; (2) mutual obligations are the basis of all group relationships; (3) each member behaves as his position in the group dictates; (4) the leader of each group acts as its representative and directs its activities.

C.60 Wittenberg, Rudolph M., and Janie Berg. "The Stranger in the Group," American Journal of Orthopsychiatry, XXII (January, 1952), 89–97.
PROBLEM: To determine how the small group affects the development of social attitudes.
METHOD: Critical analysis and discussion of published materials in some of which a girl scout troop was part of the sample.
CONCLUSIONS: At the time when the adolescent vacillates between adult and peer values, rejecting his parents, his siblings, and his old friends, the peer group greatly increases in importance as one of the decisive supports and aids in the adolescent's breaking with his family. How the adolescent realigns his peer group contacts will later be significant in his formation of adult social attitudes and in his discerning of appropriate group attitudes.

C.61 Zuk, Gerald H. "Sex Appropriate Behavior in Adolescence," Journal of Genetic Psychology, XCIII (September, 1958), 15–32.
PROBLEM: To ascertain the direction of trends in and the broad characteristics of sex-appropriate behavior for adolescents 15–17 years old, and to discover if there is any relationship between this behavior and possible psychological-biological components.
METHOD: Sociometric questionnaires were given to 99 boys and girls from which data were collected.
CONCLUSIONS: (1) Although Sex Appropriate Behavior increased in girls from 16–17, it seemed to be more stable in girls from year to year; (2) the Sex Appropriate Behavior appears to fluctuate broadly from one area into another, with the most stability for both sexes noted in the sixteenth year.

C.62 Marshall, Helen R., and Boyd R. McCandless. "Relationships Between Dependence on Adults and Social Acceptance by Peers," Child Development, XXVIII (December, 1957), 413–419.
PROBLEM: "Is the degree of the preschool child's dependence on adults in free play situations related to his participation with and acceptance by his peers? If so, is

this relationship affected by length and progress of acquaintanceship?"

METHOD: Data were gathered from sociometric tests and observations of two 19 member groups of preschool children, group one averaging 4.4 years and group two, 4.11 years.

CONCLUSIONS: These data indicate that dependence on adults in the preschool situation accompanies relatively low social status and participation within the peer group. No conclusions were drawn concerning the effect of length of acquaintanceship on peer acceptance.

C.63 Wardlow, Mary E., and James E. Greene. "An Exploratory Sociometric Study of Peer Status Among Adolescent Girls," Sociometry, XV (1952), 311–318.

PROBLEM: "To what extent is measured peer status a function of the measuring instruments employed? What measurable traits and characteristics are significantly related to each of the five measures of peer status?" (311).

METHOD: The Ohio Social Acceptance Scale and the Ohio Social Recognition Scale plus a mental and physical test of projection were administered to 37 adolescent girls enrolled in a class of first-year homemaking in the University of Georgia Demonstration School (311).

CONCLUSIONS: "Sociometric research dealing with correlates of peer status must recognize that peer status is per se situational or specific in character. ... The relatively low relationships established between the five measures of peer status and the 35 variables suggest the need for further research to determine what characteristics are significantly related to peer status" (318).

D / ADOLESCENT IN PREPARATION FOR ADULTHOOD

D.1 Ausubel, David P., and Herbert M. Schiff. "A Level of Aspiration Approach to the Measurement of Goal Tenacity," Journal of General Psychology, LII (1955), 97–100.

PROBLEM: The problem in this study was to develop a measurement of goal tenacity through the use of a standard level of aspiration experiment. Goal tenacity is taken to be the individual's ability to maintain a high level of aspiration in the face of failure or series of failures. It was felt that such a measure of goal tenacity would reflect a stable personality trait in the area of aspirational behavior.

METHOD: Four types of speed tests were applied to a group of 50 members of the junior class at University High School in Urbana, Illinois. The mean age of the 24 boys and 26 girls involved in the experiment was 15.8 years. Most of the subjects came from professional homes.

CONCLUSIONS: Analysis of the data suggested that the developed measure of goal tenacity did reflect a stable personality trait relating to aspirational behavior. Support was also given to the conception of the goal tenacity score as a reflection of the individual's typical response pattern in the face of a series of successes and failures.

D.2 Ausubel, D. P., H. M. Schiff, and H. P. Zeleny. " 'Real Life' Measures of Level of Academic and Vocational Aspiration in Adolescents: Relation to Laboratory Measures and to Adjustment," Child Development, XXIV (1953), 155–168.

PROBLEM: The purpose of this study was to compare the usefulness of " real life" (subjective individual responses) measures of academic and vocational aspiration levels to standard laboratory measures.

METHOD: Academic grade reports and a series of tests and scales were examined to obtain data on a group of 50 students in the junior class at University High School, Urbana, Illinois. The mean age of the 24 boys and 26 girls involved in the experiment was 15.8 years. Most of the subjects came from professional homes.

CONCLUSIONS: There was generally found to be little or no significant relationship between "real life" and laboratory measures of the level of vocational and academic aspirations. This absence of significant relationships was attributed to the greater degree of ego-involvement in the "real life" measures as opposed to the typical laboratory experimental measures.

D.3 Bordin, Edward S. "A Theory of Vocational Interests as a Dynamic Phenomenon," Educational and Psychological Measurement, III (1943), 49–65.

PROBLEM: Assuming that an individual's responses to the Strong Vocational Interest Test reflects his acceptance of a particular self-image in terms of occupational stereotypes, the author hypothesizes: (1) that the degree of interest shown will vary positively with the individual's acceptance of the stereotype as self-descriptive; (2) that the degree of interest shown will vary positively with the individual's knowledge of the true (i.e., most applicable as opposed to most widely held) occupational stereotype.

METHOD: Analysis was made on the basis of a survey of existing research involving the Strong Vocational Interest Test.

CONCLUSIONS: The results of the analysis seemed to support the hypotheses and enabled the author to make further predictions and hypotheses, including: (1) the relationship between the expressed interest and the specific occupation will vary according to the social status connected with the father's occupation, the length of time the father has held the occupation, and the quality of the relationship between the father and the son; (2) the differences between claimed and measured interest will be reduced as the individual's knowledge and experience of the occupational stereotype increases.

D.4 Brown, James C. "An Experiment in Role-Taking," American Sociological Review, XVII (October, 1952), 587—597.
PROBLEM: This study is a preliminary investigation into the effects of the sex of the role-taker, the sex of the person whose role is taken, and the sexual orientation, male or female, of the specific situation on the act of role-taking. Based on the proposition that the cultural disjunctions of the world of males and females will be reflected in the partial failure of their ability to take the opposite-sex role in specific situations, it was expected that, in the experimental situation, same-sex role-taking would be superior to cross-sex role-taking and that in male oriented situations the males would be more skillful than the females.
METHOD: The nonrandom sample of 16 middle-class, white, thirteen-year-olds was taken from a freshman class at University High School, Bloomington, Indiana. This group was divided into 8 mixed pairs which participated in a series of 4 sociodramas. Data on same-sex and cross-sex role taking was gathered from the subjects' evaluations of the performances in the plays.
CONCLUSIONS: (1) The sexual orientation of the specific situation had little influence on the role-taking with the exception that male roles in female-oriented situations and female roles in male-oriented situations were most readily perceived; (2) regardless of the sexual orientation of the situation, males were slightly better at perceiving the roles of others than were females. Generally speaking, both of the expected results mentioned above were present.

D.5 Centers, Richard. "Children of the New Deal: Social Stratification and Adolescent Attitudes," International Journal of Opinion Attitude Research, IV (1950), 315—335.
PROBLEM: The purpose of this paper was to see if the attitudes of adolescents on labor and collectivism would conform to observed adult patterns at different occupational strata.
METHOD: The analysis was made on the basis of question-

naires administered to more than 1000 high-school students in a small city in New York.

CONCLUSIONS: The results of the analysis tended to conform the hypothesis that adolescent attitudes toward labor and collectivism would conform to previously observed adult patterns.

6 Chapman, Dwight W., and John Volkmann. "A Social Determinant of the Level of Aspiration," in E. E. Maccoby, T. M. Newcomb, and E. L. Hartley (eds.), Readings in Social Psychology, (New York: Henry Holt and Company, 1958), pp. 281—290.

PROBLEM: This paper investigates the influence of knowledge on the aspiration level of individuals performing a given task. In one case knowledge is taken to mean knowledge of the performance of other groups rather than knowledge of the specific task. In the other case, knowledge refers to firsthand experience with the given task.

METHOD: Two groups of college students were given tests of ability in specific areas. The first group had no previous experience with the test but were told how other groups of varying ability had performed on the test. The second group was given extensive knowledge of the test as well as knowledge of the past performance of other groups. Both groups were asked to estimate their score on the test.

CONCLUSIONS: Analysis showed that the first group had a significant rise in level of aspiration while for the second group actual knowledge of the task to be performed overcame the influence of the knowledge of the performance of other groups and the resultant level of aspiration was not affected by estimations of others' performance. The results are explained by the author in terms of the differing frames of reference of the two groups.

7 Dyer, William G. "Parental Influence on the Job Attitudes of Children from Two Occupational Strata," Sociology and Social Research, XLII (January—February 1958), 203—206.

PROBLEM: This study was conducted to test the hypotheses that, within occupational strata, children's attitudes toward jobs will parallel their parents' attitudes and that the children of white collar parents will be more favorably disposed toward the father's occupation than will the children of blue collar families.

METHOD: Eighty-seven families were selected at random from the population of Ames, Iowa. Forty-two of these families were white collar families and 45 were blue collar families. All family members over 10 years of age were interviewed. Fifty-one children between the ages of 10 and 22 were thus in the sample.

CONCLUSIONS: Analysis of the interviews showed that, while the white collar families were more satisfied with the father's occupation than were the blue collar families, neither the parents nor the children from either level wanted the children to follow the father's occupation. Since both groups fell in the lower categories of occupations, it was felt that the prestige value of the father's occupation played an important part in the evaluation of job and its influence on his children.

D.8 Dynes, R. R., A. C. Clarke, and S. Dinitz. "Levels of Occupational Aspiration: Some Aspects of Family Experience as a Variable," American Sociological Review, XXI (1956), 212—215.
PROBLEM: The authors set out to see if individuals with high aspirations are also characterized by more interpersonal difficulties in their families than are those with low aspirations.
METHOD: A questionnaire incorporating a measure of aspiration and a measure of family relations was administered to 350 university students. The sample was predominantly urban, middle-class, Midwestern, and Protestant.
CONCLUSIONS: Analysis revealed that the high aspires felt their parents showed favoritism toward some child in the family, felt more feelings of rejection, and felt less attachment to their parents. Evidence, then, supported the hypothesis.

D.9 Elwood, Robert H. "The Role of Personality Traits in Selecting a Career," Journal of Applied Psychology, XI (1927), 199—201.
PROBLEM: Considering the intellectual and emotional aspects of selecting a career, the author compared two groups of females with respect to their degree of extroversion.
METHOD: On the basis of a standard intelligence test and two parts of the Colgate Mental Hygiene Tests, a group of nurses entering a New York City Training School were compared to a group of girls entering a liberal arts college.
CONCLUSIONS: (1) The average nurse in the group tested was more extroverted than 94 per cent of all the college girls. (2) The nurses were found to be more stable than 77 per cent of the college girls.

D.10 Empey, LaMar T. "Social Class and Occupational Aspiration: A Comparison of Absolute and Relative Measurement," American Sociological Review, XXI (December, 1956), 703—709.
PROBLEM: The author tests three hypotheses in this study: (1) The absolute occupational status aspirations of male high-school seniors from middle and upper classes

are significantly higher than those of seniors from lower classes; (2) the relative occupational status aspirations of lower-class seniors will indicate that they prefer and anticipate significantly higher occupational status than their fathers; (3) lower-class seniors will be more inclined to reduce their occupational aspirations significantly when faced with the necessity of choosing their preferred and anticipated occupations.

METHOD: Questionnaires were administered to one-tenth of all the male high-school seniors in Washington state in the Spring of 1954.

CONCLUSIONS: The findings supported hypotheses 1 and 2, but failed to support hypothesis 3.

D.11 Engel, Mary. "The Stability of the Self-Concept in Adolescence," in J. M. Seidman (ed.), The Adolescent (New York: Holt, Rinehart and Winston, Inc., 1960), pp. 646—663.
PROBLEM: To investigate the stability of the self-concept in adolescence over a two-year period.
METHOD: Analysis was made on data from five instruments administered to 172 eighth- and tenth-grade students in 1954. Two years later, the same adolescents were re-tested with the same instruments.
CONCLUSIONS: Among the findings were read: (1) "subjects whose self-concept was negative at the first testing were significantly less stable in self-concept than subjects whose self-concept was positive"...; (2) subjects who persisted in a negative self-concept over the two-year period gave evidence of significantly more maladjustment than subjects who persisted in a positive self-concept..." (654).

D.12 Ezell, Lonnie B., and Henry H. Tate. "High School Students Look to the Future," Journal of Educational Research, XLIX (November, 1955), 217—222.
PROBLEM: The purpose of this study was to gather data on high-school students' expectations for the future.
METHOD: Analysis was made on the basis of questionnaires administered to 1572 high-school boys and girls.
CONCLUSIONS: The findings reveal: (1) most of the students expected to go to college and felt that their high-school courses were preparing them for their anticipated occupations; (2) one-quarter of the boys and one-half of the girls, however, planned to go to work directly after high school; (3) there were very few students who planned to marry as soon as they graduated; (4) 10 per cent of the boys and 1 per cent of the girls were doubtful as to their future occupations; (5) 20 per cent of the boys and 5 per cent of the girls selected occupations similar to those of their parents.

D.13 Havighurst, Robert J., and Audrey F. Rieger. "The Role of Adults Outside the Family in Character Formation," in Havighurst, R. J. and Taba, H., Adolescent Character and Personality. (New York: John Wiley and Sons, Inc., 1949), pp. 70—80.
COMMENTS: This chapter discusses two related studies that investigated what type of adults were chosen by sixteen-year-olds as ideals and what adults were most visible to them. There is no discussion of how these adults actually influence character formation.
In conclusion the authors state, "The 'ideal self' seems to be increasingly influenced during adolescence by adults outside the family, and especially by attractive and visible young adults. The data indicate that, if imitation takes place, the objects of imitation tend to be attractive young adults and successful middle-aged citizens. They also show that a small number, probably not exceeding 1 per cent of the adult population, are unusually visible to boys and girls and that perhaps these persons play an influential role in the character formation of adolescents in the community" (80).

D.14 Havighurst, R. J., M. Z. Robinson, and M. Door. "The Development of the Ideal Self in Childhood and Adolescence," Journal of Educational Research, XL (1946), 241—257.
PROBLEM: The purpose of this study was to describe the development of the ideal self, as revealed by self-reports from children and adolescents.
METHOD: 539 boys and 608 girls in the age range 8 to 12 were asked to write essays on "The Person I Would Like to Be Like." All of the subjects were from the Midwest and were distributed by educational, economic, and ethnic background.
CONCLUSIONS: In general, by the period of late adolescence, the ideal self has developed from the childhood identification with a parent figure to a composite of the parental figure and attractive, successful young adults.

D.15 Hill, George E., and Richard M. Hole. "Comparison of the Vocational Interests of Tenth-Grade Students with Their Parents' Judgments of These Interests," Educational and Psychological Measurement, XVIII (Spring, 1958), 173—187.
PROBLEM: "Are parents of tenth-grade students able to respond to the Kuder Preference Record in such a way as to produce interest patterns similar to those of their children" (173).
METHOD: The Kuder questionnaires was administered to 40 pairs of parents of tenth-grade students. They were instructed to attempt to match their childrens' responses.

CONCLUSIONS: 80 per cent of the parents were able to match two or three of their child's top three interests, the mothers estimating their children's interests slightly better than fathers. In general, parents tended to estimate their child's interests best in the literary, artistic, and clerical areas for girls, and in the musical, artistic, and outdoor areas for boys (183).

D.16 Himmelweit, Hilde T. "Socio-Economic Background and Personality," International Social Science Bulletin, VII (Fall, 1955), 29—35.
COMMENTS: In this study of 600 English students, ages 13—14 years old, the author found that the middle-class boys had higher aspirations than the lower-class boys; the upwardly mobile boys had stronger middle-class values than the middle-class boys; and the teachers seemed to be biased in favor of the middle-class boys.

D.17 Hurlock, Elizabeth B. "A Study of Self-Ratings by Thir-teen-Year-Old Children," Journal of Applied Psychology, XI (1927), 490—502.
PROBLEM: This study describes the results of applying a check list of desirable and undesirable character traits to a group of children to determine how they would respond to the undesirable traits.
METHOD: The Downey Group Will Temperament Test was administered to a group of 423 Negro and white boys and girls in the seventh and eighth grades of a public school in New York City.
CONCLUSIONS: The findings revealed that, not only did the thirteen-year-olds overestimate the presence of desirable traits and underestimate the presence of undesirable traits, but they also did this to a greater extent than was typical of college students.

D.18 Jones, Mary C., and N. Bayley. "Physical Maturing Among Boys as Related to Behavior," Journal of Educational Psy-chology, XLI (1950), 129—148.
PROBLEM: This study is an investigation of the relation-ship between the physical and psychological phases of de-velopment in adolescent boys.
METHOD: Two groups of sixteen boys each were examined for this study. One group was selected on the basis of retarded physical development, the other on the basis of accelerated physical development. Physical development was judged from cumulative X-rays and the Todd Standards for hand and knee.
CONCLUSIONS: It was found that the physically advanced boys held more positions of leadership in the school, were accepted by adults as more mature, and had little need to

strive for status among their peers. On the other hand, the physically retarded boys revealed more status striving and a higher degree of immature behavior. However, some of the retarded boys had achieved status in other areas and some of the advanced boys revealed characteristics which offset their presumed advantages. The authors stress the importance of the interaction of various physical, psychological, and cultural factors that influence personality formation.

D.19 Jones, Mary C., and Paul Mussen. "The Behavior-Inferred Motivations of Late and Early Maturing Boys," Child Development, XXIX (March, 1958), 61—67.
PROBLEM: This study examines the motivations for late and early maturing as inferred from behavior.
METHOD: The sample consisted of 34 subjects, 16 of whom were physically advanced. The remaining 18 were physically retarded. Interviews were held with professionals intimately known to the subjects. These judges were asked to describe what they felt were the individual's motives based in the context of a larger study on his overt behavior.
CONCLUSIONS: Significant differences between the early and late maturers was established in two of the nine questioned motives, social acceptance and aggression. In both of these areas, the late maturers were significantly higher than the early maturers. This was attributed, by the authors, to the feelings of insecurity, rejection, and dependency found in the late maturers.

D.20 Jones, Mary C., and P. H. Mussen. "Self-Conceptions, Motivations and Interpersonal Attitudes of Late and Early Maturing Boys," Child Development, XXVIII (June, 1957), 243—256.
PROBLEM: To investigate the relationship between manifested aspects of personality and physical development in late maturing adolescent boys.
METHOD: The Thematic Apperception Test was administered to a group of 33 seventeen-year-old male students. Sixteen of the subjects were advanced in physical maturity and 17 were retarded.
CONCLUSIONS: The physically retarded boys were found to have negative self-conceptions, feelings of inadequacy, feelings of rejection, and negative attitudes toward their parents. While an earlier study (D.18) indicated that the early maturers had a more favorable environment than the late maturers, this study shows that the relatively poor environment of the late maturers may have adverse effects on their personality structure.

D.21 Jones, Mary C., and P. H. Mussen. "Self-Conceptions, Motivations, and Interpersonal Attitudes of Early and Late Maturing Girls," Child Development, XXIX (December, 1958), 491—501.
PROBLEM: To see if early maturing girls reveal more negative self feelings and less satisfactory interpersonal attitudes than do late maturing girls.
METHOD: The Thematic Apperception Test was administered to a group of 34 seventeen-year-old girls. Sixteen of the subjects were advanced in physical maturity (early maturers) and eighteen were retarded (late maturers).
CONCLUSIONS: It was found that the early maturing girls: (1) had better scores on total adjustment; (2) had lower scores on negative characteristics; (3) reflected less of a desire for personal recognition than did the late maturing girls.

D.22 Kahl, Joseph A. "Educational and Occupational Aspirations of 'Common-Man' Boys," Harvard Educational Review, XXIII (Summer, 1953), 186—203.
PROBLEM: This study was concerned with investigating why only 12 of a group of 24 upper-lower class boys, were aspiring to higher educational and occupational levels.
METHOD: The sample of 24 boys to be interviewed was drawn from a larger group of 3971 boys who had been subjects in "The Mobility Project" at Harvard University.
CONCLUSIONS: In general, it was found that the "common man" boys who aspired to higher educational and occupational status came from families which were relatively unsatisfied with their position and encouraged their sons to improve themselves. Those boys who did not plan to attend college came from families which did not stress the advantages of education and did not encourage their sons to improve themselves.

D.23 Lane, Lenora C. "Self-Realization: An Exploratory Study of the Self Concept in a Group of College Students," Journal of Human Relations, LVII (spring, 1957), 106—116.
PROBLEM: To investigate the relationship between self-concept, self-realization, and religious development.
METHOD: 63 college students (30 freshmen and 33 sophomores) were asked to tell what they liked most about themselves and what they liked least.
CONCLUSIONS: In general, the best-liked characteristics were related to the self in successful relations with others. Disliked characteristics were related to poor interpersonal relations. The self was felt to be wanting when it did not meet the expectations of the culture. Interpreting awareness of cultural expectations as a concern over the "common good" and asserting that the kingdom of God is

grounded in the "common good," the author concludes
that these students are oriented toward the religious life.

D.24 Lodge, Helen C. "The Influence of the Study of Biography
on the Moral Ideology of the Adolescent at the Eighth Grade
Level," Journal of Educational Research, L (1956) 241—255.
PROBLEM: The purpose of this research was to study the
effect of a course on biography on the value system of
eighth-grade students.
METHOD: Prior to a course in biography, a group of
eighth-grade students were requested to write a paper
entitled, "The Person I Would Like to Be Like." A second
and third rewriting were requested following the course.
Interviews were also utilized.
CONCLUSIONS: Analysis revealed that the course in biography had little influence on the value system of the students. A marked influence in the relationship of personally
known adults to the students and a strong vein of realism
concerning life expectancies was found.

C.25 Miyamoto, S. Frank, and Stanford M. Dornbusch. "A Test
of Interactionist Hypotheses of Self-Conception," American
Journal of Sociology, LXI (March, 1956), 399—403.
PROBLEM: To study the influence of the response of
others in shaping self-definitions and the "response of the
other" G. H. Mead, Mind, Self and Society [Chicago: University of Chicago Press, 1934] broken down into the actual
response of the other and the subject's perception of the
response of the other.
METHOD: 195 subjects in ten groups ranging in size from
8—84 persons were asked to complete questionnaires.
CONCLUSIONS: Analysis of the data indicated that: (1)
some degree of relationship between the response of others
and self-conception; (2) a greater degree of relationship
between the subject's perception of the response of the
other and the self-concept. In general, the findings support
the interactionist hypotheses of self-conception.

D.26 Nosow, Sigmund. "Educational Values and Orientations of
College Students," Journal of Educational Research, LII
(December, 1958), 123—128.
PROBLEM: This study was based on the assumption that
college students' objectives will be reflected in their at-
titudes toward instructors, the content of the curriculum,
and other areas of the educational process.
METHOD: Analysis of a poll taken on a sample of 169
Michigan State University students who were in their first
term of Social Science.
CONCLUSIONS: It was found that socio-economic back-
ground, success in school, sex of the subject, or the sub-

jects' attitudes toward the instructor played little part in the students' attitudes toward the class. It was concluded that students were oriented more toward achievement than content (or substance). Students with favorable attitudes toward the course were less achievement-oriented than were those of unfavorable attitudes.

D.27 Pearson, Gerald H. J. Adolescence and the Conflict of Generations (New York: W. W. Norton and Co., Inc., 1958). COMMENTS: A nonempirical discussion of the development of the ego to meet new strains placed on it by the growth and maturation processes found in adolescence. The conflict of generations arises from the emerging ego development of the adolescent in interaction with an older generation that manifests a stubborn resistance to the development of his personal identity and assumption of adult roles.

D.28 Pierce, J. J. "Socio-Economic Status and Adolescent Interests," Psychological Reports, V (October, 1959), 683ff. PROBLEM: The purpose of this study was to test the hypothesis that significant relationships exist between socioeconomic status and interest behavior. METHOD: The sample consisted of 185 males and 185 females chosen at random from the eleventh-grade population in a city of 40000. This sample was given the Home Index Test and the Kuder Preference Record. Item analysis was used on the data. CONCLUSIONS: The findings tended to support the hypothesis. It was found that: (1) low socio-economic status students preferred mechanical, domestic, service, and clerical tasks; (2) high socio-economic status students preferred complex social activity, and occupations demanding high ability and offering responsbility and prestige; (3) each group tended to reject the items that the other group accepted.

D.29 Rivlin, Leanne G. "Creativity and the Self-Attitudes and Sociability of High School Students," Journal of Educational Psychology, L (August, 1959), 147—152. PROBLEM: To see if creative and noncreative high-school students of equal ability differ with regard to self-attitude and sociability. METHOD: 14 criteria of creativity were applied to 126 tenth and eleventh graders in the New York City high schools. The subjects were nominated by teachers as creative or uncreative. CONCLUSIONS: Analysis revealed that: (1) the over-all self-attitudes of the creative and noncreative students did not differ; (2) two factors, social confidence and higher

educational level of parents, were found to be associated
with creativity. The author suggests that a number of other
trait combinations might be equally conducive to creativity.

D.30 Rosen, Bernard C. "The Achievement Syndrome: A Psychocultural Dimension of Social Stratification," American
Sociological Review, XXI (April, 1956), 203—211.
PROBLEM: From the proposition that social mobility can
be explained in terms of the differing psychological motives and cultural values of the social classes, the author
hypothesizes that social strata are dissimilar with respect
to achievement motivation and value orientation.
METHOD: 120 male, white high-school students, 14—16
years old, in the New Haven area were given a Thematic
Apperception Test type projective test. The sample was
stratified by the social position of the major wage-earner
in the family.
CONCLUSIONS: The findings supported the hypothesis of
differences in value orientation and achievement motivation
between social classes. It was generally found that high
motivation scores were related to high grades but value
orientations were not. It was also found that educational
aspiration was related to value orientation but not to motivation score. The author suggests that middle-class
children are more likely to be taught both the motives
and the values that make achievement possible.

D.31 Roth, Robert M. "The Role of Self-Concept in Achievement," Journal of Experimental Education, XXVII (June,
1959), 265—281
PROBLEM: To examine the relationship between self-
concept and achievement. It was felt that the self-concepts
would vary with achievement.
METHOD: The subjects were drawn from reading improvement classes at the University of Texas. In these classes
students were repeatedly tested for improvement.
CONCLUSIONS: The findings supported the notion that
achievement or non-achievement is a function of the needs
of the student's self-concept. The improver group showed
the least general defensiveness, while the attrition group
showed the greatest amount of defensiveness. The non-
improver group fell in between the other two groups.

D.32 Schmidt, John L., and John W. Rothney. "Variability of
Vocational Choices of High School Students," Personnel and
Guidance Journal, XXXIV (November, 1955), 142—146.
PROBLEM: The purpose of this study was to examine the
consistency of vocational choice in the high school period
and its possible relation to vocational activity after high
school.

METHOD: Data for this study were drawn from the Wisconsin Counseling Study which began in 1948. For this study, a sample of 347 sophomore students were chosen at random from four Wisconsin high schools.
CONCLUSIONS: Analysis of the findings suggests that consistency is the exception while variability is the rule in vocational choice in the high-school years.

D.33 Sewell, W. H., A. O. Haller, and M. A. Straus. "Social Status and Educational and Occupational Aspiration," American Sociological Review, XXII (February, 1957), 67—73.
PROBLEM: This examination rests on the testing of a series of null hypotheses based on the general hypothesis that, when the factor of intelligence is controlled, the aspiration levels of youth, whether male or female, are associated with the social status of their families.
METHOD: Questionnaires were administered to a random sample of all nonfarm seniors in public and private high school in Wisconsin in 1947. The sample size was 4167. Of the null hypotheses, two related to males and two related to females. The second variable in the hypotheses was educational or occupational aspirations.
CONCLUSIONS: All four of the null hypotheses were rejected. This finding supports the position that values in different status positions are important influences on educational and occupational aspirations.

D.34 Simpson, Richard L., and Ida H. Simpson. "The School, the Peer Group, and Adolescent Development," Journal of Educational Sociology, XXXII (1958), 37—41.
COMMENTS: This article is a nonempirical analysis of the peer group social needs and status of the adolescent in the U.S., and the role of the school in adolescent development. The lack of well defined status position for the adolescent in the U.S. may be reflected in the adolescent's lack of an all-pervasive self-concept. The peer group, through its acceptance of the individual on personal grounds, defends him against the formal structure and the lack of status. The author feels that the school can aid the adolescent through its extracurricular activities, which serve to draw together the separate roles of "student" and "member of the peer group."

D.35 Stephenson, Richard M. "Mobility Orientation and Stratification of 1000 Ninth Graders," American Sociological Review, XXII (April, 1957), 204—212.
PROBLEM: This paper is concerned with three variables: mobility orientation, mobility resources, and mobility skill,

in the determination of social mobility within the class structure.

METHOD: Questionnaires were administered to a sample of 1000 ninth-grade students in four semi-industrial, medium-sized communities in New Jersey.

CONCLUSIONS: The findings reveal that students do make a distinction between aspirations and expectations. There was relative agreement in aspirations, but expectations varied considerably with position in the class structure. This is explained by regarding aspirations to be generally culture based while expectations are influenced more by class differences in opportunity and life chances.

D.36 Strang, Ruth. The Adolescent Views Himself (New York: McGraw-Hill Book Co., 1957).

COMMENTS: Concerning the adolescent's anxiety over educational and occupational goals the author writes in Chapter 11, "The anxiety so many adolescents feel concerning their inability to make educational and vocational choices arises from their general struggle to become psychologically independent. This anxiety is augmented by their parents' conflicts, insecurity, and unfulfilled ambitions, and by social and economic conditions which limit their choice or make it impossible for them to carry out appropriate plans. Added to these causes of anxiety are the earlier feelings of insecurity and inadequacy many adolescents bring with them into the teens."

D.37 Strang, Ruth. "Gifted Adolescents" Views of Growing Up," Exceptional Children, XXIII (October, 1956), 10—15.

PROBLEM: To obtain more information on the way in which adolescents (gifted ones in particular) perceive themseves and their world, how they feel about growing up, and to what extent their perceptions differ with I.Q.

METHOD: Data was obtained from compositions on "How it Feels to be Growing Up" written by 1124 pupils in grades 7—12 inclusive. The sample was divided into 883 students with average I.Q. of 95, and 241 students with I.Q.'s 120 or greater.

CONCLUSIONS: (1) The gifted students are more satisfied with their physical growth and social status than the average students; (2) the gifted group expressed more satisfaction with their relations with their parents; (3) fewer of the gifted students were indecisive about their vocations; (4) the gifted group was not much less concerned with scholastic success or grades than the average students; (5) an overwhelming concern for world peace was expressed by the gifted student.

D.38 Stratton, Dorothy C. "Interpretations of the Findings of the National Study of Adolescent Girls," Journal of the National

Association of Women Deans and Counselors, XXI (October, 1957), 18—20.

PROBLEM: To discuss the findings of the survey of girls' hopes, worries, relations with parents and friends, dating, plans for education, work and marriage sponsored by the National Girl Scout Organization.

METHOD: Interviews were held with 2000 girls in the age range from 11—18.

CONCLUSIONS: Among the findings, we see that: (1) while most of the girls started dating around the age of 14, only 10 per cent of the total girls "go steady" and only about 20 per cent even like the idea; (2) most of the girls felt that the rules laid down by parents were fair and necessary, but occasionally conflicts arose over clothing, dating, and hours; (3) the girls appeared to have resolved the possibly conflicting aspirations of marriage and career by a desire for a period of work followed by marriage.

D.39 Wilson, Alan B. "Residential Segregation of Social Classes and Aspirations of High School Boys," American Sociological Review, XXIV (December, 1959), 836—845.

PROBLEM: To examine the role played in the formation of aspirations by the values of membership groups.

METHOD: Questionnaire data collected from the male populations of 13 high schools in the San Francisco-Oakland Bay area.

CONCLUSIONS: It is shown that the values of the membership groups do affect the formation of aspirations and, further, that the ethics of the school affect academic achievement, political preferences, and occupational aspirations. Residential segregation of social classes in an urban area affects the climate of the school, the membership groups, and thereby influences the motivations of the child.

D.40 Youmans, E. Grand. "Social Factors in the Work Attitudes and Interests of 12th Grade Michigan Boys," Journal of Educational Sociology, XXVIII (September, 1954), 35-48.

PROBLEM: To investigate the influence of socio-economic factors on the attitudes toward work of a group of adolescent boys.

METHOD: Data were collected from questionnaire responses of a group of 1279 twelfth-grade school boys in Michigan.

CONCLUSIONS: The following hypotheses were confirmed in whole or in part: (1) Social stratification is significantly related to the differential socialization of youth in the home, in the school, and in the community. (2) The value orientations of the social strata are more important in forming work attitudes than are school work experience or type of community. (3) Actual work experience produces changes in behavior which are reflected in work attitudes. (4) The school is not successful in removing class-centered attitude differences concerning work.

E / ADOLESCENT AND THE WORLD IN WHICH HE LIVES

E.1 Aberle, David F. "Shared Values in Complex Societies," American Sociological Review, XV (August, 1950), 495—502. PROBLEM: The purpose of this article is to discuss possible approaches to the analysis of value-systems in complex societies other than searching for the most general or the most universal values. Special attention is given to the matter of the integration of subsystems with diverse values, within the total social system.
CONCLUSIONS: (1) Analysis of the various value-systems within a society should account for the necessary integration of the value-systems with one another and that every individual participates in a number of subsystems; (2) the various interactional situations involving value-systems should be studied so to ". . . see what values must be shared in each situation, and how this impinges on the value-systems shared in other situations" (502); (3) there should be a ". . . more precise formulation of role-systems and their component value-elements, and their integration with one another through certain common value-elements from one system to the next" (502).

E.2 Boyer, William H. "A Survey of the Attitudes, Opinions and Objectives of High School Students in the Milwaukee Area," Journal of Educational Sociology, XXXII (February, 1959), 344—348.
From the analysis of questionnaires administered to 569 adolescents in the Milwaukee area (69 per cent of the respondents were from the upper high-school grades) the author concludes: (1) most of these students are unaware of the critical problems of the day. The author regards this as an indication that they are generally unaware of the realities of their world; (2) most of the students felt that education is vocational preparation and are unable to realize its non-vocational values; (3) it was found that students are willing to accept the advice of their parents, especially their mothers.

E.3 Cahman, Werner J. "Attitudes of Minority Youth: A
Methodological Introduction," American Sociological Review,
XIV (August, 1949) 543—548.
PROBLEM: To discover (1) "how Jewish and Negro youth
look at themselves; (2) and how they formulate their cultural
and intercultural interests" (543).
METHOD: Interviews and questionnaires plus regular attendance at the meetings of a current events club were used
to gather information from two groups of Jewish adolescents. Two similar groups of Negro young people were
tested at an all-Negro "Y" in the neighborhood.
CONCLUSIONS: (1) In general, in terms of interest, Jews
appear as social actionists; Negroes as musical actionists.
Both groups, if confronted with the same stimulus, resort to
a different response, thus the basis for formulation of their
cultural and intercultural interests, the responses of Jews
reflecting their socially oriented interests while the responses of Negroes reflect their musically oriented interests. (2) Jewish views stress "narrowness of outlook, clan-
nishness, competitiveness, defensiveness, inhibition,
anti-Semitism of Jews, feelings of insecurity"; (3) the views
of the Negroes stress as their weak points: "drinking,
fighting, physical violence, economic jealousy, carelessness,
lack of foresight, lack of community spirit, of political organization, inferiority complex" (546).

E.4 Carroll, Rebecca E. "Relation of Social Environment to the
Moral Ideology and the Personal Aspirations of Negro Boys
and Girls," School Review, LIII (1945), 30—38.
PROBLEM: The purposes of this study were to determine
the relation of the socio-economic status of boys and girls
in a Negro community: (1) to their conception of what is
right or wrong; (2) to their ideas of the person they would
most like to resemble.
METHOD: 300 Negro adolescents were divided into two
groups (lower and middle classes). The median I.Q. for the
middle-class group was 105, while that for the lower-class
group was 95. The median age for each group was 13. Each
individual wrote an essay on "The Person I Would Most
Like to Be Like" and essay answers on their ideas on lying,
cheating, and stealing.
CONCLUSIONS: (1) middle-class adolescents tended to
choose "successful" adults while the lower-class adolescents preferred the "glamorous" adults; (2) the ideal self
of the middle-class adolescents was characterized by moral
and intellectual qualities, but the lower-class ideal self reflected personal beauty and fame; (3) in this sample, the
middle-class adolescents seemed to have a higher degree
or moral development than the lower-class individuals. In

general, this study supported the theory that the environment has a strong effect on the formation of moral and social values in adolescents.

E.5 Chapman, Ames W. "Attitudes Toward Legal Authorities by Juveniles," Sociology and Social Research, XL (1956), 170—175.
PROBLEM: The purpose of this study was to determine if the attitudes toward legal authorities differed between delinquents and nondelinquents.
METHOD: Questionnaires designed to measure these attitudes were given to a group of 160 boys between the ages of 13 and 17.
CONCLUSIONS: It was found that delinquents held more negative attitudes toward police and other legal agencies of authority than did the nondelinquents.

E.6 Dixon, Marguerite M. "Adolescent Girls Tell About Themselves," Marriage and Family Living, XX (November, 1958), 400—401.
PROBLEM: To determine the personal, social interests, and aspirations of girls, ages 11—18.
METHOD: The data was gathered by means of interviews and questionnaires from 200 girls from grades six to twelve. This is the first section of a two-part survey by the National Girl Scout Organization on the needs of the adolescent girl and how they can be met.
CONCLUSIONS: (1) Adolescent girls are under the most stress between the ages of 14 and 16 when they are beginning to make important contacts outside of their families; (2) although most of the girls started dating at age 14, the majority do not like the idea of going steady. Personality rather than physical appearance is seen as determining popularity with boys; (3) in their family relationships, most girls felt that the rules laid down by the family were fair, necessary, and helpful. Up to 14 years old, most family disagreements centered around clothes and make-up, from 14 to 16 driving and dating were the major disagreements, but after the age of 16 family conflicts were centered in ideas; (4) most of the respondents planned to work before and after marriage and preferred white-collar jobs both for themselves and their husbands.

E.7 Durkin, Delores. "Children's Concept of Justice: A Further Comparison With the Piaget Data, "Journal of Educational Research LII (March, 1959), 252—257.
PROBLEM: This study deals with children's concept of justice in a situation of physical aggression between children.
METHOD: Case histories and interviews on 119 boys and

girls from grades two, five, eight, and eleven in a large
West Coast city were examined.
CONCLUSIONS: The older children showed more concern
over possible mitigating factors in the particular situation
and tended to turn to an authority person for a judgment.

E.8 Frenkel-Brunswick, Else. "A Research Project on Ethnic
Prejudice in Children and Adolescents," Human Relations, I
(1948), 295—306.
PROBLEM: This study discussed the determinants of children's and adolescents' susceptibility to ethnic and racial
prejudice.
METHOD: Attitude and personality tests and interviews with
parents and children were utilized. The original sample of
1500 boys and girls was reduced to 120 on the basis of extremely prejudiced or lack of prejudice. Ages ranged from
11 to 16.
CONCLUSIONS: The author found a somewhat consistent
patterning of responses to statements about men and society,
which, in turn, were related to certain personality features.
The parents of the prejudiced children were found to be very
concerned with status and harsh in their discipline. The
parents of the unprejudiced children were less rigid and
more loving and understanding. The formation of prejudiced
attitudes is seen to be a function of the child's attitude toward authority as influenced by the attitudes of the parents.

E.9 Harmin, Merrill, et al. "General Characteristics of Participating Youth Groups," Journal of Educational Sociology,
XXX (October, 1956), 49—57.
COMMENTS: This volume of the Journal of Educational Sociology is devoted entirely to various discussions of the
Youth Community Participation Project at New York University. This project was concerned with ". . . studying the
achievement of freedom and significance by youth in community life" (44). This selection describes the general
characteristics of the 11 youth groups involved in the larger
study. It illustrates the importance of adult direction in
youth clubs which are desirous of relating to the larger
community. Those clubs with little direction or desire to
relate to the community as a whole seem to develop or de-
generate on different grounds than do the sponsored clubs.

E.10 Hess, Robert D., and Irene Goldblatt. "The Status of Adolescents in American Society: A Problem of Social Identity," Child Development, XXVIII (December, 1957), 459—
468.
PROBLEM: In this study the attitudes of teen-agers and
parents toward adolescents were investigated. In addition,

the relationship between the attitudes of parents and teens within the same family was investigated.

METHOD: The sample was comprised of 32 adolescents and 54 parents. A set of rating scales as well as interviews were used. The families in this sample were upper-middle and middle class in a metropolitan area.

CONCLUSIONS: It was found that: (1) while parents and adolescents express a mildly favorable opinion of teen-agers, the parents tend to feel that teens have an extremely high opinion of themselves and that teen-agers tend to undervalue adults; (2) on the other hand, adolescents feel that, while adults evaluate themselves relatively accurately, they tend to undervalue adolescents. Adolescents see a relatively greater status difference between teen-agers and adults than do the parents, but both adolescents and parents believe that the status differences between teen-agers and adults will be distorted to approximately the same extent by the other group.

E.11 Hill, David S. "Personification of Ideals by Urban Children," Journal of Social Psychology, I (1930), 379—393.

PROBLEM: The purpose of this paper is to ascertain age and sex differences in the selection of personages that are considered by youth as "ideals."

METHOD: Questionnaires were administered to 8812 white students in grades two through twelve in the public school system of Birmingham, Montgomery, and Mobile, Alabama.

CONCLUSIONS: Age and sex differences: (1) the largest number of ideals were historical and public characters. Frequency of this selection was found to increase with age; (2) the second largest number of ideals were selected (all ages combined) from the immediate environment (i.e., father, mother, teacher), but the influence of these ideals was seen to decline with age; (3) at every age, more boys than girls selected ideals from the remote environment while more girls selected ideals from the immediate environment.

E.12 Kluckhohn, Florence R. "Dominant and Variant Value Orientations," in C. Kluckhohn and H. A. Murray (eds.), Personality in Nature, Society and Culture (2nd ed. New York: Alfred A. Knopf, 1959), pp. 342—357.

COMMENTS: While the aim of this paper is the development of a conceptual scheme which will permit the ordering of cultural value orientations in a framework of common human problems, it can be interpreted as having value for the understanding of variant value orientations within a given group such as the adolescent group. Considering the role, ethnic and class differences within a society, the expression of variant values is understandable.

E.13 Kuhlen, Raymond G., and H. S. Bretsch. "Sociometric
Status and Personal Problems of Adolescents," Sociometry, X (May, 1947), 122—132.
PROBLEM: This study was a search for data on the kinds
of personal problems which characterize adolescents who
are socially unacceptable as contrasted with the problems
of those who are acceptable to their peers.
METHOD: A questionnaire incorporating the Mooney Problems Check List, Junior High Form, was administered to a
sample of 692 ninth-grade students in a city in central New
York State. The mean age of the subjects was 14.6 years.
CONCLUSIONS: The general finding was that the unaccepted children have more problems than the accepted children. The accepted group checked problems that related to
social activities and the educational and occupational future
while the unaccepted group checked problems that related
to concern over social skills, dislike of school, family
problems, unhappiness, and lack of status.

E.14 Logan, R. F. L., and E. M. Goldberg. "Rising Eighteen in
a London Suburb," British Journal of Sociology, IV (December, 1953), 323—345.
PROBLEM: To study the physical, mental, and social health
of a group of London adolescents.
METHOD: A group of 85 males (age 18) were given questionnaires, focused interviews, and physical exams in 1949.
CONCLUSIONS: (1) The chosen occupation of the son was
strongly influenced by the social class of the father; (2)
there was a striking lack of interest in constructive leisure
pursuits; (3) a great deal of family-centered emotional disturbance was found; there was little observable guilt in the
area of premarital sexual relations.

E.15 McKee, John P., and Alex C. Sheriffs. "Men's and
Women's Beliefs, Ideals, and Self-Concepts," American
Journal of Sociology, XLIV (1959), 356—363.
PROBLEM: To study aspects of the attitude and belief
system which may reflect role changes in, and disequilib-
rium between the sex groups.
METHOD: 100 single men and 100 single women at the
University of California were given Sarbin's Adjective
Check List.
CONCLUSIONS: In general, the findings show that the roles
of men and women are changing and that there is a disequi-
librium between the groups. Investigation of the content
and implications of the stereotypes of males and females
revealed: (1) women's Real Self is more sex-typed and
seen as more unfavorable than men's; (2) women's Ideal
Self is a little less sex-typed than men's; (3) women, in

describing their Ideal Man, select favorable female characteristics as often as they select favorable male characteristics. Men, however, include favorable male characteristics considerably less often in describing their Ideal Woman.

E.16 Mooney, Ross L. "Surveying High-School Students' Problems by Means of a Problem Check List," Educational Research Bulletin, XXI (March, 1942), 57-69.
PROBLEM: In this study, the author has applied the Problem Check List to one school in order to illustrate the nature and uses of the data obtainable with this instrument.
METHOD: The Problem Check List was administered to 603 students in the Stephens-Lee High School in Ashville, North Carolina.
CONCLUSIONS: In general, the findings revealed that the problems could be divided by grade level and sex in many cases. Predominant problem areas by grade level were generally as follows: (1) Freshman, more than any other class, were concerned with health problems while sophomores, to a small degree, favored problems in the classification of "social and recreational activities" and juniors led other classes in their emphasis on problems related to "adjustment to school work." Seniors were most concerned with problems in the area of "the future: vocational and educational"; (2) the girls at all grade levels led the boys in the mention of problems in the areas of "home and family" and "social-psychological relations" while the boys led the girls in the areas of "adjustment to school work" and "the future, vocational and educational."

E.17 Newcomb, Theodore M. "Community Roles in Attitude Formation," American Sociological Review, VII (October, 1942), 621—630.
PROBLEM: This study deals with individual attitude changes and the influence of the community setting. It is based on the thesis that the personality processes involved in attitude formation are closely related to the processes by which a role is assumed in reference groups which have a characteristic attitude toward a given issue.
METHOD: An attitude scale entitled "Political and Economic Progressivism" was administered to the student body of Bennington College from 1935 to 1939. The scale was constructed to emphasize issues of importance in the community.
CONCLUSIONS: Full assimilation into this college community demands the assumption of less conservative attitudes. The trend of attitude change ran from freshman conservatism to senior nonconservatism. The explanation

for the exceptions to this trend in particular and the process of attitude change and personality formation in general is felt to lie in the interaction of the individual's response to the total community (his response to membership in a community with certain approved attitudes) and the effect of membership in one or more reference groups, which may or may not be contained in and reflect the immediate community.

E.18 Pierce, J. J. "Interest Correlates of Socio-Economic Status in Adolescence," Educational and Psychological Measurement, XIX (Fall, 1959), 65—67.
PROBLEM: The purpose of this study was: (1) to construct new scales which would measure socio-economic status indirectly through teen-agers' responses to an interest inventory; (2) to see if the results of conventional interest scales were comparable to the results of the new scales and to objective socio-economic status.
METHOD: The scales were constructed from data obtained from two random samples of eleventh-grade pupils in a city of 50,000.
CONCLUSIONS: (1) The new scales were found to be reliable measures of the socio-economic status of the sample; (2) investigation revealed that interest status was positively related to I.Q., grade-point average, and literary, musical, scientific, and persuasive interests.

E.19 Pierce, J. J., J. B. Reid, and F. J. King. "Adolescent Racial and Ethnic Group Differences in Social Attitudes and Adjustment," Psychological Reports, V (October, 1959), 549—552.
PROBLEM: The hypothesis of this study was that Negro and white children with similar levels of intellectual ability differ in several important social attitudes and in certain areas of personal and social adjustment. It was felt that there would also be differences between ethnic groups.
METHOD: Data were taken from a sample of 252 adolescents (84 Negroes, 84 Latin-Americans, and 84 Anglo-Americans). This group was selected from a population of about 1600 seventh-grade pupils under study in the Human Talent Research Projects at the University of Texas.
CONCLUSIONS: (1) The only significant relationship found within racial groups was that Negro children were more negatively oriented to society; (2) feelings of social ill-ease were reported more by Latin-Americans than by Anglo-Americans or Negroes. No significant difference in the self-report of feelings of social inadequacy was found between Negroes and Anglo-Americans.

E.20 Ramsey, Charles E., and Lowry Nelson. "Change in Values and Attitudes Toward the Family," American Sociological Review, XXI (October, 1956), 605—609.

PROBLEM: Considering the increase in the divorce rate from 1939 to 1952 and the surrender of functions of the family to other institutions, the authors expect to see a change in attitudes toward the family as expressed by adolescents.

METHOD: The data for this study were taken from a study done in 1939 and replicated in 1952. The questionnaire, controlled for sex, father's occupation and residence, was administered in 1939 to 58 females and 33 males. In the 1952 replication, 71 females and 71 males received the questionnaire. All the subjects were juniors and seniors in high school.

CONCLUSIONS: With the exception that in 1952 the girls felt less obligation to the family of origin, there was no supporting evidence that there would be a change in adolescents' attitudes toward the family.

E.21 Remmers, H. H., and A. J. Drucker. "Teen-Age Attitudes Toward Problems of Child Management," Journal of Educational Psychology XLII (1951), 105—113.

PROBLEM: The purpose of this study was to assess teenagers' attitudes and behavior in the area of child management. The variability of attitudes, future orientation to the role of parent, and education for child management are among the topics discussed.

METHOD: Form A and Form B of the Stedman-Remmers Scale were administered to a sample of 1132 high-school students. The sample was stratified with respect to high-school grade, geographical region, religion, and level of parents' education. The sample was randomly selected with respect to sex, size of community, and home environment. This scale was administered to the national sample of Poll No. 24 of the Purdue Opinion Panel.

CONCLUSIONS: The findings show that girls score higher than boys on the Stedman-Remmers Scale of attitudes and that attitudes improve with age, maturation, and educational influence. The authors conclude that the high-school years are appropriate for education and training in child-management.

E.22 Remmers, H. H., and D. H. Radler. "Teenage Attitudes," Scientific American, CXCVIII (June, 1958), 25—29.

PROBLEM: In 1941, H. H. Remmers began a study of adolescents. In 1957, Remmers and Radler published The American Teenager. This book was a summary and interpretation of the findings of the first 45 polls conducted by the Purdue Opinion Panel, by Remmers formed in 1941.

This article brings the polling results up to date and discusses interpretations found in the book.

METHOD: The samples of the Purdue Opinion Panel are drawn from various high schools throughout the nation in such a way as to accurately represent all the high-school grades, the various sections of the country, and rural and urban dwellers. The results of the polls lead the authors to the conclusion that the main characteristic of adolescents in 1958 is a drive toward conformity. They note, among other things, a strong tendency to drift with the crowd, a type of passive intellectualism, and a strong drive to be liked by one's peers.

E.23 Rose, Arnold M. "Attitudes of Youth Toward Mental Health Problems," Sociology and Social Research, XLI (June, 1957), 343—348.

PROBLEM: The purpose of this paper is to compare adolescent girls' and boys' attitudes and knowledge on mental health problems.

METHOD: The original sample for the study consisted of 1400 students (the entire sophomore class) of three Minneapolis high schools. The original sample included all ethnic groups and socio-economic classes in the city. The final sample, 100 students from each school, was drawn at random from the original sample.

CONCLUSIONS: The major finding was that the girls revealed a greater knowledge and held better attitudes toward the problems of mental health than did the boys. It was hypothesized that the difference in attitudes and knowledge was a function of the generally higher scholastic performance of the girls. Since girls study more, they will have more accurate knowledge of the problem. No evidence was offered in support of this hypothesis.

E.24 Rothman, Philip. "Socio-Economic Status and Values of Junior High School Students," Journal of Educational Sociology, XXVIII (November, 1954), 126—130.

PROBLEM: This study is concerned with the relationship between the social class position and the value systems of students in the lower-middle and upper-lower classes.

METHOD: The findings are based on an investigation of a sample of 56 ninth-grade students, 28 in the lower-middle class and 28 in the upper-lower class.

CONCLUSIONS: Of the eight areas examined (purposes, feelings, attitudes, interests, beliefs, thinking, action, and aspirations), only the areas of purposes, actions, and aspirations showed a slight differentiation between classes. While the study was generally unable to show a significant relation between value differences and class differences,

175

the author felt that the slight differentiation which did exist indicated the need for the teacher to deal with the student as an individual.

E.25 Schenk, Quentin F., and A. Kimball Romney. "Some Differential Attitudes Among Adolescent Groups as Revealed by Bogardus' Social Distance Scale," Sociology and Social Research, XXXV (September—October, 1950), 38—45.
PROBLEM: This study analyzes the attitudes of four residentially homogeneous groups of adolescents regarding the effects of social isolation and ecology upon attitudes of social distance.
METHOD: The Social Distance Scale was administered to 89 adolescent boys (24 of whom were Negro), ages 12—18, who lived in three different areas of one city.
CONCLUSIONS: "The influence of differences in residential area did not show up as important as did the differences in age and race" (45).

E.26 Strang, Ruth. "Adolescents' Views on One Aspect of Their Development," Journal of Educational Psychology, XLVI (1955), 423—432.
PROBLEM: To analyze adolescents' attitudes on growing up.
METHOD: 277 adolescents were asked to write an essay on "How It Feels to Be Growing Up." These essays were then examined to determine the range of attitudes.
CONCLUSIONS: It was found that many of the statements made by the adolescents supported what is generally known about adolescent life, but some of them suggested attitudes and feelings which have not been sufficiently explored. Among these are: (1) the adolescent's satisfaction in successful completion of adolescent tasks; (2) the adolescent's recognition that freedom should be accompanied by responsibility; (3) the adolescent's eagerness to assume responsibility; (4) the adolescent's insight into adult's point of view.

E.27 Symonds, Percival M. "Sex Differences in the Life Problems and Interests of Adolescents," School and Society, XLIII (May, 1936), 751—752.
PROBLEM: This paper presents the results of a study of the more important life problems and interests of adolescents.
METHOD: Questionnaires were administered to a sample of 784 boys and 857 girls of the high schools in Tulsa, Oklahoma, and the Grover Cleveland High School in New York.
CONCLUSIONS: In the area of interests: (1) boys indicate a greater interest in safety, health, money, civic affairs,

recreation, and study; (2) girls indicate a greater interest in personal attractiveness, etiquette, and getting along with other people. In the area of problems, boys rank money as a problem more highly than do girls. Girls rank personal attractiveness and etiquette more highly as problems.

E.28 Taba, Hilda. "The Moral Beliefs of Sixteen-Year-Olds," in The Adolescent, Jerome Seidman (ed.) (New York: Holt, Rinehart and Winston, Inc., 1960), pp. 592—596.
COMMENTS: This article was taken from a cooperative study, Adolescent Character and Personality (See General Bibliography) on the character and personality of 16-year-olds in a Midwestern community. In the article the author gives us some understanding of the adolescents' code of morals with respect to qualities of friendliness, honesty, loyalty, moral courage, and responsibility. Generally, she finds that adolescents of this age group tend to rely on stereotyped slogans rather than their value judgments in the resolutions of conflicts arising in their daily experience. In other words, adolescents lack maturity in applying moral beliefs to daily experience.

E.29 Tryon, Caroline M. "Evaluations of Adolescent Personality by Adolescents," Child Behavior and Development (New York: McGraw-Hill Book Co., 1943).
PROBLEM: To investigate the factors involved in peer status maintenance in junior high school and to analyze children's notions of what are prestige-lending characteristics and behaviors.
METHOD: Two testings, six months apart, were used in this study. The average age of the first group was 12.1 while the average age of the second group was 14.9. All of the children attended public schools in Oakland, California. About three-fourth of the subjects were common to both testings (260 out of 350).
CONCLUSIONS: (1) twelve-year-old boys: children of this age emphasized, in general, aggressiveness, boisterousness, and competence in group games as important characteristics in boys; (2) fifteen-year-old boys: in this group, generalized activity had lost its appeal as a prestige factor and skill in games, self assertion, social ease, and poise in heterosexual relations are important prestige factors; (3) twelve-year-old girls: in this group, prestige attributes include such items as attractive appearance, friendly social manner, good sense of humor, and controlled behavior conforming to adult standards; (4) fifteen-year-old girls: two channels of prestige are noted for this group: light-hearted good-fellowship with both boys and girls, and glamorous qualities appealing to the boys.

In the younger group, the differences between boys and girls lie in the areas of aggressive and generalized behavior. In the older group, the boys feel that attractiveness to the opposite sex includes the approval of other boys while the girls at this age feel that attractiveness is independent of their relations with other girls.

E.30 Turner, Ralph H. "Moral Judgment: A Study in Roles," American Sociological Review, XVII (February, 1952), 70—77.
PROBLEM: "This paper is concerned with the way in which an individual conceives his role in a situation in which a close friend has violated a moral norm" (70).
METHOD: Of 120 written projective questionnaires administered to students at the University of California, Los Angeles, 105 responses were used in the analysis. From the analysis of this data, the author formulates a typology of role-playing in the questionnaire situations.
CONCLUSIONS: "In summary, a typology of role-playing . . . has been shown to be associated in some respects with patterns of role-taking, views of the friendship relation, and the individual's view of the norm. There is some suggestion of personality types reflected in the roles, including individuals who feel personally implicated in the misdeeds of others, individuals with high ' social responsibility' orientation, and moralistic individuals with high personal loyalty" (76).

E.31 Whitlow, C. M. "Attitudes and Behavior of High School Students," American Journal of Sociology, XL (January, 1935), 489—494.
PROBLEM: This study is an attempt to discuss moral attitudes and ethical behavior of high-school students on the basis of data gathered directly from them.
METHOD: Questionnaires were administered to a sample of 603 male and female students in a six-year high school. The questionnaire was concerned with potential offenses. The subjects were asked to select, from the 26 items listed, the five worst and the five most committed offenses.
CONCLUSIONS: From the analysis of the responses the author concludes that the school has little or no direct influence upon the formation of ethics or conduct. A hypothetical "typical student" extrapolated from the data (1) believes that stealing, drinking, and lying, in that order, are the worst offenses, but he most frequently commits the offenses of swearing, disobedience, and lying; (2) has never failed a grade, is affiliated with some church, never drinks, and has little patience with a "flunker." Girls were found to be more consistent than boys in relating attitudes to behavior.

F / ADOLESCENT AND
DEVIANT BEHAVIOR

F.1 Benedict, Ruth. "Continuities and Discontinuities in Cultural Conditioning," Psychiatry, I (1938), 161—167.
COMMENTS: In this discussion of the interrelationships between biological factors, group membership, and role as determinants of personality, the author contends that maladjustment and personality upheavals may be, in part, due to the discontinuities in the society's cultural conditioning. She notes that many primitive societies assume the presence of strain in the shift of roles and the physiological changes inherent in the transition from childhood to adulthood. These societies minimize the disruptive influences of such changes by the use of specifically defined age groups (secret groups) and ceremonies that serve to support the individual and define the situation. In our society, with no well defined and supported period of transition, the shift from childhood to adulthood may easily produce anxiety that is expressed in the fixation of personality development at an earlier stage.

F.2 Davids, A., and A. N. Parenti. "Personality, Social Choice and Adults' Perception of These Factors in Groups of Disturbed and Normal Children," Sociometry, XXI (1958), 212—224.
PROBLEM: To examine the sociometric patterns of normal and disturbed groups in order to describe the similarities and differences in group structure.
METHOD: Sociometric investigation of three mixed groups: (1) 48 emotionally disturbed children at Bradley Hospital, Riverside, R.I.; (2) 80 normal children at a summer camp in Kingston, N.Y.; (3) 57 normal children attending public school in East Providence, R.I.
CONCLUSIONS: In both groups social popularity was found to be associated with good emotional adjustment, possession of positive personality traits, and absence of negative personality traits. In the disturbed group, the disliked tended to be more disturbed than were the ignored.

F.3 Demerath, N. J. "Adolescent Status Demands and the Student Experiences of Twenty Schizophrenics," American Sociological Review, VIII (October, 1943), 513—518.
PROBLEM: To investigate the hypothesis that successful adjustment to adult demands depends greatly on the individual's participation in the informal group life of adolescence.

METHOD: Investigation of the case histories of ten male and ten female white, native born, Protestants who were hospitalized for schizophrenia.

CONCLUSIONS: Investigation of the case history material revealed that the twenty subjects had little participation in the informal life of their age mates and seemed to be precocious adults in their desire to conform to adult standards. It was found also that the subjects' experiences as students were not essentially different from the experiences of many nonpsychotics.

F.4 Fromm, Erich. "Individual and Social Origins of Neurosis," American Sociological Review, IX (August, 1944), 380—384.

PROBLEM: To discuss the concern of the psychoanalyst: Beyond the readjustment of the individual, the psychoanalyst must be aware that the individual's ideal of normalcy may work against readjustment.

METHOD: Theoretical discussion.

CONCLUSIONS: One of the points made in this discussion is that the crux of neurosis often lies in the defeat of the individual will in its struggle against authority; contributing to the breakdown of the individual will is the cultural stigma attached to sex rather than the child's own specific incestuous wish.

F.5 Furfey, Paul H. "The Group Life of the Adolescent," Journal of Educational Sociology, XIV (December, 1940), 195–204.

PROBLEM: To point out a general trend in research on the adolescent.

METHOD: Discussion, using secondary sources, of delinquent behavior in terms of cultural behavior patterns. Delinquency patterns in Chicago are used to illustrate the discussion. No sample.

CONCLUSIONS: The authors point out that there is a tendency to study group behavior more in terms of the cultural behavior patterns of the group and less in terms of the individual. The adolescent is being studied more as a member of a group than as an individual.

F.6 Gibbons, Don C., and Manzer J. Griswold. "Sex Differentials Among Juvenile Court Referrals," Sociology and Social Research, XLII (November—December, 1957), 106—110.

PROBLEM: To determine sex differentials in delinquency.

METHOD: Data was based on records from 35 counties in the state of Washington and concerned with children referred to the juvenile courts between 1953 and 1955. Over 18,000 cases were examined. Ratio of males to females was approximately 3.5 to 1; 7 per cent of the cases were nonwhite.

CONCLUSIONS: (1) Female cases were more likely to be nonwhite than were male cases. (2) Most female cases involved running away from home. (3) More girls than boys were either from broken homes or were out of school. (4) More girls than boys were committed if their cases were not dismissed.

F. 7 Gough, Harrison G. "A Sociological Theory of Psychopathy," American Journal of Sociology, LIII (March, 1948), 359—366.
PROBLEM: A sociological approach to the concept of the psychopathic personality.
METHOD: Theoretical discussion; no empirical data.
CONCLUSIONS: The author contends that the sociological concept of role-playing is of particular importance in the diagnosis of psychopathy and that role-playing inability is a more valuable diagnostic element than social maladjustment.

F.8 Kobrin, Solomon. "The Conflict of Values in Delinquency Areas," American Sociological Review, XVI (October, 1951), 653—661.
PROBLEM: To discuss delinquency as the result of personality or psychological processes rather than as the result of cultural processes.
METHOD: Discussion of existing statistical data and secondary sources.
CONCLUSIONS: The author feels that available statistics support the proposition that urban areas with high delinquency rates manifest a duality of conduct norms rather than a dominant conventional or delinquent culture. This conflict of values is useful in explaining the variability of boys' behavior in delinquent areas and in formulating a model of delinquency areas based on the interaction of opposing value schemes.

F.9 Levy, John. "The Impact of Cultural Forms Upon Children's Behavior," Mental Hygiene, XVI (April, 1932), 208—221.
PROBLEM: To discuss the hypothesis that the specific society into which a child is born has an influence on the specific conflicts and disturbances the child will face.
METHOD: Nonstatistical discussion of the problem.
CONCLUSIONS: The sources of conflict in childhood arise both from the conscious instruction of the social group in the form of discipline and from the unconscious emotional stress placed on the child by his culture. Since inherently the training of the child induces conflicts of authority and the structure of family life, sex codes, and religious beliefs and the conflicts within them influence his emotional development, the author feels that problem children are, in part, a product of our social organization.

F.10 Lexton, Donald A. "A Study of the Validity of Parent Attitude Measurement," Child Development, LVIII (December,
1958), 515—520.
PROBLEM: To determine if there are differences between
the attitudes of parents of problem children and the attitudes of parents of nonproblem children toward their
respective children.
METHOD: Twenty pairs of parents of children from each
grade of two Los Angeles grade schools were given the
Shoben Parent Attitude Survey and the Minnesota Teachers
Attitude inventory.
CONCLUSIONS; The author found: (1) a significant similarity between mother's and father's attitudes toward
children within a given family, (2) no significant difference
between scores of parents whose children had excellent
adjustment ratings and of parents whose children had poor
adjustment ratings, and (3) a wider disagreement between
parents and poorly adjusted children than between parents
of well adjusted children.

F.11 Mayo, Elton. "Psychiatry and Sociology in Relation to
Social Disorganization," American Journal of Sociology,
LXII (May, 1937), 825—831.
PROBLEM: To relate sociology and psychiatry to each
other in the field of social disorganization.
METHOD: Discussion of problem with reference to secondary sources.
CONCLUSIONS: "In adolescence the insufficiently conditioned individual may develop perverse or promiscuous
practices, or, if he endeavors to repress such a tendency
and to live like more normal persons, he will instantly
develop psychoneurotic symptoms. The psychoneurosis
is the negative of the perversion. It is not the repression
of a normal sexual impulse that leads to psychoneurosis,
but the attempt to impose a normal expression upon an abnormal attitude" (828).

F.12 Miller, Derek H. "Family Interaction in the Therapy of
Adolescent Patients," Psychiatry, XXI (August, 1958),
277—284.
PROBLEM: To describe the steps taken to minimize potentially disturbing family interactions in hospitalized adolescents.
METHOD: Analysis of the case histories of 25 male and
female adolescents under two-year treatment at Menninger
Memorial Hospital.
CONCLUSIONS: Since each of the patients was in the hospital as a result of the apparently destructive or unhealthy
interaction with his family, further contact was strictly
controlled until the precise nature of the relationship was

established. As the patient progressed to the point where
he could handle the contact, increased interaction was per-
mitted and encouraged.

F.13 Olson, V. J., F. I. Nye, and J. F. Short. "Socio-Economic
Status and Delinquent Behavior," American Journal of
Sociology, LXII (January, 1958), 381—389.
PROBLEM: To see if a measure of reported delinquency
as opposed to official records would show delinquency to be
more prevalent in the lower classes. It was also felt that
there would be no difference in delinquency rates between
boys and girls at the various socio-economic levels.
METHOD: Questionnaires were administered to 2350 boys
and girls in three Western communities and to 250 boys and
265 girls in three Midwestern communities.
CONCLUSIONS: The study found: (1) no significant difference in delinquency rate of boys and girls at the same
socio-economic level; (2) when status was held constant
by two independent measures, no significant relation between status and delinquency was found.

F.14 Philip, B. R., and H. E. Peirotto. "An Objective Evaluation
of Brief Group Psychotherapy on Delinquent Boys," Canadian Journal of Psychology, XIII (December, 1959), 273—280.
PROBLEM: To see if projective tests would be more easily
applicable to delinquent boys than questionnaire tests (of
which they are often suspicious).
METHOD: A sample of 86 delinquent boys, 14 to 16 years
old, committed for minor misdemeanors to St. John's
Training School, Uxbridge, Ontario, was divided into eight
groups: four control and four experimental. The experimental groups received the projective tests and were expected to show a reduction of hostility.
CONCLUSIONS: Reduction of hostility in the experimental
group reached the 5 per cent level of confidence and the
hypothesis was supported. Changes in four other variables
were noted but did not reach an accepted level of significance.

F.15 Polk, Kenneth. "Juvenile Delinquency and Social Areas,"
Social Problems, V (1957), 214—217.
PROBLEM: To see if delinquency rates varied between
census tracts (where tracts reflected differences in exhibited culture).
METHOD: Study done in San Diego, California, within the
framework of social area analysis. Group behavior comparison of all delinquency in census tracts was based on
economic status, family status, and ethnic status.
CONCLUSIONS: (1) Areas of low economic status, low
family status, and high ethnic status reflected the highest

rates of delinquency; (2) with family status and ethnic status held constant, no evidence could be found to show that the rate of delinquency was based on a class system. This also held true for ethnic and family status when the two other variables were held constant.

F.16 Reckless, W. C., S. Dinitz, and E. Murray. "Self-Concept as an Insulator Against Delinquency," American Sociological Review, XXI (December, 1956), 744—746.
PROBLEM: In a high delinquency rate area in Columbus, Ohio, what insulates some early teen-age boys against delinquency?
METHOD: 125 boys, evaluated by teachers as "good," were given a series of four self-administered scales.
CONCLUSIONS: "Insulation against delinquency on the part of these boys may be viewed as an outgoing process reflecting an internalization of non-delinquent values and conformity to the expectations of significant others" (746). Their continued "goodness" will depend on their ability to maintain their present self-image.

F.17 Reeves, J. M., and L. Goldman. "Social Class Perceptions and School Maladjustment" Personnel and Guidance Journal, XXXV (March, 1957), 414—419.
PROBLEM: To examine the internal and external definitions of social class and to explore whether possible discrepancies between them may be factors in school maladjustment. Close agreement of definitions was expected from the adjusted students.
METHOD: Three questionnaires were administered to a sample of 385 students in the ninth through the twelfth grades of a high school in western New York. All social classes were represented.
CONCLUSIONS: The findings offered some support for the proposition that maladjustment is associated with discrepancies between internal and external measures of social class level.

F.18 Reiss, Albert J., Jr. "Social Correlates of Psychological Types of Delinquency," American Sociological Review, XVII (December, 1952), 710—718.
PROBLEM: To attempt to isolate social correlates of psychological types, which may operate in the formation of personal controls of delinquents.
METHOD: Discussion of problem with reference to published materials and documents. No sample.
CONCLUSIONS: Three psychological types and a series of associations for these types were isolated. The three types were: (1) delinquents of relatively integrated personality, (2) the delinquent with markedly weak ego controls; and (3) those with relatively weak super-ego controls.

F.19 Robin, Lee N., and P. O'Neal. "The Marital History of Former Problem Children," Social Problems, V (Spring, 1958), 347—357.
PROBLEM: To test the hypothesis that socially disapproved marital history is related to socially disapproved premarital history.
METHOD: Interviews were obtained from 524 consecutive patients of the St. Louis Municipal Psychiatric Clinic located after 30 years.
CONCLUSIONS: (1) Religious background was found to be less important than early behavior problems in predicting divorce. (2) Broken homes were found to be less related to divorce in later life than the fact that the patients had been problem children.

F.20 Stolz, H. R., and L. M. Stolz. "Adolescent Problems Related to Somatic Variations," Forty-third Yearbook of the National Society for the Study of Education, Pt. 1 (1944) (University of Chicago Press), pp. 81—99.
PROBLEM: To attempt to analyze some of the somatic conditions that may be involved as causes and/or effects of adjustment problems which adolescents face.
METHOD: Discussion of the problem with reference to secondary sources and personal knowledge as physician and educator. No sample.
CONCLUSIONS: The authors conclude that in matters of individual guidance an adjustment problem exists only where the individual recognizes the existence of the problem. It is up to the guidance counselor to determine the significance of actual or imagined somatic conditions.

F.21 Vold, George B. "Discussion of Solomon Kobrin's Paper 'The Conflict of Values in Delinquency Areas,' " American Sociological Review, XVI (October, 1951), 671—672.
PROBLEM: To discuss the above-mentioned hypothesis of simultaneous existence in delinquency areas of two conflicting value systems and its implications for delinquency theory.
METHOD: Discussion.
CONCLUSIONS: Vold supports Kobrin's hypothesis but feels that the significant theoretical problem in this area is determining why a person identifies with one of these systems rather than the other. Vold feels that motivation for identification rather than existence of the systems is the critical point.

F.22 Wattenberg, William W., and James J. Balistrieri. "Gang Membership and Juvenile Misconduct," American Sociological Review, XV (December, 1950), 744—752.
PROBLEM: (1) "In a group of boys, all having police

records, those belonging to gangs would show a higher proportion coming from poorly supervised homes and from unfavorable socioeconomic conditions; (2) the differentials between gang and non-gang boys on items reflecting socioeconomic conditions and home supervision would be sharper among boys repeatedly in trouble than among those whose police records were limited to a single incident; (3) items reflecting weak home supervision and poor neighborhood conditions would be more highly predictive of repeating among gang boys than non-gang boys" (746).

METHOD: Analysis of the case histories of 5878 boys between the ages of 10 and 16 who were "interviewed on complaint" by Detroit police officers in 1946 and 1947.

CONCLUSIONS: "Those boys who belonged to gangs differed from non-gang boys in showing evidence of coming from easy-going homes and living in socioeconomically low neighborhoods. The non-gang boys gave indications of coming from tense or depriving families. In predicting repeating by these boys, socioeconomic indices had greater value in the case of gang members, and family indices in the case of non-gang boys" (752).

F.23 Witmer, Helen L. "The Influence of Parental Attitudes on the Social Adjustment of the Individual," American Sociological Review, II (October, 1937), 756—763.

PROBLEM: To discuss the parent-child relationship and its influence on the later adjustment of the individual.

METHOD: Nonstatistical analysis of case histories, interviews and secondary sources.

CONCLUSIONS: Well adjusted children are less likely to have had poor parent-child relationships than problem children, delinquents, prepsychotics, manic-depressives, and schizophrenics. The treatment of children with poor parent-child relationships is rarely successful unless parental attitudes improve.

F.24 Bloch, Herbert Aaron. The Gang (New York: Philosophical Library, 1958).

PROBLEM: To discuss the hypothesis that when society does not provide ways for the indoctrination of the adolescent members into the status of adults, forms of behavior which supply the necessary psychological reinforcement arise. In our society the formation of gangs is an attempt of adolescents to obtain support in this transitional period.

METHOD: Discussion of published material on this subject. No sample.

CONCLUSIONS: (1) From an understanding of the role of the adolescent gang, it is possible to gain understanding of the role of the adolescent in any given culture; (2) the findings indicate that the phenomenon of adolescence contains certain basic similarities in all cultures, irrespective of other cultural differences; (3) it seems expedient to regard adolescent gangs as a normal manifestation of that particular age level.

IV. General Bibliography

Abbott, M. A. "A Sampling of High-School Likes and Dislikes in Motion Pictures," Secondary Education, 6 (1937), 74—76.

Aberle, David F. "Shared Values in Complex Societies," American Sociological Review, 15 (August, 1950), 495—502. (E.1)

Abrahamson, Stephen. "Our Status System and Scholastic Rewards," Journal of Educational Sociology, 25 (April, 1952), 441—450. (B.1)

Abt, L. E., P. Mendenhall, and E. P. Partridge. "The Interests of Scouts and Non-Scouts," Journal of Educational Sociology, 14 (1940), 178—182.

"Adolescence," Forty-third Yearbook of the National Society for the study of Education, Part I (1944), University of Chicago Press, Chap. 12.

Aichorn, August. Wayward Youth (New York: Viking Press, 1938).

Alcorn, Bruce K. "Some Psychological Effects of Paternal Deprivation Upon Children from Ten to Sixteen," Journal of Educational Sociology, 35 (April, 1962), 337—345.

Allen, Philip J. "The Leadership Pattern," American Sociological Review, 17 (February, 1952), 93—96.

Altman, Esther Royal. "The Effect of Rank in Class and Size of High School on the Academic Achievement of Central Michigan College Seniors Class of 1957," Journal of Educational Research, 52 (April, 1959), 307—309.

Anastasi, A., and S. Miller. "Adolescent 'Prestige Factors' in Relation to Scholastic and Socio-Economic Variables," Journal of Social Psychology, 29 (February, 1949), 43—50. (C.1)

Anderson, C. C. "A Developmental Study of Dogmatism During Adolescence With Reference to Sex Differences," Journal of Abnormal and Social Psychology, 65 (August, 1962), 132—135.

————, and R. E. Traub. "A General Factor of Social Desirability in the High School," Educational and Psychological Measurement, 22 (Autumn, 1962), 463—472.

Anderson, Esther M. "A Study of Leisure-Time Reading of Pupils in Junior High School," Elementary School, 48 (1948), 258—267. (A.1)

Anderson, John E. "The Development of Social Behavior," American Journal of Sociology, 44 (May, 1939), 839—857.

Anderson, J. P. "A Study of the Relationships Between Certain

Aspects of Parental Behavior and Attitudes and Behavior of
Junior High School Pupils," Teachers College Contributions
to Education, No. 809, Teachers College, Columbia University (1940).

Anderson, W. A. "High-School Youth and the Values in Rural
Living," Rural Sociology, 18 (June, 1953), 156—163.

Anderson, William F., Jr. "Attitudes of University Students
Toward Cheating," Journal of Educational Research, 50
(April, 1957), 581—588.

Andrews, Robert O., and Harold T. Christensen. "Relationship
of Absence of a Parent to Courtship Status: A Repeat
Study," American Sociological Review, 16 (August, 1951),
541—545.

Angelino, Henry, Lenorah A. Barnes, and Charles L. Shedd.
"Attitudes of Mothers and Adolescent Daughters Concerning Clothing and Grooming," Journal of Home Economics,
48 (December, 1956), 779—782. (A.2)

Angell, Robert Cooley. The Campus: A Study of Contemporary
Undergraduate Life in the American University (New York:
D. Appleton and Company, 1928).

Anshen, Ruth. The Family, Its Function and Destiny (New York:
Harper & Bros., 1949).

Apple, Dorrian. "Learning Theory and Socialization," American Sociological Review, 16 (February, 1951), 23—27.

Arlitt, Ada Hart. Adolescent Psychology (New York: American
Book Co., 1933).

—————. The Adolescent (New York: McGraw-Hill Book Co.,
Inc.; London: Wittlesey House, 1938).

Armstrong, David W. "The Adolescent Boy," Journal of Human
Relations, 3 (1955), 41—57.

Armstrong, Marion E. "A Comparison of the Interests and Social Adjustment of Under-Achievers and Normal Achievers
at the Secondary School Level," Dissertation Abstracts, 15
(1955), 1349.

Arsenian, Seth. "Change in Evaluative Attitudes During Four
Years of College," Journal of Applied Psychology, 27
(1943), 338—349. (B.2)

Ausubel, David P. "Prestige Motivation of Gifted Children,"
Psychological Monographs, 43 (1951), 53—117.

—————. "Reciprocity and Assumed Reciprocity of Acceptance
Among Adolescents, A Sociometric Study," Sociometry, 16
(November, 1953), 339—348.

—————. The Theory and Problems of Adolescent Development
(New York: Grune and Stratton, 1954). (C.4)

—————. "Sociempathy as a Function of Sociometric Status in
an Adolescent Group," Human Relations, 8 (Spring, 1955),
75—84. (C.3)

—————, and Herbert M. Schiff. "A Level of Aspiration Approach to the Measurement of Good Tenacity," Journal of

General Psychology, 52 (1955), 97—110. (D.1)
————, Herbert M. Schiff, and E. B. Gasser. "A Preliminary Study of Developmental Trends in Sociempathy: Accuracy of Perception of Own and Others' Sociometric Status," Child Development, 23 (1952), 111—118. (C.2)
————, Herbert M. Schiff, and H. P. Zeleny. "'Real Life' Measures of Level of Academic and Vocational Aspiration in Adolescents: Relation to Laboratory Measures and to Adjustment," Child Development, 24 (1953), 155—168. (D.2)
Averill, Lawrence Augustus. Adolescence: A Study in the Teen Years (New York: Houghton Mifflin Company, 1936).

Baer, Clyde J. "The School Progress and Adjustment of Underage and Overage Students," Journal of Educational Psychology, 49 (February, 1958), 17—19.
Bagley, Henry L. "Don't Fight Them—Educate Them!" School and Community, 46 (December, 1959), 8 ff.
Baisley, Gene. "The Hot Rod Culture," American Quarterly, 2 (1950), 353—359. (A.4)
Baker, H. L. "High-School Teachers' Knowledge of Their Pupils," School Review, 46 (1938), 175—190. (B.3)
Ball, John C. "Comparison of M.M.P.I. Profile Differences Among Negro—White Adolescents," Journal of Clinical Psychology, 16 (July, 1960), 304—307.
Balogh, K. Joseph. "Television Viewing Habits of High-School Boys," Educational Research Bulletin, 38 (1959), 66—71. (A.3)
Bancker, J. Digressive Behavior in Middle- and Lower-Class Organized Youth Groups (Unpublished Master's Thesis, University of Chicago, 1951).
Bandura, Albert. Adolescent Aggression (New York: Ronald Press Co., 1959).
Banning, Evelyn I. "Social Influences on Children and Youth," Review of Educational Research, 25 (1955), 36—47.
Barbe, Walter B. "Peer Relationships of Children of Different Intelligence Levels," School and Society, 80 (1954), 60—62. (C.5)
Bardis, Panos D. "Attitudes Toward Dating Among High School Students," Sociology and Social Research, 42 (1958), 274—277. (C.46)
————. "Attitudes Toward the Family Among College Students and Their Parents," Sociology and Social Research, 43 (May—June, 1959), 352—358.
Barker, Roger G., and Herbert F. Wright. Midwest and Its Children: The Psychological Ecology of an American Town (Evanston, Illinois: Row, Peterson and Co., n.d.; Preface is dated "June, 1954").
Barnes, Melvin W. "The Nature and Nurture of Early Adolescents," Teachers College Record, 57 (May, 1956), 513—521.

Barron, Milton L. The Juvenile in Delinquent Society (New York: Alfred A. Knopf, 1954. Especially Chapter XII).

Barry, Charles A., and Arlynne L. Jones. "A Study of the Performance of Certain Freshman Students," Journal of Educational Research, 52 (January, 1959), 163—166.

Bartlett, Claude J. "Dimensions of Leadership Behavior in Classroom Discussion Groups," Journal of Educational Psychology, 50 (December, 1959), 280—284.

————, and John E. Horrocks. "A Study of the Needs Status of Adolescents from Broken Homes," Journal of Genetic Psychology, 93 (September, 1958), 153—159. (B.4)

Barwick, Janice M., and D. S. Arbuckle. "A Study of the Relationship Between Parental Acceptance and the Academic Achievement of Adolescents," Journal of Educational Research, 56 (November, 1962), 148—151.

Bassett, Raymond E. "Cliques in a Student Body of Stable Membership," Sociometry, 7 (1944), 290—302. (B.100)

Becker, Howard S. "Social-Class Variations in the Teacher-Pupil Relationship," Journal of Educational Sociology, 25 (April, 1952), 451—465. (B.5)

Bedoian, Vagarsh H. "Social Acceptability and Social Rejection of the Underage, at Age and Overage Pupils in the Sixth Grade," Journal of Educational Research, 47 (March, 1954), 513—520.

Beilin, Harry, and Emmy Werner. "Sex Role Expectations and Criteria of Social Adjustment for Young Adults," Journal of Clinical Psychology, 13 (1957), 341—343.

Bell, Earl H. "Age Group Conflicts and Our Changing Culture," Social Forces, 13 (December, 1933), 237—243.

Bell, G. B., and H. E. Hall. "The Relationship Between Leadership and Empathy," Journal of Abnormal and Social Psychology, 49 (1954), 156—157.

Bell, Howard M. Youth Tell Their Story (Washington, D.C.: American Council on Education, 1938).

Bell, Robert R. "The Adolescent Subculture," Education, 81 (March, 1961), 427—429.

Bellingrath, G. C. "Qualities Associated with Leadership in the Extra-Curricular Activities of the High-School," Teachers College Contributions to Education, No. 399, Teachers College, Columbia University (1930).

Benedict, Ruth. "Continuities and Discontinuities in Cultural Conditioning," Psychiatry, 1 (1938), 161—167. (F.1)

————. "Transmitting Our Democratic Heritage in the Schools," American Journal of Sociology, 48 (May, 1943), 722—727. (B.6)

Benson, Leonard G. "Family Social Status and Parental Authority Evaluations Among Adolescents," Southwestern Social Science Quarterly, 36 (June, 1955), 46—54.

Berdie, Ralph F. "Skilled Manpower from the High Schools,"

School and Society, 86 (January 4, 1958), 8—9.

Bereiter, Carl. "Verbal and Ideational Fluency in Superior Tenth Grade Students," Journal of Educational Psychology, 51 (December, 1960), 337—345.

Berg, Irwin A. "Expressed Standards of High-School Students, Teachers, and Parents," Personnel and Guidance Journal, 34 (1956), 261—267. (B.7)

Bernard, Harold W. Adolescent Development in American Culture (Yonkers, New York: World Book Co., 1957).

Bernard, Jessie. "The Neighborhood Behavior of School Children in Relation to Age and Socioeconomic Status," American Sociological Review, 4 (October, 1939), 652—662. (B.8)

Bernard, William S. "Student Attitudes on Marriage and the Family," American Sociological Review, 3 (June, 1938), 354—361.

Bernstein, Alvin J. "Absence of Primary Interest Patterns in Adolescent Boys," Dissertation Abstracts, 14 (1954), 181—182.

Berry, Elizabeth. "About Teaching Writing in High School," School and Community, 45 (January, 1959), 12—13.

Bertrand, Alvin L. "School Attendance and Attainment: Function and Dysfunction of School and Family Social Systems," Social Forces, 40 (March, 1962), 228—233.

Best, Elise Sebille. "Johnny Enters High School," Education, 79 (November, 1958), 157—158.

Bettelheim, Bruno. Truants From Life: Rehabilitation of Emotionally Disturbed Children (New York: The Free Press of Glencoe, 1955).

————. Love Is Not Enough: The Treatment of Emotionally Disturbed Children (New York: The Free Press of Glencoe, 1959).

Biddulph, Lowell G. "Athletic Achievement and the Personal and Social Adjustment of High School Boys," Research Q Quarterly of the American Association for Health, Physical Education, and Recreation, 25 (1954), 1—7. (B.9)

Birney, Robert C., and Marc J. Taylor. "Scholastic Behavior and Orientation to College," Journal of Educational Psychology, 50 (December, 1959), 266—274.

Bishton, Rodger. "A Study of Some Factors Related to Achievement of Intellectually Superior Eighth-Grade Children," Journal of Educational Research, 51 (November, 1957), 203—207.

Blanchard, Phyllis. The Child and Society: An Introduction to the Social Psychology of the Child (New York: Longmans, Green and Co., 1928).

Bleckner, Janet E. "The Responses of Average and Gifted Students on the Group Rorschach," California Journal of Educational Research, 10 (November, 1959), 200—206.

Bledsoe, Joseph C. "An Investigation of Six Correlates of Stu-

dent Withdrawal from High School," Journal of Educational
Research, 53 (September, 1959), 3—6. (B.10)
Bloch, Herbert A. The Gang (New York: Philosophical Library,
1958). (F.24)
Blocksma, Douglas D. "The Adolescent: His Characteristics,"
Review of Educational Research, 24 (February, 1954), 11—
18.
Blodgett, H. E. An Experimental Approach to the Measurement
of Self-Evaluation Among Adolescent Girls (Unpublished
Doctoral Dissertation, University of Minnesota, 1953).
Blood, Robert O., Jr. "A Retest of Waller's Rating Complex,"
Marriage and Family Living, 17 (February, 1955), 41—47.
———. "Uniformities and Diversities in Campus Dating Pref-
erences," Marriage and Family Living, 18 (February,
1956), 46—51.
Blos, Peter. The Adolescent Personality: A Study of Individual
Behavior for the Commission on Secondary School Curricu-
lum (New York: D. Appleton-Century Co., 1941).
———. On Adolescence: A Psychoanalytic Interpretation (New
York: The Free Press of Glencoe, 1962).
Bock, Elmer W., and L. G. Burchinal. "Social Status, Hetero-
sexual Relations and Expected Ages of Marriage," Journal
of Genetic Psychology, 101 (September, 1962), 43—51.
Boehm, Leonore. "The Development of Independence: A Com-
parative Study," Child Development, 28 (1957), 85—92.
(B.11)
Bogardus, Ruth, and Phyllis Otto. "The Social Psychology of
Youth," Sociology and Social Research, 20 (1936), 260—270.
(C.6)
Bonney, Merle E. "Sociometric Study of Agreement Between
Teacher Judgements and Student Choices, in Regard to the
Number of Friends Possessed by High School Students,"
Sociometry, 10 (May, 1947), 133—146. (B.12)
———. "Popular and Unpopular Children, A Sociometric
Study," Sociometric Monographs, No. 9 (Beacon House,
1947). (C.7)
Bonsall, Marcella R. "Reactions of Gifted High School Pupils
to Elementary Education," California Journal of Educational
Research, 6 (May, 1955), 107—109.
———. "Introspections of Gifted Children," California Journal
of Educational Research, 11 (September, 1960), 159—166.
———, and B. Stefflre. "The Temperament of Gifted Chil-
dren," California Journal of Educational Research, 6 (September, 1955), 162—165.
Bordin, Edward S. "A Theory of Vocational Interests as a Dynamic Phenomena," Educational and Psychological Measurement, 3 (1943), 49—65. (D.3)
Bossard, James H. S. The Sociology of Child Development (New
York: Harper and Bros., 1948. Especially Part VI, Chapter
XXI). (C.8)

————, and Eleanor S. Boll (eds.). Adolescents in Wartime (Philadelphia: American Academy of Political and Social Science, 1944).

————, and Eleanor S. Boll. "The Role of the Guest: A Study in Child Development," American Sociological Review, 12 (April, 1947), 192—201.

Bowman, Howard A. "Differences in Academic Achievement Between Pupils Who Left and Pupils Who Entered Los Angeles High Schools, 1948-50," California Journal of Educational Research, 3 (November, 1952), 216—223.

Bowman, P. H., and M. Pellman. "Socially Underprivileged Youth and the Schools," High School Journal, 41 (May, 1958), 331—335. (B.13)

Boyer, William H. "A Survey of the Attitudes, Opinions and Objectives of High School Students in the Milwaukee Area," Journal of Educational Sociology, 32 (February, 1959), 344—348. (E.2)

Bretsch, Howard S. "Social Skills and Activities of Socially Accepted and Unaccepted Adolescents," Journal of Educational Psychology, 43 (December, 1952), 449—458. (C.9)

Brim, Orville G., Jr. "Family Structure and Sex Role Learning by Children: A Further Analysis of Helen Koch's Data," Sociometry, 21 (1958), 1—16.

————, and R. Forer. "A Note on the Relation of Values and Social Structure to Life Planning," Sociometry, 19 (January, 1956), 54—60.

Broderick, Carlfred B., and Stanley E. Fowler. "New Patterns of Relationships Between the Sexes among Preadolescents," Marriage and Family Living, 23 (February, 1961), 27—30.

Brogan, Denis W. The American Character (New York: Alfred A. Knopf, 1944).

Bronfenbrenner, Urie. "Toward an Integrated Theory of Personality," in R. R. Blake and G. V. Ramsey, Perception: An Approach to Personality (New York: Ronald Press, 1951), pp. 206—257.

Brookover, Wilbur. "The Social Roles of Teachers and Pupil Achievement," American Sociological Review, 8 (August, 1943), 389—393.

Brown, James C. "An Experiment in Role-Taking," American Sociological Review, 17 (October, 1952), 587—597. (D.4)

Brown, Willis C. "What About Extra-Class Activities?" Education, 78 (October, 1957), 94—99.

Buchner, Leonard J. "Personality Repair Through Reading Improvement," Education, 78 (October, 1957), 107—113.

Burchinal, Lee G. "Social Status, Measured Intelligence Achievement, and Personality Adjustment of Rural Iowa Girls," Sociometry, 22 (1959), 75—80.

————. "Adolescent Role Deprivation and High-School Age Marriage," Marriage and Family Living, 21 (November, 1959), 378—384. (B.14)

————. "Differences in Educational and Occupational Aspirations of Farm, Small Town, and City Boys," Rural Sociology, 26 (June, 1961), 107—121.

————, Glenn R. Hawkes, and Bruce Gardner. "Adjustment Characteristics of Rural and Urban Children," American Sociological Review, 21 (February, 1957), 81—87.

Burgess, Ernest W. "The Family as a Unity of Interacting Personalities," The Family, 7 (March, 1926), 1—9.

————, and Harvey J. Locke. "Comment on Lowrie's 'Dating Theories and Student Responses'" (letter to the Editor), American Sociological Review, 16 (December, 1951), 843—844.

Burks, Frances. The Adolescent in Social Groups (Stanford, California: Stanford University Press, 1946).

Burma, John H. "Self-Tattooing Among Delinquents," Sociology and Social Research, 43 (May, 1959), 341—345. (A.5)

Butler, Broadus N. "High School Students and College Credit," School and Society, 87 (December 5, 1959), 499—500.

Butler, Ruth M. "Mothers' Attitudes Toward the Social Development of Their Adolescents," Part I, Social Casework, 37 (1956), 219—226. (B.15)

————. "Mothers' Attitudes Toward the Social Development of Their Adolescents," Part II, Social Casework, 37 (1956), 280—288. (B.16)

Butterfield, O. M. "Love Problems of Adolescence," Teachers College Contributions to Education, No. 768, Teachers College, Columbia University (1939).

Byers, Joe L. "A Study of the Level of Aspiration of Academically Successful and Unsuccessful High School Students," California Journal of Educational Research, 13 (November, 1962), 209—216.

Cahman, Werner J. "Attitudes of Minority Youth: A Methodological Introduction," American Sociological Review, 14 (August, 1949), 543—548. (E.3)

Callender, Wesley P., Jr. "Thoughts With Expression—The Values of Debate in Schools," Education, 78 (October, 1957), 117—120.

Calvin, A. D., P. B. Koons, Jr., S. L. Fingham, and H. H. Fink. "A Further Investigation of the Relationship Between Manifest Anxiety and Intelligence," Journal of Consulting Psychology, 19 (1955), 280—282. (B.17)

Cameron, M. Y. "An Enquiry into the Factors Governing Membership of Youth Clubs and Juvenile Organizations," British Journal of Educational Psychology, 18 (February, 1948), 48—52. (B.101)

Cameron, W. Jaffray. "A Study of Early Adolescent Personality," Progressive Education, 25 (November, 1938), 553—563. (C.10)

Cannon, Kenneth L. "Stability of Sociometric Scores of High School Students," Journal of Educational Research, 52 (October, 1958), 43—48.

——, R. Staplos, and H. Carlson. "Personal Appearance as a Function in Social Acceptance," Journal of Home Economics, 44 (1952), 710—713.

Caravello, S. J. "The Drop-Out Problem," High School Journal, 41 (May, 1958), 335—340.

Carroll, Rebecca E. "Relation of Social Environment to the Moral Ideology and the Personal Aspirations of Negro Boys and Girls," School Review, 53 (1945), 30—38. (E.4)

Cassel, Russel N., and Robert Brauckle. "Level of Aspiration and Ego-Strength Comparisons for Student Council Members and a Matched Group of Students from a Select High School in South Texas," High School Journal, 42 (October, 1958), 29—32.

——, and B. Lynn Harriman. "A Comparative Analysis of Personality and Ego-Strength Test Scores for In-Prison, Neuro-Psychiatric and Typical Individuals," Journal of Educational Research, 53 (October, 1959), 43—52.

——, and R. A. Sanders. "A Comparative Analysis of Scores from Two Leadership Tests for Apache Indian and Anglo American Youth," Journal of Educational Research, 55 (September, 1961), 19—23.

Cava, Esther L., and H. L. Raush. "Identification and the Adolescent Boy's Perception of His Father," Journal of Abnormal and Social Psychology, 47 (1952), 855—856. (B.18)

Cavan, Ruth Shonle. "The Relation of Home Background and Social Relations to Personality Adjustment," American Journal of Sociology, 40 (September, 1934), 143—154. (B.19)

Centers, Richard. "Children of the New Deal: Social Stratification and Adolescent Attitudes," International Journal of Opinion Attitude Research, 4 (1950), 315—335. (D.5)

——. "Social Class Identification of American Youth," Journal of Personality, 18 (1950), 290—302. (C.11)

Chapin, F. S. "Sociometric Stars as Isolates," American Journal of Sociology, 56 (1950), 263—267.

Chapman, Ames W. "Attitudes Toward Legal Authorities by Juveniles," Sociology and Social Research, 40 (1956), 170—175. (E.5)

Chapman, Dwight W., and John Volkmann. "A Social Determinant of the Level of Aspiration," in E. E. Maccoby, T. M. Newcomb, and E. L. Hartley (eds.), Readings in Social Psychology (New York: Henry Holt and Co., 1958), pp. 281—290. (D.6)

Christensen, Harold T. "Dating Behavior as Evaluated by High-School Students," American Journal of Sociology, 57 (May, 1952), 580—586. (C.12)

Christian, Charles O. "Student Council in Action," School and Community, 45 (November, 1958), 19—20.

Clark, Willis W. "Sex Differences in Mental Abilities Among Students of High Intelligence," California Journal of Educational Research, 5 (March, 1954), 90—93.

Clausen, John A., and Melvin L. Kohn. "The Ecological Approach in Social Psychiatry," American Journal of Sociology, 60 (September, 1954), 140—149.

Cliffe, Marian C. "Reactions of Recent High School Graduates with Implications for Guidance," California Journal of Educational Research, 2 (November, 1951), 223—226.

Cline, E. C. "Social Implications of Modern Adolescent Problems," School Review, 49 (1941), 511—514.

Cobb, Henry V. "Role-Wishes and General Wishes of Children and Adolescents," Child Development, 25 (September, 1954), 161—172.

Coffin, Thomas E. "Television's Effect on Leisure-Time Activities," Journal of Applied Psychology, 32 (1949), 550—558. (A.6)

Cohen, Albert K. Delinquent Boys: The Culture of the Gang (New York: The Free Press of Glencoe, 1955).

Cohen, Eli E., and Lila Rosenblum. "Are Jobs the Answer to Delinquency?" School and Society, 86 (May 10, 1958), 215—216.

Cole, Luella W., and Irma Nelson Hall. Psychology of Adolescence (5th Ed. New York: Rinehart and Co., 1959).

Coleman, James S. "The Adolescent Subculture and Academic Achievement," American Journal of Sociology, 65 (January, 1960), 337—347. (B.20)

————. The Adolescent Society (New York: The Free Press of Glencoe, 1961).

"College Success May Depend on School Student Attended," School and Community, 46 (December, 1959), 20.

Collier, R. M., and H. P. Lawrence. "The Adolescent Feeling of Psychological Isolation," Educational Theory, 1 (1951), 106—115.

Connor, Ruth, Theodore B. Johannes, Jr., and James Walters. "Parent-Adolescent Relationships," Journal of Home Economics, 46 (March, 1954), 183—186.

Consumer Reports. "Teen-Age Consumer," Consumer Reports, 22 (March, 1957), 139—142. (A.7)

Cook, Edward S., Jr. "An Analysis of Factors Related to Withdrawal from High School Prior to Graduation," Journal of Educational Research, 50 (November, 1956), 191—196. (B.21)

Cook, Lloyd A. "An Experimental Sociographic Study of a Stratified Tenth Grade Class," American Sociological Review, 10 (April, 1945), 250—261. (B.22)

Cooper, Joseph B., and J. H. Lewis. "Parent Evaluation as Related to Social Ideology and Academic Achievement," Journal of Genetic Psychology, 101 (September, 1962), 135—143.

Coster, John K. "Attitudes Toward School of High School Pupils from Three Income Levels," Journal of Educational Psychology, 49 (April, 1958), 61—66.

———. "Some Characteristics of High School Pupils from Three Income Groups," Journal of Educational Psychology, 50 (April, 1959), 55—62. (B.23)

Costin, Frank. "The Effect of Child Psychology on Attitudes Toward Parent-Child Relationships," Journal of Educational Psychology, 49 (February, 1958), 37—42.

Cottrell, Leonard S., Jr. "Roles and Marital Adjustment," Publications of the American Sociological Society, 27 (1933), 107—113.

———. "The Analysis of Situational Fields in Social Psychology," American Sociological Review, 7 (June, 1942), 370—382.

———. "The Adjustment of the Individual to His Age and Sex Roles," American Sociological Review, 7 (October, 1942), 617—620. (C.13)

———. "The Present Status and Future Orientation of Research on the Family," American Sociological Review, 13 (April, 1948), 123—129.

———. "Some Neglected Problems in Social Psychology," American Sociological Review, 15 (December, 1950), 707—712.

Cowley, W. H. "Student Personnel Services in Retrospect and Prospect," School and Society, 85 (January, 1957), 19—22.

Crane, A. R. "Stereotypes of the Adult Held by Early Adolescents," Journal of Educational Research, 50 (November, 1960), 227—230.

Crawford, Paul R., Daniel I. Malamud, and James R. Dumpson. Working with Teen-Age Groups: A Report on the Central Harlem Street Clubs Project (New York: Welfare Council of New York City, 1950).

Crist, John R. "High School Dating as a Behavior System," Marriage and Family Living, 15 (1953), 23—28. (C.14)

Croft, Joyce E. "Prediction of Clothing Construction Achievement of High School Girls," Educational and Psychological Measurement, 19 (Winter, 1959), 653—655. (A.8)

Crow, Alice. "Three R's for Teenagers," High School Journal, 41 (May, 1958), 365—372.

Crow, Lester P. "The Expanding Interests of Adolescents," High School Journal, 46 (October, 1962), 23—34.

———, and Alice Crow. Adolescent Development and Adjustment (New York: McGraw-Hill Book Co., 1956).

Crowell, David H., and Arthur A. Dole. "Animism and College Students," Journal of Educational Research, 50 (January, 1957), 391—395.

Cruze, Wendell Wayne. Adolescent Psychology and Development (New York: Ronald Press Co., 1953).

Cuber, John F. "Changing Courtship and Marriage Customs," Annals of the American Academy of Political and Social Science, 229 (September, 1943), 30—38.

Cunningham, Ruth. "Understanding Group Behavior of Boys and Girls," New York Bureau of Publications, Teachers College, Columbia University (1951).

Curtin, Thomas J. "What Kind of Education Leads People to Behave as Good Citizens?" Education, 77 (February, 1957), 353—357.

Cutright, Phillip. "Students' Decision to Attend College," Journal of Educational Sociology, 33 (February, 1960), 292—299.

Cutts, Norma E., and Nicholas Moseley. "The Disorderly Underachiever," High School Journal, 42 (December, 1958), 79—83.

Daane, Calvin J., and Louis G. Schmidt. "Empathy and Personality Variables," Journal of Educational Research, 51 (October, 1957), 129—135.

Dahlke, H. Otto. Values in Culture and Classroom (New York: Harper and Bros., 1958).

Dales, Ruth J. "A Method for Measuring Developmental Tasks: Scales for Selected Tasks at the Beginning of Adolescence," Child Development, 26 (June, 1955), 111—122. (B.24)

Daly, Maureen (ed.). Profile of Youth (New York: J. B. Lippincott Company, 1951).

D'Amico, Louis A. "Characteristics of Students Admitted to Xavier University in 1951 and a Follow-Up of Their Achievement," Journal of Educational Research, 51 (January, 1958), 361—366.

Davids, A., and A. N. Parenti. "Personality, Social Choice and Adults' Perception of These Factors in Groups of Disturbed and Normal Children," Sociometry, 21 (1958), 212—224. (F.2)

Davis, A. "Socialization and Adolescent Personality," Forty-Third Yearbook of the National Society for the Study of Education, Part I (1944) (University of Chicago Press), 198—216. (B.25)

————. "Social Class and Color Differences in Child-Rearing," American Sociological Review, 11 (December, 1946), 698—710.

————. Father of the Man: How Your Child Gets His Personality (Boston: Houghton Mifflin Co., 1947).

————, and Robert Havighurst. "American Status Systems and the Socialization of the Child," American Sociological Review, 6 (June, 1941), 345—356.

Davis, Clyde B. The Age of Indiscretion (Philadelphia: J. B. Lippincott Co., 1950).

Davis, Junius A. "Returns Sought From Adult Work by Early

Adolescents in Relation to Sociometric Status Among Peers," Dissertation Abstracts, 16 (1956), 1232.

———. "Correlates of Sociometric Status Among Peers," Journal of Educational Research, 50 (April, 1957), 561—569.

Davis, Kingsley. "The Sociology of Parent-Youth Conflict," American Sociological Review, 5 (August, 1940), 523—535. (B.26)

———. "The Child and the Social Structure," Journal of Educational Sociology, 14 (December, 1940), 217—229. (B.27)

———. "Adolescence and the Social Structure," Annals of the American Academy of Political and Social Science, 235 (November, 1944), 8—16. (B.28)

Davis, O. L., Jr. "The Effect of a School Camp Experience on Friendship Choices," Journal of Educational Sociology, 33 (1960), 305—313. (C.15)

Demerath, N. J. "Adolescent Status Demands and the Student Experiences of Twenty Schizophrenics," American Sociological Review, 8 (October, 1943), 513—518. (F.3)

Demos, George D. "Attitudes of Student Ethnic Groups on Issues Related to Education," California Journal of Educational Research, 11 (November, 1960), 204—206, 224.

Dennis, Wayne. "Animistic Thinking Among College and High School Students in the Near East," Journal of Educational Psychology, 48 (April, 1957), 193—198.

———. "The Adolescent," Leonard Carmichael (ed.) in Manual of Child Psychology (New York: John Wiley and Sons, Inc., 1946), pp. 663—667.

Deno, Evelyn. "Self-Identification Among Adolescent Boys," Child Development, 24 (September—December, 1953), 269—274.

Dentler, Robert A., and L. J. Monroe. "Social Correlates of Early Adolescent Theft," American Sociological Review, 26 (October, 1961), 732—743.

Deutsch, Morton. "Discussion and Critique of Some Variables in the Social Psychology of School to College Transition," Journal of Educational Sociology, 33 (February, 1960), 300—304.

Dewey, John. Human Nature and Conduct: An Introduction to Social Psychology (New York: The Modern Library, 1930).

Dewey, Richard. "The Neighborhood, Urban Ecology, and City Planners," American Sociological Review, 15 (August, 1950), 502—507.

Dexter, E. S. "Three Items Related to Personality: Popularity, Nicknames, and Homesickness," Journal of Social Psychology, 30 (1949), 155—158.

Diemer, June. "Good Buy, Mr. Chips?" High School Journal, 42 (November, 1958), 45—49.

Dimock, H. S. "A Research in Adolescence: The Social World of the Adolescent," Child Development, 6 (1935), 285—302.

————. "Rediscovering the Adolescent (New York: Association Press, 1937).

Dinitz, Simon, F. R. Scarpitti, and W. C. Reckless. "Delinquency Vulnerability: A Cross Group and Longitudinal Analysis," American Sociological Review, 27 (August, 1962), 515—517.

Dintzer, Lucien. Le jeu d'adolescence (Adolescent Play). (Paris: Presses Universitaires de France, 1956).

Dixon, Marguerite M. "Adolescent Girls Tell About Themselves," Marriage and Family Living, 20 (November, 1958), 400—401. (E.6)

Doane, Kenneth R. "Differences Between Pupils With Good Sitting Posture and Pupils With Poor Sitting Posture," Journal of Educational Research, 52 (May, 1959), 315—317.

Dodson, Leigh M. "Analysis of Student Personnel Problems on Counseling Practices at Junior College Level," California Journal of Educational Research, 3 (May, 1952), 118—121.

Doll, Edgar A. "Evaluating Social Maturity," Education, 77 (March, 1957), 409—413.

Dollard, John. "Culture, Society, Impulse, and Socialization," American Journal of Sociology, 45 (July, 1939), 50—63.

Douvan, E. Character Process in Adolescence. Paper read at the American Psychological Association (1957).

————. "Independence and Identity in Adolescents," Children, 4 (September, 1957), 186—190.

Douvan, Elizabeth, and Joseph Adelson. "The Psychodynamics of Social Mobility in Adolescent Boys," Journal of Abnormal and Social Psychology, 56 (January, 1958), 31—44.

Drasgow, James. "Problems of Progeny Related to Paternal Education," Journal of Educational Psychology, 48 (December, 1957), 521—524.

Dreger, Ralph M., and Lewis R. Aiken, Jr. "The Identification of Number Anxiety in a College Population," Journal of Educational Psychology, 48 (October, 1957), 344—351.

Drucker, Arthur J. "Relationships Between Citizenship Attitudes, Parental Education and Other Variables," Purdue University Studies in Higher Education, No. 71 (1950).

Duel, Henry J. "Effect of Periodical Self-Evaluation on Student Achievement," Journal of Educational Psychology, 49 (August, 1958), 197—199.

Dugan, Ruth. "An Investigation of the Personal, Social, Educational and Economical Reasons for Success and Lack of Success in School as Expressed by 105 Tenth Grade Biology Students," Journal of Educational Research, 55 (August, 1962), 544—553.

Durkin, Delores. "Children's Concept of Justice: A Further Comparison With the Piaget Data," Journal of Educational Research, 52 (March, 1959), 252—257. (E.7)

DuToit, J. B. "Work and Leisure Roles of Young People," Sociology and Social Research, 44 (March—August, 1960), 235—243.

Dwyer, Robert J. "A Report on Patterns of Interaction in Desegregated Schools," Journal of Educational Sociology, 31 (March, 1958), 253—256.

Dyer, William G. "Parental Influence on the Job Attitudes of Children from Two Occupational Strata," Sociology and Social Research, 42 (1957), 203—206. (D.7)

Dynes, R. R., A. C. Clark, and S. Dinitz. "Levels of Occupational Aspiration: Some Aspects of Family Experience as a Variable," American Sociological Review, 21 (1956), 212—215. (D.8)

Edwards, Martha. "Guiding the Junior High School Student," School and Community, 45 (May, 1959), 13.

Edwards, Newton, and Herman G. Richey. "The School in American Society," Review of Educational Research, 28 (February, 1958), 29—42.

Edwards, T. Bently, and Allen B. Wilson. "The Association Between Interest and Achievement in High School Chemistry," Educational Psychological Measurement, 19, (Winter, 1959), 601—610. (B.29)

Egner, Robert E., and Alvan J. Obelsky. "Effect of Stereotyped Attitudes on Learning," Journal of Educational Psychology, 48 (April, 1957), 207—212.

Ehrmann, Winston W. "Dating Behavior of College Students," in J. M. Seidman (ed.), The Adolescent (New York: Holt, Rinehart and Winston, Inc., 1960).

————. Premarital Dating Behavior (New York: Henry Holt and Co., 1959).

————. "Influence of Comparative Social Class of Companion Upon Premarital Heterosexual Behavior," Marriage and Family Living, 17 (February, 1955), 48—53.

Eisenstadt, S. N. "Youth Activities and Social Stratification," Explorations in Entrepreneurial History, 8 (Winter Supplement, 1956), 58—60.

————. From Generation to Generation (New York: The Free Press of Glencoe, 1956).

Elkin, David. "Quantity Conceptions in Junior and Senior High School Students," Child Development, 32 (September, 1961), 551—560.

Elkin, Frederick, and William A. Westley. "The Myth of Adolescent Culture," American Sociological Review, 20 (December, 1955), 680—684. (B.30)

Ellis, Albert. "Love and Family Relationships of American College Girls," American Journal of Sociology, 55 (May, 1950), 550—556. (B.31)

Elwood, Robert H. "The Role of Personality Traits in Selecting a Career," Journal of Applied Psychology, 11 (1927), 199—201. (D.9)

Empey, LaMar T. "Social Class and Occupational Aspiration: A Comparison of Absolute and Relative Measurement," American Sociological Review, 21 (December, 1956), 703—709. (D.10)

————, and J. Rabon. "The Provo Experiment in Delinquency Rehabilitation," American Sociological Review, 26 (October, 1951), 679—696.

Engel, Mary. "The Stability of the Self-Concept in Adolescence," in J. M. Seidman (ed.), The Adolescent (New York: Holt, Rinehart and Winston, Inc., 1960), pp. 646—663. (D.11)

English, O. Spurgeon, and Gerald H. J. Pearson. Emotional Problems of Living: Avoiding the Neurotic Pattern (New York: W. W. Norton and Co., 1945).

Ericson, Martha C. "Child-Rearing and Social Status," American Journal of Sociology, 52 (November, 1946), 190—192.

Erikson, Erik H. Childhood and Society (New York: W. W. Norton and Co., 1950).

————. Adolescence and Identity. Paper read at 5th Annual Symposium, Committee on Human Development, University of Chicago, February 6, 1954.

————. Identity and the Life Cycle (New York: International Universities Press, 1959).

Eversole, Mrs. John. "Teenagers Need Encouragement," School and Community, 45 (October, 1958), 37.

Ezell, Lonnie B., and Henry H. Tate. "High School Students Look to the Future," Journal of Educational Research, 49 (November, 1955), 217—222. (D.12)

Farber, Bernard. "Marital Integration as a Factor in Parent-Child Relations," Child Development, 33 (March, 1962), 1—14.

Faris, Ellsworth. The Nature of Human Nature and Other Essays in Social Psychology (New York: McGraw-Hill Book Co., 1937).

Farnham, Marynia F. The Adolescent (New York: Harper and Bros., 1951).

Faust, Margret S. "Developmental Maturity as a Determinate in Prestige of Adolescent Girls," Child Development, 31 (March, 1960), 173—184.

Faw, Volney. "Learning to Deal with Stress Situations," Journal of Educational Psychology, 48 (March, 1957), 135—144.

Fifer, Gordon. "Grade Placement of Secondary School Pupils in Relation to Age And Ability," California Journal of Educational Research, 3 (January, 1952), 31—35.

Fink, Howard H., and Theodore C. Kahn. "A Comparison of Normal and Emotionally Ill Children on the Kahn Test of Symbol Arrangement," Journal of Educational Research, 53 (September, 1959), 35—36.

Fink, Morton B. "Self-Concept as It Relates to Academic Underachievement," California Journal of Educational Research, 13 (March, 1962), 57—62.

Fleege, Urban H. Self-Revelation of the Adolescent Boy (Milwaukee: The Bruce Publishing Company, 1945).

Fleming, C. M. The Social Psychology of Education (New York: Oxford University Press, 1944).

————. Adolescence, Its Social Psychology (New York: International Universities Press, 1949).

————. Studies in the Social Psychology of Adolescence (London: Routledge & Kegan Paul, 1951).

Folsom, Joseph K. "Changing Values in Sex and Family Relations," American Sociological Review, 2 (October, 1937), 717—726.

Foote, Nelson N. "Identification as the Basis for a Theory of Motivation," American Sociological Review, 16 (February, 1951), 14—21.

————, and Leonard S. Cottrell, Jr. Identity and Interpersonal Competence: A New Direction in Family Research (Chicago: University of Chicago Press, 1955).

Forer, Raymond. "The Impact of a Radio Program on Adolescents," Public Opinion Quarterly, 19 (Summer, 1955), 184—194. (A.9)

Forman, Edna. "For Holding Power—A 'Home' in High School," Education, 79 (November, 1958), 144—146.

Frank, Lawrence K. "Adolescence as a Period of Transition," Adolescence, Forty-third Yearbook of the National Society for the Study of Education, Part I. Edited by Nelson B. Henry (Chicago: The Department of Education, The University of Chicago, 1944), pp. 1—7.

————. "The Adolescent and the Family," Adolescence, Forty-third Yearbook of the National Society for the Study of Education, Part I. Edited by Nelson B. Henry. (Chicago: The Department of Education, The University of Chicago, 1944), pp. 240—254.

————. Society as the Patient: Essays on Culture and Personality (New Brunswick, N. J.: Rutgers University Press, 1948).

Frank, Mary, and Lawrence K. Frank. Your Adolescent at Home and in School, (New York: The Viking Press, 1956).

Frankel, Edward. "A Comparative Study of Achieving and Underachieving High School Boys of High Intellectual Ability," Journal of Educational Research, 53 (January, 1960), 172—180.

Franzblau, Abraham N. "Religious Belief and Character Among Jewish Adolescents," Teachers College Contributions to Education, Teachers College, Columbia University (1934). (B.32)

Freidson, Eliot. "Adult Discount: An Aspect of Children's Changing Taste," Child Development, 24 (March, 1953), 39—49. (A.10)

Frenkel-Brunswick, E. "A Research Project on Ethnic Prejudice in Children and Adolescents," Human Relations, 1 (1948), 295—306. (E.8)

Frick, Willard. "The Adolescent Dilemma: An Interpretation," Peabody Journal of Education, 32 (1955), 206—210. (B.33)

Friedenberg, Edgar Z. The Vanishing Adolescent (Boston: Beacon Press, 1959). (B.34)

Fromm, Erich. Escape from Freedom (New York: Rinehart and Co., 1941).

————. The Art of Loving (New York: Harper and Bros., 1956).

————. "Individual and Social Origins of Neurosis," American Sociological Review, 9 (August, 1944), 380—384. (F.4)

Frymier, Jack R. "Acceptance and Rejection as Related to Length of School Attendance," Journal of Educational Research, 53 (November, 1959), 112—114.

————. "Analysis of Adolescents' Responses to the F Scale," Journal of Experimental Education, 29 (September, 1960), 73—79.

Furfey, Paul H. "The Group Life of the Adolescent," Journal of Educational Sociology, 14 (December, 1940), 195—204. (F.5)

Gabriel, Anne. "A Study of the Attitudes of Parents of Adolescents," Researches in Parent Education, 4 (University of Iowa Studies in Child Welfare, Vol. 17). Edited by George D. Stoddard (Iowa City: The University of Iowa Press, 1939).

Galdston, Iago M. (ed.). The Family in Contemporary Society (New York: International Universities Press, 1958).

Gardner, George E. "Sex Behavior of Adolescents in Wartime," Annals of the American Academy of Political and Social Science, 236 (November, 1944), 60—66.

————. "Present-Day Society and the Adolescent," American Journal of Orthopsychiatry, 27 (1957), 508—517.

————. "A Study of Student Disciplinary Practices in Two Georgia High Schools," Journal of Educational Research, 53 (December, 1959), 153—156.

Garrison, Karl C. The Psychology of Adolescence (New York: Prentice-Hall, 1956).

Geist, Harold. "A Comparison of Observations of Parents of Their Children's Interests and Scores on a Picture Interest Inventory," California Journal of Educational Research, 11 (November, 1960), 207—212.

George, Jane Pippin. "A Study of the Patterns of Social Interaction at the Senior High School Level and Their Relationship to Certain Selected Factors," Dissertation Abstracts, 17 (1957), 1705—1706.

Gesell, Arnold, Frances L. Ilg, and Louise Bates Ames. Youth: The Years From 10 to 16 (New York: Harper and Bros., 1956).

Getzels, J. W., and P. W. Jackson. "Occupational Choice and

Cognitive Functioning: Career Aspirations of Highly Intelligent and of Highly Creative Adolescents," Journal of Abnormal and Social Psychology, 61 (July, 1960), 119—123.

Gibbons, Don C., and Manzer J. Griswold. "Sex Differentials Among Juvenile Court Referrals," Sociology and Social Research, 42 (1957), 106—110. (F.6)

Gilfoy, Lewis W. "Educating the Most Able High School Students at Indianapolis," Education, 78 (September, 1958), 25—27.

Glaser, Daniel. "Criminality Theories and Behavioral Images," American Journal of Sociology, 61 (March, 1956), 433—444.

————, and Kent Rice. "Crime, Age, and Employment," American Sociological Review, 24 (October, 1959), 679—686.

Glick, Paul C., and Emanuel Landau. "Age as a Factor in Marriage," American Sociological Review, 15 (August, 1950), 517—529.

Glicksberg, Charles I. "Student Ethics and the Honor System," School and Society, 85 (May, 1957), 181—183.

Goda, Sidney, and B. C. Griffith. "Spoken Language of Adolescent Retardates and its Relation to Intelligence, Age and Anxiety," Child Development, 33 (September, 1962), 489—498.

Gold, Martin. "Power in the Classroom—Leadership," Sociometry, 21 (1958), 50—60.

Goldberg, Harriet L. Child Offenders: A Study in Diagnosis and Treatment (New York: Grune and Stratton, 1948).

Goodykoontz, Bess. "How School Services Help to Prevent Delinquency," Juvenile Delinquency and the Schools, Forty-seventh Yearbook, Part I (1948) (National Society for the Study of Education, University of Chicago Press), 100—125.

Gorden, Wayne. "The Role of the Teacher in the Social Structure of the High School," Journal of Educational Sociology, 29 (September, 1955), 21—29.

————. The Social System of the High School (New York: The Free Press of Glencoe, 1957). (B.35)

Gordon, Ira J. "A School's Values and Classroom Behavior," School and Society, 87 (February 28, 1959), 90—92.

Gorer, Geoffrey. The American People: A Study in National Character (New York: W. W. Norton and Co., 1948).

Gough, Harrison G. "A Sociological Theory of Psychopathy," American Journal of Sociology, 53 (March, 1948), 359—366. (F.7)

Grace, Harry A., and L. W. Lewellyn. "The No-Man's-Land of Youth," Journal of Educational Sociology, 33 (November, 1959), 135—140.

Graham, Ray. "Evaluating Programs for the Underachieving Pupil," High School Journal, 42 (December, 1958), 75—79.

Grambs, Jean D. "The Community and the Self-Governing Adolescent Group," Journal of Educational Sociology, 30 (October, 1956), 94—105. (B.36)

Gredler, Gilbert Rugg. "Ethnocentrism in Adolescents: A Study of Certain Aspects of Cognitive and Affective Characteristics," Dissertation Abstracts, 17 (1957), 302.

Green, Arnold W. "The Social Situation in Personality Theory," American Sociological Review, 7 (June, 1942), 388—393.

——. "The Middle Class Male Child and Neurosis," American Sociological Review, 11 (February, 1946), 31—41.

Green, Leah Ann. "A Study of Creativity and the Self-Attitudes and Sociability of High School Students," Dissertation Abstracts, 17 (1957), 1807—1808.

Green, T. L. "A Comparison of Status on Two Tests of Social Acceptability," Journal of Educational Research, 51 (March, 1958), 493—503.

Greenberg, H. M., Louise Allison, Mildred Fewell, and Charles Rich. "The Personality of Junior High and High School Students Attending Residential School for the Blind," Journal of Educational Psychology, 48 (November, 1957), 406—410.

Greene, James, and S. L. Daughtry. "Factors Associated with School Mobility," Journal of Educational Sociology, 35 (September, 1961), 36—40.

——, and Mary E. Wardlow. "An Exploratory Sociometric Study of Peer Status Among Adolescent Girls," Sociometry, 15 (August—November, 1952), 311—318.

Gronlund, Norman E., and Loren Anderson. "Personality Characteristics of Socially Accepted, Socially Neglected, and Socially Rejected Junior High School Pupils," Educational Administration and Supervision, 43 (October, 1957), 329—338. (C.16)

——, and Algard P. Whitney. "Relation Between Pupils' Social Acceptability in the Classroom, in the School, and in the Neighborhood," School Review, 64 (September, 1956), 267—271. (C.17)

Gustard, J. W. "Changes in Social Attitudes and Behavior: A Review of the Literature," Educational and Psychological Measurement, 11 (1951), 87—102.

——. "Factors Associated with Social Behavior and Adjustment: A Review of the Literature," Educational and Psychological Measurement, 12 (1952), 3—19.

Gustav, Alice, and A. M. Crosman. "College Grades of Underage Students," School and Society, 90 (September, 1962), 298—299.

Hacker, Frederick J., and Elisabeth R. Geleerd. "Freedom and Authority in Adolescence," American Journal of Orthopsychiatry, 15 (October, 1945), 621—630.

Hadley, L. S. "New College Students Lack Study Techniques," School and Society, 85 (November 23, 1957), 353—354.

Hale, Creighton J. "Changing Growth Patterns of the American Child," Education, 78 (April, 1958), 467—470.

Hale, Lincoln B. From School to College: A Study of the Transition Experience (New Haven: Yale University Press, 1939).

Hall, Granville S. Adolescence: Its Psychology and Its Relations to Physiology, Anthropology, Sociology, Sex, Crime, Religion and Education (New York: D. Appleton and Co., 1924).

Haller, Archibald O., and S. Thomas. "Personality Correlates of the Socioeconomic Status of Adolescent Males," Sociometry, 25 (December, 1962), 398—406.

———, and C. E. Wolff. "Personality Orientations of Farm, Village and Urban Boys," Rural Sociology, 27 (September, 1962), 275—293.

Hallworth, H. J. "Sociometric Relations Among Grammar School Boys and Girls Between the Ages of 11 and 16 Years," Sociometry, 16 (February, 1953), 37—70. (B.37)

Hamlin, Richard E. "The Relationship of Certain Adolescent Developmental Tasks to Hi-Y Membership," Dissertation Abstracts, 17 (1957), 807—808.

Hanley, Charles. "Physique and Reputation of Junior High School Boys," Child Development, 22 (December, 1951), 247—260.

Harmin, Merrill, et al. "General Characteristics of Participating Youth Groups," Journal of Educational Sociology, 30 (October, 1956), 49—57. (E.9)

Harper, Robert A. "Is Conformity a General or a Specific Behavior Trait?" American Sociological Review, 12 (February, 1947), 81—86. (C.18)

Harris, Dale B. "Sex Differences in the Life Problems and Interests of Adolescents—1935 and 1957," Child Development, 30 (1959), 453—459.

———, and Sing Chu Tseng. "Children's Attitudes Toward Peers and Parents as Revealed by Sentence Completions," Child Development, 28 (1957), 401—411. (C.19)

Harris, Stanley W. "The Expressed Interests of 200 Jewish Teenagers," Journal of Jewish Communal Services, 32 (1956), 406—415.

Hartley, Ruth E. Sociality in Pre-Adolescent Boys (New York: Bureau of Publications, Teachers College, Columbia University, 1946). (C.20)

Hartshorne, Edward Y. "Undergraduate Society and the College Culture," American Sociological Review, 8 (June, 1943), 321—332.

Harvey, O. J., Muzafer Sherif, and B. Jack White. "Status in Experimentally Produced Groups," American Journal of Sociology, 60 (January, 1955), 370—379. (C.21)

Hatch, David L., and Mary A. "Criteria of Social Status as Derived From Marriage Announcements in the New York Times," American Sociological Review, 12 (August, 1947), 396—403.

208

Hathaway, Starke R., and E. D. Monachesi. "The Minnesota Multiphasic Personality Inventory In the Study of Juvenile Delinquents," American Sociological Review, 17 (December, 1952), 704—709.

————, E. D. Monachesi, and L. A. Young. "Rural-Urban Adolescent Personality," Rural Sociology, 24 (December, 1959), 331—346.

Havighurst, Robert J. "Research on the Developmental-Task Concept," School Review, 64 (May, 1956), 215—223. (B.38)

————, and Dorothy Neubaur. "Community Factors in Relation to Character Formation," in R. J. Havighurst and Hilda Taba (eds.), Adolescent Character and Personality, Chap. 4, pp. 27—46. (B.39)

————, and Bernice J. Neugarten. American Indian and White Children: A Sociopsychological Investigation (Chicago: University of Chicago Press, 1955).

————, and Bernice J. Neugarten. Society and Education (Boston: Allyn and Bacon, 1962).

————, and Audrey F. Rieger. "The Role of Adults Outside the Family in Character Formation," in R. J. Havighurst and Hilda Taba (eds.), Adolescent Character and Personality, Chap. 7, pp. 70—80. (D.13)

————, and Hilda Taba (eds.). Adolescent Character and Personality (New York: John Wiley and Sons, 1949).

————, Myra Z. Robinson, and Mildred Dorr. "The Development of the Ideal Self in Childhood and Adolescence," Journal of Educational Research, 40 (1946), 241—257. (D.14)

Hayden, James Richard. "An Analysis of the Personal-Social Problems Considered Important by the Junior-High-School Adolescent According to Sex, Grade, Age, IQ, and Bilingualism," V 1 & 2, Dissertation Abstracts, 17 (1957), 275.

Haygood, Lillian. "What Kinds of Accidents do Teenagers Have?" High School Journal, 42 (November, 1958), 53—61.

Hearn, Gordon. "Kurt Lewin on Adolescence," The Group, 17 (December, 1954). 9—15.

Heath, Clark W. What People Are: A Study of Normal Young Men (Cambridge, Mass.: Harvard University Press, 1945).

Heaton, Margaret M. "Sororities and the School Culture," Journal of Educational Sociology, 21 (1948), 527—535. (B.40)

Heinicke, Christopher, and B. Whiting. Bibliographies on Personality and Social Development of the Child. Social Science Research Council, Pamphlet 1C.

Heiss, Jerold S. "Variations in Courtship Progress Among High School Students," Marriage and Family Living, 22 (May, 1960), 165—170.

Heist, Paul. "The Entering College Student—Background and Characteristics," Review of Educational Research, 30 (October, 1960), 285—297.

Helfant, Kenneth G. Parents' Attitudes vs. Adolescent Hostility in the Determination of Adolescent Sociopolitical Attitudes (Washington: American Psychological Association, 1952).

Hemmerling, Robert L., and H. Hurst. "The Effects of Leisure Time Activities on Scholastic Achievement," California Journal of Educational Research, 12 (March, 1961), 86—90.

Hendricks, Marvin L. "Changing Mores Concerning Cheating on Examinations," School and Society, 86 (November 22, 1958), 413—414.

Henry, Andrew F. "Sibling Structure and Perceptions of the Disciplinary Roles of Parents," Sociometry, 20 (March, 1957), 67—74.

Henzie, Russell. "A Junior High Program," Education, 80 (November, 1959), 151—153.

Herberls, Rudolf. "A Note on Riesman's The Lonely Crowd," American Journal of Sociology, 57 (July, 1955), 34—35.

Herman, Robert D. "The 'Going Steady' Complex: A Re-examination," Marriage and Family Living, 17 (February, 1955), 36—40.

Herskovitz, M. J., and M. M. Wiley. "The Cultural Approach to Sociology," American Journal of Sociology, 249 (September, 1923), 188—199.

Hess, Robert D. "The Adolescent: His Society," Review of Educational Research, 30 (February, 1960), 5—12.

———, and Irene Goldblatt. "The Status of Adolescents in American Society: A Problem in Social Identity," Child Development, 28 (December, 1957), 459—468. (E.10)

Hildreth, Elon E. "A Critical Evaluation of the Student Council in the High Schools of California," California Journal of Educational Research, 3 (September, 1952), 154—158.

Hildreth, Gertrude. "The Social Interests of Young Adolescents," Child Development, 16 (March—June, 1945), 119—121. (C.22)

Hill, David Spence. "Personification of Ideals by Urban Children," Journal of Social Psychology, 1 (1930), 379—393. (E.11)

Hill, George E., and Richard M. Hole. "Comparison of the Vocational Interests of Tenth Grade Students with Their Parents' Judgments of These Interests," Educational and Psychological Measurement, 18 (Spring, 1958), 173—187. (D.15)

———, and Harold Rogge. "The Relation of Kuder Preference Record Scores in High School," Journal of Educational Research, 51 (March, 1958), 545—548.

Hill, Patty Smith. "The Home and the School as Centers of Child Life," Progressive Education, 115 (July—August, 1928), 211—217.

Hill, R. "An Experimental Study of Social Adjustment," American Sociological Review, 9 (1944), 481—494.

Hill, Thomas J. "Dating Patterns and Family Position," Clearing House, 29 (May, 1955), 552—554. (C.23)

Himmelweit, Hilde T. "A Study of the Attitudes, Value Systems and Behavior of Young Adolescents Belonging to Different Social Status Groups," Bulletin of the British Psychological Society, 20 (1953), 7.

———. "Socio-Economic Background and Personality," International Social Science Bulletin, 7 (Fall, 1955), 29—35. (D.16)

———, A. N. Oppenheim, and P. Vince. T.V. and the Child (London: Oxford University Press, 1958). (Book Review by Edward Blishen, Sociological Review, 7 (1959), 273—274.)

Hindman, Baker, M. "The Emotional Problems of Negro High School Youth Which Are Related to Segregation and Discrimination in a Southern Urban Community," Journal of Educational Sociology, 27 (November, 1953), 115—127.

Hobart, Charles W. "Emancipation From Parents and Courtship in Adolescents," Pacific Sociological Review (Spring, 1958), 25—29.

———. "Some Effects of Romanticism During Courtship on Marriage Role Opinions," Sociology and Social Research, 42 (May—June, 1958), 336—343. (C.24)

———. "Some Changes in Parent-Offspring Interaction During Courtship and Marriage," Pacific Sociological Review, 5 (Spring, 1962), 54—59.

Hocker, Louis M. "New Kinds of Students and New Ways of Testing Achievements," School and Society, 85 (September 28, 1957), 261—263.

Hollingshead, A. B. "The Concept of Social Control," American Sociological Review, 6 (April, 1941), 217—224. (C.25)

———. Elmtown's Youth: The Impact of Social Classes on Adolescents (New York: John Wiley and Sons, 1949). (B.41)

Holmes, Darrell. "An Investigation of Student Attitudes Which May Be Related to Leaving College," Journal of Educational Research, 52 (September, 1958), 17—21.

Holmes, Jack A., and Carmen J. Finley. "Under- and Over-Age Grade-Placements and School Achievement," Journal of Educational Psychology, 48 (November, 1957), 447—456.

Holzner, Burkart. "Institutional Change, Social Stratification, and the Direction of Youth Movements," Journal of Educational Sociology, 37 (October, 1962), 49—56.

Horrocks, John E., and Mae E. Becker. "A Study of the Friendship Fluctuations of Preadolescents," Journal of Genetic Psychology, 10 (June, 1951), 131—144.

Horton, Donald. "The Dialogue of Courtship in Popular Songs," American Journal of Sociology, 62 (May, 1957), 569—578.

Hoult, Thomas F., and Charles W. Peckham. "Religion as a Cultural Factor in One Aspect of the Personality of Selected College Students," Journal of Educational Sociology, 31 (October, 1957), 75—82.

Hunt, J. T. "Special Education: Segregation," Education, 77 (April, 1957), 475—479.

——. "Emotional Development in Childhood and Adolescence," Review of Educational Research, 28 (December, 1958), 401—410.

——. "The Adolescent: His Characteristics and Development," Review of Educational Research, 30 (February, 1960), 13—22.

Hurlock, Elizabeth B. "A Study of Self-Ratings by Thirteen-Year-Old Children," Journal of Applied Psychology, 11 (1927), 490—502. (D.17)

——. Adolescent Development (New York: McGraw-Hill Book Co., 1955). (B.42)

——, and L. C. McDonald. "Undesirable Behavior Traits in Junior High School Students," Child Development, 5 (1934), 278—290. (B.102)

Hussmann, L. A., and Gene Levine. "Social Class and Sociability in Fraternity Pledging," American Journal of Sociology, 65 (January, 1960), 391—399. (C.26)

Hutson, P. W., and D. R. Kovar. "Some Problems of Senior High School Pupils in Their Social Recreation," Educational Administration and Supervision, 28 (1942), 503—519.

Hutt, Max L., and Daniel R. Miller. "Value Interiorization and Democratic Education," Journal of Social Issues, 5 (1949), 31—43.

Ireland, Ralph R. "The Significance of Recreational Maturation," Journal of Educational Sociology, 32 (February, 1959), 356—364. (A.11)

Jackson, Philip W., and Jacob W. Getzels. "Psychological Health and Classroom Functioning: A Study of Dissatisfaction with School among Adolescents," Journal of Educational Psychology, 50 (December, 1959), 295—300.

——, Jacob W. Getzels, and George A. Kajolis. "Psychological Health and Cognitive Functioning in Adolescents: A Multivariate Analysis," Child Development, 31 (June, 1940), 285—298.

James, H. E. O., and F. T. Moore. "Adolescent Leisure in a Working Class District," Occupational Psychology, 14 (1940), 132—145.

Jantzen, J. Marc. "An Opinionaire on Why College Students Choose to Teach," Journal of Educational Research, 53 (September, 1959), 13—17.

Jenkins, Wesley W. "An Experimental Study of the Relationship of Legitimate and Illegitimate Birth Status to School and Personal and Social Adjustment of Negro Children," American Journal of Sociology, 64 (September, 1958), 169—173.

Jennings, Joe. "Leisure Reading of Junior High School Boys and Girls," Peabody Journal of Education, 6 (1929), 343—347. (A.12)

Jerome, Sister Agnes. "A Study of Twenty Slow Learners,"
  Journal of Educational Research, 53 (September, 1959),
  23—27.
Jersild, Arthur T. The Psychology of Adolescence (New York:
  The Macmillan Company, 1957).
Jex, F. B., and R. M. Merrill. "Intellectual and Personality
  Characteristics of University of Utah Students," Journal of
  Educational Research, 53 (November, 1959), 118—120.
Johannis, Theodore B., Jr. "Participation by Fathers, Mothers
  and Teenage Sons and Daughters in Selected Social Activ-
  ity," The Coordinator, 7 (December, 1958), 24—25. (B.43)
———, and James Rollins. "Attitudes of Teen-Agers Towards
  Family Relationships and Characteristics of Their Par-
  ents," Sociology and Social Research, 43 (July—August,
  1959), 415—420. (B.44)
Johnson, Orville. "The Problem of the Low Achiever in the
  High School," High School Journal, 42 (December, 1958),
  72—75.
Johnson, Ronald C. "A Study of Children's Moral Judgments,"
  Dissertation Abstracts, 20 (October, 1959), 1430—1431.
Johnson, Thomas F. "Conceptions of Parents Held by Adoles-
  cents," Journal of Abnormal and Social Psychology, 47
  (1952), 783—789. (B.45)
Johnstone, John, and Elihu Katz. "Youth and Popular Music: A
  Study in the Sociology of Taste," American Journal of So-
  ciology, 62 (May, 1957), 563—568. (A.13)
Jones, Edward E., and Richard deCharms. "Changes in Social
  Perception as a Function of the Personal Relevance of Be-
  havior," in E. E. Maccoby, T. M. Newcomb, and E. L. Hart-
  ley (eds.), Readings in Social Psychology (New York: Henry
  Holt and Co., 1958), pp. 102—109. (C.27)
Jones, H. E. "Adolescence in Our Society," in J. M. Seidman
  (ed.), The Adolescent: A Book of Readings (New York:
  Holt, Rinehart and Winston, Inc., 1960), pp. 50—60. (C.28)
Jones, Mary Cover. "Adolescent Development and the Junior
  High School Program," High School Journal, 33 (Novem-
  ber—December, 1949), 237—239.
———. "A Study of Socialization Patterns at the High School
  Level," Journal of Genetic Psychology, 93 (September,
  1958), 87—111. (B.46)
———. "A Comparison of the Attitudes and Interests of Ninth-
  Grade Students Over Two Decades," Journal of Educational
  Psychology, 51 (August, 1960), 175—186.
———. "The Later Careers of Boys Who Were Early or Late
  Maturing," Child Development, 28 (March, 1957), 113—128.
———, and N. Bayley. "Physical Maturing Among Boys as Re-
  lated to Behavior," Journal of Educational Psychology, 41
  (1950), 129—148. (D.18)
———, and P. H. Mussen. "Self-Conceptions, Motivations and

Interpersonal Attitudes of Late and Early Maturing Boys,"
Child Development, 28 (June, 1957), 243—256. (D.20)
————, and P. H. Mussen. "The Behavior-Inferred Motivations
of Late and Early Maturing Boys," Child Development, 29
(March, 1958), 61—67. (D.19)
————, and P. H. Mussen. "Self-Conceptions, Motivations, and
Interpersonal Attitudes of Late and Early Maturing Girls,"
Child Development, 29 (December, 1958), 491—501. (D.21)
Joseph, Alice, Rosamond B. Spicer, and Jane Chesky. The Des-
ert People: A Study of the Panago Indians (Chicago: Uni-
versity of Chicago Press, 1949).
Josselyn, Irene M. "Social Pressures in Adolescence," Social
Casework, 33 (May, 1952), 187—193. (C.29)
————. The Adolescent and His World (New York: Family
Service Association of America, 1952).

Kahl, Joseph A. "Educational and Occupational Aspirations of
'Common-Man' Boys," Harvard Educational Review, 23
(Summer, 1953), 186—203. (D.22)
Kanin, Eugene J. "Male Aggression in Dating-Courtship Rela-
tions," American Journal of Sociology, 63 (September,
1957), 197—204. (C.30)
Karpf, Fay Berger. "American Social Psychology—1951,"
American Journal of Sociology, 58 (September, 1952), 187—
193.
Kasdon, Lawrence M. "Early Reading Background of Some Su-
perior Readers Among College Freshman," Journal of Edu-
cational Research, 52 (December, 1958), 151—154. (B.47)
Katz, Irwin. Conflict and Harmony in an Adolescent Interracial
Group (New York: New York University Press, 1955).
Kay, Barbara, Simon Dinitz, and Walter C. Reckless. "Delin-
quency Proneness and School Achievement," Educational
Research Bulletin, 36 (December, 1957), 131—136. (B.48)
Keinhart, William E., and Lionel R. Olsen. "Foreign Student
Reactions to American College Life," Journal of Educa-
tional Sociology, 31 (March, 1958), 277—280.
Keislar, Evan R. "A Distinction Between Social Acceptance and
Prestige Among Adolescents," Child Development, 24
(1953), 275—283. (C.31)
————. "Girls' Social Groups Rate Each Other," California
Journal of Educational Research, 4 (November, 1953), 227—
232.
————. "Differences Among Adolescent Social Clubs in Terms
of Members' Characteristics, Journal of Educational Re-
search, 48 (December, 1954), 297—303. (A.14)
————. "Peer Group Ratings of High School Pupils with High
and Low Grades," Journal of Experimental Education, 23
(June, 1955), 375—378. (C.32)
————. "The Generalization of Prestige Among Adolescent

Boys," <u>California Journal of Educational Research</u>, 10 (September, 1959), 153—156. (C.33)

Kelley, Janet A. "Varying Mores in School and College Culture," <u>Journal of Educational Sociology</u>, 31 (March, 1958), 244—253.

Kelly, Harold H., and Martin M. Shapiro. "An Experiment on Conformity to Group Norms, Where Conformity Is Detrimental to Group Achievement," <u>American Sociological Review</u>, 19 (December, 1954), 667—677.

————, and Edmund H. Volkhart. "The Resistance to Change of Group-Anchored Attitudes," <u>American Sociological Review</u>, 17 (August, 1952), 453—465.

Kennedy, Wallace A. "M.M.P.I. Profiles of Gifted Adolescents," <u>Journal of Clinical Psychology</u>, 18 (April, 1962), 148—149.

Kiell, Norman, "Behavior of Five Adolescent Poker Players," <u>Journal of Human Relations</u>, 5 (1957), 79—89. (A.15)

————. <u>The Adolescent Through Fiction</u> (New York: International Universities Press, 1959).

Killian, Lewis M. "The Significance of Multiple-Group Membership in Disaster," <u>American Journal of Sociology</u>, 57 (January, 1952), 309—314.

Kinch, John W., and C. E. Bowerman. "Changes in Family and Peer Orientation of Children Between Fourth and Tenth Grades," <u>Social Forces</u>, 37 (March, 1951), 206—211. (B.49)

Kirkpatrick, Clifford, and Theodore Caplow. "Courtship in a Group of Minnesota Students," <u>American Journal of Sociology</u>, 51 (September, 1945), 114—125.

————, and Charles Hobart. "Disagreement, Disagreement Estimate, and Non-Empathetic Imputations for Intimacy Groups Varying from Favorite Date to Married," <u>American Sociological Review</u>, 19 (February, 1954), 10—19.

————, and Eugene Kanin. "Male Sex Aggression on a University Campus," <u>American Sociological Review</u>, 22 (1957), 52—58.

Kitsuse, John I., and David C. Dietrick. "Delinquent Boys: A Critique," <u>American Sociological Review</u>, 24 (April, 1959), 208—215.

Klapp, Orrin E. "The Creation of Popular Heroes," <u>American Journal of Sociology</u>, 54 (September, 1948), 135—141.

Kluckhohn, Florence Rockwood. "Dominant and Variant Value Orientation," in C. Kluckhohn and H. A. Murray (eds.), <u>Personality in Nature, Society and Culture</u> (2nd ed. New York: Alfred A. Knopf, 1959), pp. 342—357. (E.12)

Kluge, Robert Botts. "Development Tasks: Middle Adolescent Peer Culture Tasks as Observed in Two Selected Environments, a High School and a Community Youth Center," <u>Dissertation Abstracts</u>, 17 (1957), 565.

Klugh, Henry E., and Robert Birely. "High School and College Ability Test and High School Grades as Predictors of College Achievement," Education and Psychological Measurement, 19 (Spring, 1959), 625—626.

Kobrin, Solomon. "The Conflict of Values in Delinquency Areas," American Sociological Review, (October, 1951), 653—661. (F.8)

Kohn, Melvin L. "Social Class and Parental Authority," American Sociological Review, 24 (1959), 352—366.

——. "Social Class and Parental Values," American Journal of Sociology, 64 (1959), 337—351.

Komarovsky, Mirra. "Cultural Contradictions and Sex Roles," American Journal of Sociology, 52 (November, 1946), 184—189. (C.35)

——. "Functional Analysis of Sex Roles," American Sociological Review, 15 (August, 1950), 508—516. (C.36)

Koopman, Norbert E. "Some Causes of Under-Achievement," High School Journal, 42 (December, 1958), 87—90.

Kornegay, William G. "Family Life Education and the Junior High School," High School Journal, 40 (April, 1957), 258—262.

Krumboltz, John D., Raymond E. Christal, and Joe H. Ward, Jr. "Predicting Leadership Ratings From High School Activities," Journal of Educational Psychology, 50 (June, 1959), 105—110.

Kuhlen, Raymond G., and B. J. Lee. "Personality Characteristics and Social Acceptability in Adolescence," Journal of Educational Psychology, 34 (1943), 321—340. (C.37)

——, and Martha Arnold. "Age Differences in Religious Beliefs and Problems During Adolescence," Journal of Genetic Psychology, 65 (1944), 291—300. (B.50)

——, and H. S. Bretsch. "Sociometric Status and Personal Problems of Adolescents," Sociometry, 10 (May, 1947), 122—132. (E.13)

Kvaraceus, William. "The Delinquent," Review of Educational Research, 28 (December, 1958), 545—553.

Landis, Judson T. "Attitudes and Policies Concerning Marriages Among High School Students," Marriage and Family Living, 18 (May, 1956), 128—136. (B.103)

Landis, Paul H. Adolescence and Youth: The Process of Maturing (2nd ed. New York: McGraw-Hill Book Co., 1952).

——. "The Ordering and Forbidding Technique and Teen-Age Adjustment," School and Society, 80 (October, 1954), 105—106. (B.51)

——. "The Families That Produce Adjusted Adolescents," Clearing House, 29 (May, 1955), 537—540. (B.52)

——, and Carol Stone. "The Relationship of Parental Authority to Teenage Adjustment," Bulletin 538, Washington Agricultural Experiment Station, Pullman, Washington, 1952.

Lane, Lenora C. "Self-Realization: An Explanatory Study of the

Self Concept in a Group of College Students," Journal of Human Relations, 57 (Spring, 1957), 106—116. (D.23)

Lane, Robert E. "Fathers and Sons: Foundations of Political Belief," American Sociological Review, 24 (August, 1959), 502—511.

Langworthy, Russell L. "Community Status and Influence in a High School," American Sociological Review, 24 (August, 1959), 537—539. (B.53)

Lansky, Leonard M., et al. "Sex Differences in Aggression and Its Correlates in Middle-Class Adolescents," Child Development, 32 (March, 1961), 45—58.

Lapierre, Richard T. "The Sociological Significance of Measurable Attitudes," American Sociological Review, 3 (April, 1938), 175—182.

Latham, Albert J. "The Relationship Between Pubertal Status and Leadership in Junior-High-School Boys," Journal of Genetic Psychology, 78 (June, 1951), 185—194. (B.54)

Layton, W. L. "The Relation of Ninth Grade Test Scores to Twelfth Grade Test Scores and High School Rank," Journal of Applied Psychology, 38 (1954), 10—11.

Lee, Alfred McClung. "Attitudinal Multivalence in Relation to Culture and Personality," American Journal of Sociology, 60 (November, 1954), 294—299.

Lee, Dorothy. "Some Implications of Culture for Interpersonal Relations," Social Casework, 31 (November, 1950), 355—360.

Lemert, Edwin M. "The Folkways and Social Control," American Sociological Review, 7 (June, 1942), 394—399.

Lerner, Eugene. "The Problem of Perspective in Moral Reasoning," American Journal of Sociology, 43 (September, 1937), 249—269.

Lessing, Elise Elkins. "Mother-Daughter Similarity on the Kuder Vocational Interest Scales," Educational and Psychological Measurement, 19 (Fall, 1959), 395—400. (C.38)

Leston, Charles. "The Relative Influence of Material and Purpose on Reading Rate," Journal of Educational Research, 52 (February, 1959), 238—240.

Leton, Donald A. "Personality Ratings of High-School Students," Journal of Educational Research, 56 (November, 1962), 160—163.

Levi, I. J. "Student Leadership in Elementary and Junior High School and Its Transfer to Senior High School," Journal of Educational Research, 22 (1930), 185—189.

Levinson, Boris M. "Traditional Jewish Cultural Values and Performance on the Wechsler Tests," Journal of Educational Psychology, 50 (August, 1959), 177—181.

———. "The Problems of Jewish Religious Youth," Genetic Psychology Monographs, 60 (1959), 311—347. (B.55)

Levitt, Morton, and Ben O. Rubenstein. "Acting Out in Adolescence: A Study in Communication," American Journal of Orthopsychiatry, 29 (July, 1959), 622—632.

Levy, David M. Maternal Overprotection (New York: Columbia University Press, 1943).

Levy, John. "The Impact of Cultural Forms Upon Children's Behavior," Mental Hygiene, 16 (April, 1932), 208—211. (F.9)

————. "Conflicts of Culture and Children's Maladjustments," Mental Hygiene, 17 (January, 1933), 41—50.

————, and Ruth Munroe. "The Adolescent and His Happy Family," in Levy and Munroe, The Happy Family (New York: Alfred A. Knopf, 1938), p. 4—17.

Lewin, Kurt. "Field Theory and Experiment in Social Psychology: Concepts and Methods," American Journal of Sociology, 44 (May, 1939), 868—896.

Lewis, W. D. "A Comparative Study of the Personalities, Interests, and Home Backgrounds of Gifted Children of Superior and Inferior Educational Achievement," Journal of Genetic Psychology, 59 (1941), 207—218. (B.56)

Lexton, Donald A. "A Study of the Validity of Parent Attitude Measurement," Child Development, 58 (December, 1958), 515—520. (F.10)

Liccione, John V. "The Changing Family Relationships of Adolescent Girls," Journal of Abnormal and Social Psychology, 51 (November, 1955), 421—426. (B.57)

Lichter, S. et al. The Drop-Outs (New York: The Free Press of Glencoe, 1962).

Lindenfeld, Frank. "A Note on Social Mobility, Religiosity, and Students' Attitudes Towards Premarital Sexual Relations," American Sociological Review, 25 (February, 1960), 81—84.

Linton, Ralph, "A Neglected Aspect of Social Organization" American Journal of Sociology, V. 45, (May, 1940), 870—886.

————. "Age and Sex Categories," American Sociological Review, (October, 1942), 589—603.

Lippitt, Ronald. "Field Theory and Experiment in Social Psychology: Autocratic and Democratic Group Atmosphere," American Journal of Sociology, 45 (July, 1939), 26—49.

————, and Ralph K. White. "An Experimental Study of Leadership and Group Life," in E. E. Maccoby, T. M. Newcomb, and E. L. Hartley, Readings in Social Psychology (New York: Henry Holt and Co., 1958), pp. 496—511. (B.58)

Livson, Norman, and D. McNeill. "Physique and Maturation Rate in Male Adolescents," Child Development, 33 (March, 1962), 145—152.

LoBuglio, Armond, Roger M. Shaw, and Earl Mullin. "Student Leadership in Operation Manhattan," Journal of Educational Sociology, 31 (February, 1958), 210—218.

Locke, Edward. "The Teaching of Morality in the Public School," High School Journal, 42 (November, 1958), 49—53.

Lodge, Helen C. "The Influence of the Study of Biography on the Moral Ideology of the Adolescent at the Eighth Grade Level," Journal of Educational Research, 50 (1956), 241—255. (D.24)

Logan, R. F. L., and E. M. Goldberg. "Rising Eighteen in a London Suburb," British Journal of Sociology, 4 (December, 1953), 323—345. (E.14)

Long, Lloyd Darl. School-Leaving Youth and Employment (New York: Bureau of Publications, Teachers College, Columbia University, 1941).

Lovejoy, Gordon W. Paths to Maturity; Findings of the North Carolina Youth Survey, 1938—1940, N.Y.A. Official Project Number 1-10934, Cooperative Personnel Study, (Chapel Hill: University of North Carolina, 1940).

Lowrie, Samuel Harman. "Dating, A Neglected Field of Study," Marriage and Family Living, 10 (Fall, 1948), 90—91, 95.

————. "Dating Theories and Student Responses," American Sociological Review, 16 (June, 1951), 334—340. (C.39)

————. "Factors Involved in the Frequency of Dating," Marriage and Family Living, 18 (February, 1956), 46—51.

————, and Lenore Dickson, "Inter-Ethnic Relations in a High-School Population," American Journal of Sociology, 58 (July, 1952), 1—10.

Lundberg, George A., and Lenore Dickson. "Selective Association Among Ethnic Groups in a High School Population," American Sociological Review, 17 (February, 1952), 23—34. (B.59)

————, and Lenore Dickson. "Inter-Ethnic Relations in a High School Population," American Journal of Sociology, 58 (July, 1952), 1—10. (B.60)

Lynd, Robert S., and Helen Merrell Lynd. Middletown (New York: Harcourt, Brace and Co., 1929). (A.16)

Lyness, Paul I. "Patterns in the Mass Communication Tastes of the Young Audience," Journal of Educational Psychology, 42 (December, 1951), 449—467. (A.17)

Lynn, David B. "A Note on Sex Differences in the Development of Masculine and Feminine Identification," Psychological Review, 66 (1959), 126—135. (B.61)

Maack, Vernon R. "Adult Distributive Education Sets the Pace for High School D E Students," High School Journal, 42 (March, 1959), 215—217.

Maas, Henry S. "Some Social Class Differences in the Family Systems and Group Relations of Pre- and Early Adolescents," Child Development, 22 (1951), 145—152.

————. "The Role of Members in Clubs of Lower-Class and Middle-Class Adolescents," Child Development, 25 (1954), 241—251. (B.68)

McArthur, Charles. "Subculture and Personality During the College Years," Journal of Educational Sociology, 33 (February, 1960), 260—268. (B.62)

McClelland, David C., A. Rindlisbacher, and Richard deCharms. "Religious and Other Sources of Parental Attitudes Toward

Independence Training," in D. C. McClelland (ed.), Studies in Motivation (New York: Appleton-Century-Crofts, 1955), pp. 389—397.

McClelland, F. M., and John A. Ratliff. "Use of Sociometry as an Aid in Promoting Social Adjustment in a Ninth Grade Home Room," Sociometry, 10 (May, 1947), 147—153. (B.63)

McClennahan, Bessie A. "Prototype in Treatment of Delinquency," Sociology and Social Research, 44 (September—October, 1959), 93—99.

McCluggage, Marston M., and Jackson L. Baur. "Drinking Patterns of Kansas High School Youth," Social Problems, 5 (Spring, 1958), 317—326. (A.18)

McCord, William, Joan McCord, and Alan Howard. "Early Familial Experiences and Bigotry," American Sociological Review, 25 (October, 1960), 717—722. (B. 64)

McCormick, Thomas C., and Boyd E. Macrory. "Group Values in Mate Selection, in a Sample of College Girls," Social Forces, 22 (March, 1944), 315—317.

MacDonald, Margherita, Carson McGuire, and R. J. Havighurst. "Leisure Activities and the Socio-Economic Status of Children," American Journal of Sociology, 54 (May, 1949), 505—519. (A.20)

McFarren, George A. "Have Student Activities Missed the Boat?" High School Journal, 40 (March, 1957), 236—238.

McGuire, Carson. Adolescent Society and Social Mobility (Ph.D. Thesis, University of Chicago, 1949).

————, and R. A. Clark. "Age-Mate Acceptance and Indices of Peer Status," Child Development 23 (1952), 141—154.

————, Monroe Lanmon, and George D. White. "Adolescent Peer Acceptance and Valuations of Role Behavior," American Psychologist, 8 (August, 1953), 397. (C.40)

MacIver, Robert M. "The Imputation of Motives," American Journal of Sociology, 46 (July, 1940), 1—12.

McKeachie, Daniel Solomon. "Students' Rating of Instructors: A Validity Study," Journal of Educational Research, 51 (January, 1958), 79—82. (B.65)

McKee, John P., and Alex C. Sherriffs. "Men's and Women's Beliefs, Ideals, and Self-Concepts," American Journal of Sociology, 44 (1959), 356—363. (E.15)

McKellar, Peter, and Ralph Harris. "Radio Preferences of Adolescents and Children," British Journal of Educational Psychology, 22 (1952), 101—113. (A.19)

MacLean, Malcolm S. "What and Why of Underachievement," High School Journal, 42 (December, 1958), 69—72.

McNeil, John D. "Changes in Ethnic Reaction Tendencies During High School," Journal of Educational Research, 53 (January, 1960), 199—200. (B.66)

McQueen, R., and K. C. Williams. "Predicting Success in Beginning High School Algebra," Psychological Reports, 4 (September, 1959), 603—606. (B.67)

Maddox, George L., Jr. "A Study of High School Drinking: A Sociological Analysis of a Symbolic Act," Dissertation Abstracts, 17 (1957), 1621.

Mainer, R. E., R. E. Horton, and H. H. Remmers. "Parents, Peers, and Problems as Viewed by Youth: Report of Poll #34," Purdue Opinion Panel, Purdue University, V. 12, No. 2 (1953).

Malm, Marguerite. Adolescence (New York: McGraw-Hill Book Co., 1952).

Mangus, A. R. "Personality Adjustment of Rural and Urban Children," American Sociological Review, 13 (October, 1948), 566—575. (B.69)

Mannino, Fortune V. "Family Factors Related to School Persistence," Journal of Educational Sociology, 35 (January, 1962), 193—202.

Marches, Joseph R. "An Empirical Study of Performance in Math and Performance on Selected Entrance Exams," Journal of Educational Research, 53 (January, 1960), 181—187.

Markert, Marlow A. "Social Status and Enrollment in Traditional Mathematics," Journal of Educational Research, 54 (October, 1960), 79.

Marks, J. B. "Interests, Leadership, and Sociometric Status Among Adolescents," Sociometry, 17 (November, 1954), 340—349. (C.41)

Marshall, Helen R. "Factors Relating to the Accuracy of Adult Leaders Judgments of Social Acceptance in Community Youth Groups," Child Development, 29 (September, 1958), 417—424. (B.70)

————, and Boyd R. McCandless. "Relationships Between Dependence on Adults and Social Acceptance by Peers," Child Development, 28 (1957), 413—419. (C.62)

Martinson, Ruth, and O. L. Thompson. "Attitudes of High School Seniors Toward Teaching," California Journal of Educational Research, 5 (May, 1954), 103—108.

Martinson, William D., and Louis C. Statmatakas. "An Attempt to Motivate Potentially Superior Students," School and Society, 87 (April 11, 1959), 173—175.

Mather, William G., Jr. "The Courtship Ideals of High-School Youth," Sociology and Social Research, 19 (November—December, 1934), 166—172.

Matza, David, and G. M. Sykes. "Juvenile Delinquency and Subterranean Values," American Sociological Review, 27 (October, 1961), 712—719.

Mayo, Elton. "Psychiatry and Sociology in Relation to Social Disorganization," American Journal of Sociology, 42 (May, 1937), 825—831. (F.11)

Mayo, George D. "Differentiating Characteristics of a Group of Students Having Psychological Problems," Journal of Educational Psychology, 48 (October, 1957), 359—370.

Mead, A. R. "Who Are the Gifted?" Education 76 (September, 1958), 1—7.

Mead, Margaret. "Administrative Contributions to Democratic Character Formation at the Adolescent Level," Journal of the National Association of Deans of Women (January, 1941). (Included in Kluckhohn and Murray (eds.), Personality in Nature, Society and Culture (2nd ed. New York: Alfred A. Knopf, 1959, pp. 523—530.)

———. "The Impact of Culture on Personality Development in the U.S. Today," Understanding the Child, V. 20, No. 1 (1951), 17—18.

———. "Changing Patterns of Parent-Child Relations in an Urban Culture," International Journal of Psycho-Analysis, 38 (1957), 369—378.

———. "Adolescence in Primitive and Modern Society," in E. E. Maccoby, T. M. Newcomb, and E. L. Hartley (eds.), Readings in Social Psychology (New York: Henry Holt and Co., 1958), pp. 341—349.

Meek, L. Hayden et al., The Personal-Social Development of Boys and Girls with Implications for Secondary Education (New York: American Education Fellowship, Progressive Educational Association, 1940). (B.71)

Menefee, Louis A., and M. M. Chambers. American Youth. (Bibliography) (Washington, D.C.: American Youth Commission of the American Council on Education, 1938).

Meredith, Cameron W. "Personality and Social Development During Childhood and Adolescence," Review of Educational Research, 25 (1955), 469—476.

Merton, Robert K. "Social Structure and Anomie," Social Theory and Social Structure (New York: The Free Press of Glencoe, 1956).

Meyer, William J. "Relations Between Social Need Strivings and the Development of Heterosexual Affiliations," Journal of Abnormal and Social Psychiatry, 59 (1959), 51—57. (C.42)

Meyers, M. S. "The Role of Certain Religious Values for High School Youth," Studies in Higher Education, No. 79, Purdue University (1951), 79—85.

Midcentury White House Conference on Children and Youth, "The Course of Healthy Personality Development," in J. Seidman (ed.), The Adolescent: A Book of Readings (New York: Holt, Rinehart and Winston, 1960), pp. 218—237. (B.72)

Middleton, George, Jr., and George M. Guthrie. "Personality Syndromes and Academic Achievement," Journal of Educational Psychology, 50 (April, 1959), 66—69.

Middleton, Russell, and C. M. Grigg. "Rural-Urban Differences in Aspirations," Rural Sociology, 24 (December, 1959), 347—354.

Miller, Daniel R., and Max L. Hutt. "Value Interiorization and Personality Development," Journal of Social Issues, V. 5, No. 4 (1949), 2—30.

Miller, Derek, H. "Family Interaction in the Therapy of Adolescent Patients," Psychiatry, 21 (August, 1958), 277–284. (F.12)

Mills, C. Wright. "Situated Actions and Vocabularies of Motive," American Sociological Review, 5 (December, 1940), 904–13.

Minehan, Thomas. Boy and Girl Tramps of America (New York: Farrar & Rinehart, 1934).

Mitchell, James V., Jr. "Goal-Setting Behavior as a Function of Self-Acceptance, Over- and Underachievement, and Related Personality Variables," Journal of Educational Psychology, 50 (June, 1959), 93–104.

Miyamoto, S. Frank, and Sanford M. Dornbusch. "A Test of Interactionist Hypotheses of Self-Conception," American Journal of Sociology, 61 (March, 1956), 399–403. (D.25)

Mohr, George J., and Marian A. Despres. The Stormy Decade: Adolescence (New York: Random House, 1958). (C.43)

Monahan, Thomas P. "On the Trend in Delinquency," Social Forces, 40 (December, 1961), 158–168.

Montague, Joel B., Jr. "A Study of Anxiety Among English and American Boys," American Sociological Review, 20 (December, 1955), 685–689. (B.73)

————. "Anxiety Among English and American Boys—An Emendation," American Sociological Review, 21 (April, 1956), 226–227.

Mooney, Ross L. "Surveying High-School Students' Problems by Means of a Problem Check List," Educational Research Bulletin, 21 (March, 1942), 57–69. (E.16)

Moore, Wilbert E., and Melvin M. Tumin. "Some Social Functions of Ignorance," American Sociological Review, 14 (December, 1949), 787–795.

Moreno, J. L., H. H. Jennings, and R. Stockton. "Sociometry in the Classroom," Sociometry, 6 (November, 1943), 425–428. (B.74)

Morris, Richard T. "A Typology of Norms," American Sociological Review, 21 (October, 1956), 610–613.

Morris, W. W. "Ontogenetic Changes in Adolescence Reflected by the Drawing-Human-Figures Techniques," American Journal of Orthopsychiatry, 25 (October, 1955), 720–728.

Morrison, Mildred M., and Pairlee J. Stinson. "Sex Differences Among High School Seniors," Journal of Educational Research, 53 (November, 1959), 103–108. (B.75)

Moss, Howard. "Standards of Conduct for Students, Teachers and Parents," Journal of Counseling Psychology, 2 (1955), 39–42.

Mott, Sina M. "Mother-Father Preference," Character and Personality, 5 (1937), 302–304.

Mulligan, Raymond A. "Theory and Juvenile Delinquency," Journal of Educational Sociology, 33 (May, 1960), 365–372.

Munger, Paul F. "Unpromising College Students Who Graduate," School and Society, 87 (February 28, 1958), 92–93.

Munro, B. C. ''The Structure and Motivation of an Adolescent
Peer Group,'' Alberta Journal of Educational Research, 3
(1953), 149–161.

Munson, Byron E. ''Personality Differentials Among Urban,
Suburban, Town, and Rural Children,'' Rural Sociology,
V. 24, No. 3 (September, 1959), 257–264.

Mussen, Paul, and Jerome Kagan. ''Group Conformity and Perceptions of Parents,'' Child Development, 29 (March, 1958),
57–60. (B.76)

Muuss, Rolf. Theories of Adolescence (Papers in Psychology,
#21) (New York: Random House, 1962).

Myers, Garry C. ''An Overlooked Cause of Mounting Juvenile
Delinquency,'' Education, 78 (October, 1957), 68–71.

Nachmanns, Barbara. ''Childhood Experience and Vocational
Choice in Law, Dentistry, and Social Work,'' Journal of
Counseling Psychology, 7 (Winter, 1960), 243–250.

Neal, Edmund R. ''A Study of the Relationship Between Prior
Experiences and the Quality of Creative Writing Done by
Seventh Grade Pupils,'' Journal of Educational Research,
51 (March, 1958), 481–492. (B.77)

Neblett, Thomas F. ''Youth Movements in the U.S.'' Annals of
the American Academy of Social and Political Science, 194
(1937), 141–151.

Neiman, Lionel J. ''The Influence of Peer Groups Upon Attitudes
Toward the Feminine Role,'' Social Problems, 2 (October,
1954), 104–111. (C.44)

Nelson, Lloyd Palm. ''Selected Factors Associated With High
School Students' Original Interest and Subsequent Development of Interest in a Favorite Leisure-Time Activity,'' Dissertation Abstracts, 16 (1956), 267–268.

Nelson, Suzanne. ''Changes in the Solution of Adolescent Tasks
by 11th Grade Boys During One Year and in Terms of Socio-
Economic Status,'' Dissertation Abstracts, 17 (1957),
1452–1453.

Neugarten, Bernice L. ''Social Class and Friendships Among
School Children,'' American Journal of Sociology, 51 (January, 1946), 305–313. (C.45)

Newcomb, Theodore. ''Community Roles in Attitude Formation,''
American Sociological Review, 7 (October, 1942), 621–630.
(E.17)

Newland, T. Ernest, ''Too Much Special Education?'' Education,
77 (February, 1957), 382–387.

Newman, F. B. ''The Adolescent in Social Groups,'' Applied
Psychology Monographs, No. 9 (1946).

———, and H. E. Jones. The Adolescent in Social Groups
(Stanford, California: Stanford University Press, 1946).

New Yorker, ''Profiles—A Caste, A Culture, A Market-II,'' New
Yorker, 34:57 (November, 29, 1958).

Noble, Gladys V., and S. E. Torsted Lund. "High School Pupils Report Their Fears," Journal of Educational Sociology, 25 (October, 1951), 97—101.

Nolan, Esther G. "School Factors Related to Delinquency," California Journal of Educational Research, 2 (May, 1951), 111—114.

Northby, Arwood S. "Sex Differences in High School Scholarship," School and Society, 86 (February 1, 1958), 63—64.

Northway, Mark L. "Outsiders: A Study of the Personality Factors of Children Least Acceptable to Their Age-Mates," Sociometry, 7 (February, 1944), 10—25.

Norton, Daniel P. "The Relationship of Study Habits and Other Measures to Achievement in 9th Grade General Science," . Journal of Experimental Education, 27 (June, 1959), 211—217.

Norton, Joseph L. "Help Wanted: The Teens Tackle Vocational Development," High School Journal, 41 (May, 1958), 357—361.

Nosow, Sigmund. "Educational Values and Orientations of College Students," Journal of Educational Research, 52 (December, 1958), 123—128. (D.26)

Nye, F. Ivan. "Adolescent-Parent Adjustment: Rurality as a Variable," Rural Sociology, 15 (December, 1950), 334—338.

————. "Adolescent-Parent Adjustment: Socio-Economic Level as a Variable," American Sociological Review, 16 (June, 1951), 341—349. (B.80)

————. "The Rejected Parent and Delinquency," Marriage and Family Living, 18 (November, 1956), 291—297.

————. "Some Family Attitudes and Psychosomatic Illness in Adolescents," The Coordinator, 6 (December, 1957), 26—30.

————, and James F. Short, Jr. "Scaling Delinquent Behavior," American Sociological Review, 22 (June, 1957), 326—331.

————, James F. Short, and Virgil J. Olson. "Socio-Economic Status and Delinquent Behavior," American Journal of Sociology, 62 (January, 1958), 381—389. (F.13)

Oppenheim, A. N. "Social Class Differences in Adolescent Values and Attitudes," Bulletin of the British Psychological Society, 20 (1953), 8.

Orlansky, Harold. "Infant Care and Personality," Psychological Bulletin, 46 (January, 1949), 1—48.

Orzack, Louis H. "Preference and Prejudice Patterns Among Rural and Urban Mates," Rural Sociology, 21 (March,1956), 29—33.

Overs, Robert P., and Norman E. St. Clair. "The Social Class Identification of 1038 Western New York Students," Journal of Educational Research, 51 (November, 1957), 185—190.

Overstreet, Pheobe L. "The High School Girl and Vocational Choice," High School Journal, 41 (May, 1958), 350—354.

Owen, John E. "The Teacher and Occupational Counseling," Education, 78 (September, 1957), 55—58.

Pangle, Roy. "Scholastic Attainment and the High School Athlete," Peabody Journal of Education, 33 (1956), 360—364.

Park, Robert E. "Symbiosis and Socialization: A Frame of Reference for the Study of Society," American Journal of Sociology, 45 (July, 1949), 141—149.

————, and Ernest W. Burgess. Introduction to the Science of Sociology (Chicago: University of Chicago Press, 1921. Especially Chap. 2,3,6,7, and 12).

Parkham, L. C. "Out of School Environment and Activities of Junior High School Pupils," Social Education, 6 (1942), 27—30.

Parsons, Talcott. "Age-Sex in the Social Structure of the U.S.," American Sociological Review, 7 (October, 1942), 604—616. (B.81)

————. "The School Class as a Social System: Some of Its Functions in American Society," Harvard Educational Review, 29 (1959), 297—318.

————, and Robert F. Bales. "Family Structure and the Socialization of the Child," in Family, Socialization, and Interaction Process (New York: The Free Press of Glencoe, 1955).

Partridge, E. De Alton. "A Study of Friendships Among Adolescent Boys," Journal of Genetic Psychology, 63 (1933), 472—476. (C.47)

————. "Leadership Among Adolescent Boys," Teachers College Contributions to Education, No. 608 (1934).

Passow, Harry A. "The Talented Youth Project: A Report of Research Underway," Educational Research Bulletin, 36 (December 11, 1957), 206—216.

Patel, A. S. "Newspaper Reading Interests of Secondary School Children," Journal of Education and Psychology, 11 (1953), 34—43. (A.21)

Patterson, Franklin K. "Adult Role in Adolescent Subculture Innovation: A Case Study," Journal of Educational Sociology, 30 (October, 1956), 58—74.

————. The Adolescent Citizen (New York: The Free Press of Glencoe, 1960).

————, Irving Tukoff, and Charles Winick. "Is Society the Patient? Research and Action Implications," Journal of Educational Sociology, 30 (October, 1956), 106—112.

Pauley, Berthold G. "The Effects of Transportation and Part-Time Employment Upon Participation in School Activities, School Offices Held, Acceptability for Leadership Positions and Grade Point Average Among High School Seniors," Journal of Educational Research, 52 (September, 1958), 3—9.

Payne, Donald E., and Paul H. Mussen. "Parent-Child Relations and Father Identification Among Adolescent Boys," Journal of Abnormal and Social Psychology, 52 (May, 1956), 358—362. (B.82)

Payne, Raymond. "Development of Occupation and Migration Expectations and Choices Among Urban, Small Town and

Rural Adolescent Boys," Rural Sociology, 21 (June, 1956), 117—125.

———. "Adolescent Attitudes Toward the Working Wife," Marriage and Family Living, 18 (November, 1956), 334—339.

———. "Rural and Urban Adolescents Attitudes Toward Moving," Rural Sociology, 22 (March, 1957), 59—61.

Pearson, Gerald H. J. Adolescence and the Conflict of Generations (New York: W. W. Norton and Co., Inc., 1958). (D.27)

Pechstein, Louis A., and A. Laura McGregor. Psychology of the Junior High School (Boston: Houghton Mifflin Co., 1924).

Peck, John R. "Terminal Education for Mentally Retarded Youth," High School Journal, 42 (April, 1959), 272—277.

Peck, Robert F. "Family Patterns Correlated with Adolescent Personality," Journal of Abnormal and Social Psychology, 57 (1958), 347—350. (B.83)

———, and C. Galliani. "Intelligence, Ethnicity, and Social Roles in Adolescent Society," Sociometry, 25 (March, 1962), 64—72.

Peckham, Charles W., and Thomas F. Howell. "Religion as a Cultural Factor in One Aspect of the Personality of Selected College Students," Journal of Educational Sociology, 31 (October, 1957), 75—81. (B.84)

Peckham, Dorothy Reed, et al., "High School Seniors' Opinions of Teaching," California Journal of Educational Research, 13 (January, 1962), 17—30.

Penny, Ronald. "Age and Sex Differences in Motivational Orientation to the Communicative Act," Child Development, 29 (June, 1958), 163—171.

Peters, Herman J. "What It Means to Grow Up," High School Journal, 41 (May, 1958), 340—347.

Phelps, Harold, and John E. Horrocks. "Factors Influencing Informal Groups of Adolescents," Child Development, 29 (March, 1958), 69—86. (C.48)

Philip, B. R., and H. E. Peirotto. "An Objective Evaluation of Brief Group Psychotherapy on Delinquent Boys," Canadian Journal of Psychology, 13 (December, 1959), 273—280. (F.14)

Pierce, Jones J. "Socio-Economic Status and Adolescent Interests," Psychological Reports, 5 (October, 1959), 683ff. (D.28)

———. "Interest Correlates of Socio-Economic Status in Adolescence," Educational and Psychological Measurement, 19 (Fall, 1959), 65—72. (E.18)

———, J. B. Reid, and F. J. King. "Adolescent Racial and Ethnic Group Differences in Social Attitudes and Adjustment," Psychological Reports, 5 (October, 1959), 549—552. (E.19)

Piers, Ellen V., J. M. Danials, and J. F. Quackenbush. "The Identification of Creativity in Adolescents," Journal of Educational Psychology, 51 (December, 1960), 346—351.

Pierson, Jerome, H. Greenburg, and S. Sherman. "The Effects of Single Session Educational Techniques on Prejudiced Attitudes," Journal of Educational Sociology, 21 (October, 1957), 82—86. (B.85)

Pihlblad, C. T., and C. L. Gregory. "The Role of Test Intelligence and Occupational Background as Factors in Occupational Choice," Sociometry, 19 (1956), 192—199.

Pinneau, Samuel R., and Harold E. Jones. "Development of Mental Abilities," Review of Educational Research, 28 (December, 1958), 375—392.

Plant, James S. Personality and the Cultural Pattern (New York: The Commonwealth Fund, 1937).

Plant, Walter T. "Changes in Ethnocentrism Associated with a Four-Year College Education," Journal of Educational Psychology, 49 (June, 1958), 162—165.

Platt, H., G. Jurgensen, and S. B. Chorost. "Comparison of Childrearing Attitudes of Mothers and Fathers of Emotionally Disturbed Adolescents," Child Development, 33 (March, 1962), 117-122.

Polk, Kenneth. "Juvenile Delinquency and Social Areas," Social Problems, 5 (1957), 214—217. (F.15)

Pope, Benjamin. "Socio-Economic Contrasts in Children's Peer Culture Prestige Values," Genetic Psychology Monographs, 48 (1953), 157—220. (C.49)

Porterfield, Austin L., and H. Ellison Salley. "Current Folkways of Sexual Behavior," American Journal of Sociology, 52 (November, 1946), 209—216.

Powell, Marvin, and Viola Bloom. "Development of and Reasons for Vocational Choices of Adolescents Through the High School Years," Journal of Educational Research, 56 (November, 1962), 126—133.

Prahl, Marie R., Louis A. D'Amico, and Howard J. Bryant. "The Relation Between MAT Scores and Achievement in Junior College Subject," Educational and Psychological Measurement, 19 (Spring, 1959), 611—616. (B.86)

Prevey, Esther E. "Family Life Education and the Needs of Boys and Girls," School and Community, 45 (April, 1959), 19—20.

"Profile of Youth Series," Ladies Home Journal (June-December, 1949).

Psathas, George. "Ethnicity, Social Class, and Adolescent Independence From Parental Control," American Sociological Review, 22 (August, 1957), 415—423. (B.87)

Racky, Donald J. "Predictions of Ninth Grade Woodshop Performance From Aptitude and Interest Measures," Educational and Psychological Measurement, 19 (Spring, 1959), 229—236. (B.88)

Rae, Philip A. "Friction Between Adolescents and Parents," Education 81 (December, 1960), 225—227.

Rainwater, Lee. A Study of Personality Differences Between Middle and Lower Class Adolescents: The Szondi Test in Culture Personality Research (Genetic Psychology Monographs, Province Town, Mass., 1956).

Rall, M. E. "Dependency and the Adolescent," Social Casework, 28 (1947), 123−130.

Ramsey, Charles E., and Lowry Nelson. "Change in Values and Attitudes Toward the Family," American Sociological Review, 21 (October, 1956), 605−609. (E.20)

────, and R. J. Smith. "Japanese and American Perceptions of Occupations," American Journal of Sociology, 65 (March, 1960), 475−482.

Raths, James. "Underachievement and a Search for Values," Journal of Educational Sociology, 34 (May, 1951), 422−424.

Rautman, Arthur L. "Youth in Search of a Standard," Mental Hygiene (October, 1946), 597−605.

Reals, Willis H. "Leadership in the High School," The School Review, 46 (1938), 523−531. (B.89)

Reckless, Walter C., Simon Dinitz, and Barbara Kay. "The Self Component in Political Delinquency and Potential Non-Delinquency," American Sociological Review, 22 (October, 1957), 566−570.

────, Simon Dinitz, and Ellen Murray. "Self-Concept as an Insulator Against Delinquency," American Sociological Review, 21 (December, 1956), 744−746. (F.16)

"Recreational Interests and Needs of High School Youth," (resume of a study conducted in New York), Recreation, 47 (January, 1954), 43−46. (A.22)

Redl, Fritz, and David Wineman. Children Who Hate: The Disorganization and Breakdown of Behavior Controls (New York: The Free Press of Glencoe, 1951).

────, and David Wineman. The Aggressive Child, contains both Children Who Hate (1951) and Controls from Within (1952) (New York: The Free Press of Glencoe, 1957).

Reeves, J. Maxson, and Leo Goldman. "Social Class Perceptions and School Maladjustment," Personnel and Guidance Journal, 35 (March, 1957), 414−419. (F.17)

Reiss, Albert J., Jr. "Social Correlates of Psychological Types of Delinquency," American Sociological Review, 17 (December, 1952), 710−718. (F.18)

────, and A. L. Rhodes. "The Distribution of Juvenile Delinquency in the Social Class Structure," American Sociological Review, 26 (October, 1961), 720−732.

Remmers, H. H., and A. J. Drucker, "Teen-Age Attitudes Toward Problems of Child Management," Journal of Educational Psychology, 42 (1951), 105−113. (E.21)

────, and D. H. Radler. "Teenage Attitudes," Scientific American, 198 (June, 1958), 25−29. (E.22)

────, and D. H. Radler. The American Teenager (New York: Bobbs-Merrill Co., 1958).

————, R. E. Horton, and Sverre Lysgaard. "Teen-Age Personality in our Culture," Report of Poll #32, Purdue Opinion Panel II, LaFayette, Indiana, Purdue University (1952).

————, M. S. Myers, and E. M. Bennett. "Some Personality Aspects and Religious Values of High School Youth," Purdue Opinion Panel, V. 10, No. 3 (1951), 30.

Resnick, J. "A Study of Some Relationships Between High School Grades and Certain Aspects of Adjustment," Journal of Educational Research, 44 (1951), 321—340.

Reuter, E. B. "The Sociology of Adolescence," American Journal of Sociology, 43 (November, 1937), 414—427. (C.50)

————. "The Education of the Adolescent," Journal of Educational Sociology, 14 (October, 1940), 67—78. (B.90)

————, et al., "Sociological Research in Adolescence," American Journal of Sociology, 42 (July, 1936), 81—94.

Rhodes, A. Lewis. "Authoritarianism and Fundamentalism of Rural and Urban High School Students," Journal of Educational Sociology, 34 (November, 1960), 97—105.

Ricciuti, Edward A. "Children and Radio: A Study of Listeners and Non-Listeners to Various Types of Radio Programs in Terms of Selected Ability, Attitude, and Behavior Measures," Genetic Psychology Monographs, 44 (1951), 69—143.

Riemer, Svend. "Courtship for Security," Sociology and Social Research, 45 (July, 1961), 423—429.

Riesman, David, et al. The Lonely Crowd (New Haven: Yale University Press, 1950).

Riley, Fay C. "Providing for the Underachiever," High School Journal, 42 (December, 1958), 91—95.

Riley, Matilda White, and Samuel H. Flowerman. "Group Relations as a Variable in Communications Research," American Sociological Review, 16 (April, 1951), 174—180. (A.23)

Rivlin, Leanne Green. "Creativity and the Self-Attitudes and Sociability of High School Students," Journal of Educational Psychology, 50 (August, 1959), 147—152. (D.29)

Robbins, Florence G. The Sociology of Play, Recreation and Leisure (Dubuque, Iowa: William C. Brown Co., 1955).

Roberts, Helen Erskine. "The Reactions of a Group of High School Sophomores to Their Experiences in Special Classes," California Journal of Educational Research, 10 (November, 1959), 220—228. (B.91)

Robin, Lee N., and P. O'Neal. "The Marital History of Former Problem Children," Social Problems, 5 (Spring, 1958), 347—357. (F.19)

Roff, Catherine. "The Self-Concept in Adolescent Girls," Dissertation Abstracts, 20 (July, 1959), 385.

Roff, Merrill, and David S. Brody. "Appearance and Choice Status During Adolescence," Journal of Psychology, 36 (1953), 347—356.

Rogers, Everett M., and A. Eugene Havens. "Prestige Rating and Mate Selection on a College Campus," Marriage and

230

Family Living, 22 (February, 1960), 55—59.

Rogoff, Natalie. "Public Schools and Equality of Opportunity," Journal of Educational Sociology, 33 (February, 1960), 252—259.

Rose, Arnold M. "Reference Groups of Rural High School Youth," Child Development, 27 (September, 1956), 351—363.

―――. "Attitudes of Youth Toward Mental Health Problems," Sociology and Social Research, 41 (June, 1957), 343—348. (E.23)

Rosen, Bernard C. "Conflicting Group Membership: A Study of Parent-Peer Group Cross-Pressures," American Sociological Review, 20 (April, 1955), 155—161. (B.92)

―――. "The Achievement Syndrome: A Psychocultural Dimension of Social Stratification," American Sociological Review, 21 (April, 1956), 203—211. (D.30)

Rosenfeld, Howard, and A. Zensler. "The Influence of Teachers on Aspirations of Students," Journal of Educational Psychology, 52 (February, 1961), 1—11.

Ross, Edward A. Principles of Sociology (1st Revision. New York: The Century Co., 1930. Especially Chapter 8).

Roth, Robert M. "The Role of Self-Concept in Achievement," Journal of Experimental Education, 27 (June, 1959), 265—281. (D.31)

―――, and J. P. Das. "A Study in Stereotype of College Freshmen," Journal of Social Psychology, 47 (1958), 373—386.

Rothman, Philip. "Socio-Economic Status and Values of Junior High School Students," Journal of Educational Sociology, 28 (November, 1954), 126—130. (E.24)

Roucek, Joseph S. "Age as a Prestige Factor," Sociology and Social Research, 42 (May—June, 1958), 349—352.

Runner, Jessie R. "Sociological Research in Adolescence," American Journal of Sociology, 42 (November, 1936), 392—393.

―――. "Social Distance in Adolescent Relationships," American Journal of Sociology, 43 (1937), 428—439.

Russell, Donald W. "A Plea to Beam in the Underachiever," High School Journal, 42 (December, 1958), 66—68.

Russell, Ivan L. "Behavior Problems of Children from Broken and Intact Homes," Journal of Educational Sociology, 31 (November, 1957), 124—130.

Ryan, F. J. "Trait Ratings of High School Students by Teachers," Journal of Educational Psychology, 49 (June, 1958), 124—128.

―――, and James S. Davie. "Social Acceptance, Academic Achievement, and Academic Aptitude Among High School Students," Journal of Educational Research, 52 (November, 1958), 101—106. (B.93)

Ryans, David G. "Some Relationships Between Pupil Behavior and Certain Teacher Characteristics," Journal of Educational Psychology, 52 (April, 1961), 82—90.

————. "Inventory Estimated Teacher Characteristics as Co-
variants of Observer Assessed Pupil Behavior," Journal of
Educational Psychology, 52 (April, 1961), 91—97.

Sadler, William S. Adolescence Problems (St. Louis: C. V.
Mosby Co., 1952).

Sagehorn, Howard. "Adolescent Reactions to Guidance," Education, 81 (December, 1960), 221—224.

Salisbury, Harrison E. The Shook-Up Generation (New York:
Harper and Brothers, 1958).

Sando, Rudolph. "This They Believe," California Journal of
Secondary Education, 31 (January, 1956), 45—49.

Sarbin, Theodore R., and Bela O. Baker. "Psychological Pre-
disposition and/or Subcultural Participation: Reply to Dr.
Glaser," Sociometry, 20 (June, 1957), 161—164.

Scandrette, Onas C. "Social Distance and Degree of Acquaintance," Journal of Educational Research, 51 (January, 1958),
367—372. (C.51)

Scarf, Robert C. "Differential Scores and Unstable Personality," Journal of Educational Psychology, 48 (May, 1957),
268—272.

Scarpitti, Frank R., E. Murray, S. Dinitz, and W. C. Reckless.
"The 'Good' Boy in a High Delinquency Area: Four Years
Later," American Sociological Review, 25 (August, 1960),
555—558.

Scheidlinger, Saul. "A Comparative Study of the Boy Scout
Movement in Different National and Social Groups," Ameri-
can Sociological Review, 13 (December, 1948), 739—750.
(B.94)

Schenk, Q. F., and A. K. Romney. "Some Differential Attitudes
Among Adolescent Groups as Revealed by Bogardus' Social
Distance Scale," Sociology and Social Research, 35 (1950),
38—45. (E.25)

Schmeidler, Gertrude R., Marjory J. Nelson, and Marjorie
Bristol. "Freshman Rorschachs and College Performance," Genetic Psychology Monographs, 59 (February,
1959), 3—44. (B.78)

Schmidt, John L., and John W. M. Rothney. "Variability of Vocational Choices of High School Students," Personnel and
Guidance Journal, 34 (November, 1955), 142—146. (D.32)

Schmitt, Robert C. "Density, Delinquency, and Crime in Hono-
lulu," Sociology and Social Research, 41 (March—April,
1957), 274—276.

Schneider, Louis, and Sverre Lysgaard. "The Deferred Gratifi-
cation Pattern: A Preliminary Study," American Sociological Review, 18 (1953), 142—149.

Schuessler, Karl, and Anselm Strauss. "A Study of Concept
Learning by Scale Analysis," American Sociological Review, 15 (December, 1950), 752—762.

232

Schullian, Dorothy M. "College Slang," School and Society, 58 (August 28, 1943), 169—170.

Schultz, Raymond E. "A Comparison of Negro Pupils Ranking High With Those Ranking Low in Educational Achievement," Journal of Educational Sociology, 31 (March, 1958), 265—271.

Schutz, Richard E. "Patterns of Personal Problems of Adolescent Girls," Journal of Educational Psychology, 49 (February, 1958), 1—5.

Sears, Robert R. "Personality Development in the Family," in R. F. Winch and R. McGinnis (eds.), Selected Studies in Marriage and the Family (New York: Henry Holt and Co., 1953), pp. 215—240.

————, et al. Patterns of Child Rearing (New York: Row, Peterson, 1957).

Seeman, Melvin. "Moral Judgement: A Study in Racial Frames of References," American Sociological Review, 12 (August, 1947), 404—411.

Segel, David. "Frustration in Adolescent Youth: Its Development and Implications for the School Program," U.S. Office of Education Bulletin No. 1 (1951).

Seidler, Murray B., and Mel J. Ravitz. "A Jewish Peer Group," American Journal of Sociology, 61 (July, 1955), 11—15. (C.52)

Seidman, Jerome (ed.). The Adolescent: A Book of Readings (Rev. ed. New York: Holt, Rinehart and Winston, Inc., 1960).

Sellin, Johan Torsten. "Culture Conflict and Crime," Social Science Research Council, Bulletin #41, New York (1938).

Sewell, William H. "Infant Training and the Personality of the Child," American Journal of Sociology, 58 (September, 1952), 150—159.

————, Archie O. Haller, and Murray Straus. "Social Status and Educational and Occupational Aspiration," American Sociological Review, 22 (February, 1957), 67—73. (D.33)

Sexton, Patricia C. "Social Class and Pupil Turn-Over Rates," Journal of Educational Sociology, 33 (November, 1959), 131—135.

Shannon, J. R. "Talent, Instruction and Motivation," Education, 78 (September, 1958), 34—38.

Shaw, Clifford. The Jack-Roller: A Delinquent Boy's Own Story (Chicago: University of Chicago Press, 1930).

Shaw, Merville C., and M. D. Black. "The Reaction to Frustration of Bright High School Underachievers," California Journal of Educational Research, 11 (May, 1960), 120—124.

————, and B. E. Dutton. "The Use of the Parent Attitude Research Inventory with the Parents of Bright Academic Underachievers," Journal of Educational Psychology, 53 (October, 1962), 203—208.

————, and J. T. McCuen. "The Onset of Academic Underachievement in Bright Children," Journal of Educational Psychology, 51 (June, 1960), 103—108.

Shaw, Robert C. "Do High School Graduation Requirements Challenge the Best Students?" School and Community, 46 (November, 1959), 13, 22.

Shay, Carleton B. "A Study of High School Students Who Completed a College Preparatory Curriculum," California Journal of Educational Research, 11 (May, 1960), 125—129.

Sheldon, Paul M. "Mexican-Americans in Urban Public Schools," California Journal of Educational Research, 12 (February, 1961), 21—26.

Sheldon, Robert B. "High School Foreign Language Study and Freshman Performance," School and Society, 85 (June, 1957), 203—205.

Sherif, Muzafer. "Integrating Field Work and Laboratory in Small Group Research," American Sociological Review, 19 (December, 1954), 759—771.

————, B. Jack White, and O. J. Harvey. "Status in Experimentally Produced Groups," American Journal of Sociology, 60 (January, 1955), 370—379. (C.21)

Shibutani, Temotsu. "Reference Groups as Perspectives, American Journal of Sociology, 60 (May, 1955), 562—569.

Shinn, Edmond O. "Interest and Intelligence as Related to Achievement in Tenth Grade," California Journal of Educational Research, 7 (November, 1956), 217—220.

Shuttleworth, Frank K. The Adolescent Period (Evanston, Ill.: Child Development Publishers, 1951).

Siggelkow, Richard A. "Were the Starkweather Murders Necessary?" School and Society, 86 (September 23, 1958), 335—336.

Silverman, Sylvia S. "Clothing and Appearance: Their Psychological Implications for Teen-Age Girls," Teachers College Contributions to Education, Teachers College, Columbia University (1945), 114—119. (A.24)

Simpson, Ansel P. "Does Student Culture Discourage Scholarship?" School and Community, 47 (January, 1961), 6—7.

Simpson, Richard L. "What Is the Importance of Peer Group Status at the High School Level?" High School Journal, 42 (May, 1959), 291—294.

————. "Parental Influence, Anticipatory Socialization and Social Mobility," American Sociological Review, 27 (August, 1962), 517—522.

————, and Ida Harper Simpson. "The School, the Peer Group, and Adolescent Development," Journal of Educational Sociology, 32 (1958), 37—41. (D.34)

Skinner, Charles E. "Some Thoughts About Children Who Have Problems," Education, 78 (February, 1958), 349—350.

————. "The ABC's of Human Adjustment," Education, 80 (December, 1959), 220—224.

Sloan, Fred A. "Developmental Characteristics of Young Adolescents and the School Program," High School Journal, 44 (April, 1961), 257—262.

Slocum, W. L. "Educational Planning by High School Seniors," Journal of Educational Research, 51 (April, 1958), 583—590.

Smith, Arthur, and Jane Josse. "Some Social-Psychological Aspects of the High School Orientation Program," Journal of Educational Sociology, 31 (November, 1957), 99—107.

Smith, Benjamin F. "Wishes of Negro High School Seniors and Social Class Status," Journal of Educational Sociology, 25 (April, 1952), 466—475.

Smith, David Wayne. "Schools and the Emotionally Disturbed," Education, 80 (December, 1959), 195—200.

Smith, Ernest A. American Youth Culture (New York: The Free Press of Glencoe, 1962).

Smith, John A., and Phillip G. Nash. "Differences in Interest Patterns According to High School Major Sequences," California Journal of Educational Research, 9 (September, 1958), 179—185.

Smith, Wayne D. "The Plot Against the Gifted," Education, 78 (February, 1958), 351—355.

Smucker, Orin. "Prestige Status Stratification on a College Campus," Applied Anthropology, 6 (1947), 20—27.

Sorelle, Zell, and Jack Walker. "What Is Television Doing to Our Children?" Journal of Educational Research, 55 (February, 1962), 236—237.

Soronson, A. G., and I. E. Morris. "Attitudes and Beliefs as Sources of Vocational Preference," Journal of Educational Research, 56 (September, 1962), 20—27.

Spaulding, Charles B., and Ruth S. Bolin. "The Clique as a Device for Social Adjustment Among Freshmen High School Girls," Journal of Educational Sociology, 24 (November, 1950), 147—153. (B.95)

Spiegel, L. "A Review of Contributions to Psychoanalytic Theory of Adolescence," Psychoanalytic Study of the Child, VI (New York: International Universities Press, 1951), pp. 375—393.

Spivak, Monroe L. "School Problems Reported by Seventh and Ninth-Grade Children Entering the Same Junior High School," Journal of Educational Research, 50 (April, 1957), 631—633.

Stanson, Pairlee J., and M. M. Morrison. "Sex Differences Among High School Seniors," Journal of Educational Research, 53 (November, 1959), 103—108.

Stefflre, Burford. "Psychological Factors Associated with Aspirations for Socio-Economic Mobility," California Journal of Educational Research, 6 (March, 1955), 55—60.

————. "Concurrent Validity of the Vocational Values Inventory," Journal of Educational Research, 52 (May, 1959), 339—341.

Stendler, Celia Burns. "A Study of Some Socio-Moral Judgments of Junior High High School Children," Child Development, 20 (March, 1949), 15—28.

Stephenson, Richard M. "Mobility Orientation and Stratification of 1000 Ninth Graders," American Sociological Review, 22 (April, 1957), 204—212. (D.35)

Sterner, Alice Parvin. "Radio, Motion Picture, and Reading Interests: A Study of High School Pupils," Teachers College Contributions to Education, No. 932, Teachers College, Columbia University (1947). (A.25)

Stewart, R. L., and G. M. Vernon. "Four Correlates of Empathy in the Dating Situation," Sociology and Social Research, 43 (March—April, 1959), 279—285.

Stockwell, Spencer L. "Sexual Experience of Adolescent Delinquent Girls," International Journal of Sexology, 7 (August, 1953), 25—27.

Stolz, H. R., and L. M. Stolz. "Adolescent Problems Related to Somatic Variations," Forty-Third Yearbook of the National Society for the Study of Education, Pt. 1 (1944) (University of Chicago Press), pp. 81—99. (F.20)

Stone, Carol L., and Paul H. Landis. "An Approach to Authority Pattern in Parent-Teen-Age Relationships," Rural Sociology, 18 (September, 1953), 233—242.

Stone, Lawrence D., and Joseph Church. Childhood and Adolescence: A Psychology of the Growing Person (New York: Random House, 1957).

Stoodley, Bartlett H. "Normative Attitudes of Filipino Youth Compared with German and American Youth," American Sociological Review, 22 (1957), 553—561.

———. "A Cross-Cultural Study of Structure and Conflict in Social Norms," American Journal of Sociology, 65 (July, 1959), 39—48.

Story, M. L. "The 'Dull Normal' Also Elect Congressmen," High School Journal, 40 (January, 1957), 159—161.

Stouffer, Samuel A. "An Analysis of Conflicting Social Norms," American Sociological Review, 14 (December, 1949), 707—717. (C.53)

Strang, Ruth. "What Discipline Means to Adolescents," Nervous Child, 9 (1951), 139—146.

———. "Adolescents' Views on One Aspect of Their Development," Journal of Educational Psychology, 46 (1955), 423—432. (E.26)

———. "Gifted Adolescents' Views of Growing Up," Exceptional Children, 23 (October, 1956), 10—15. (D.37)

———. The Adolescent Views Himself (New York: McGraw-Hill Book Co., 1957). (D.36)

———. "An Introspective Approach to Study Problems," Journal of Educational Research, 51 (December, 1957), 271—278.

———. "Reading and Study as Viewed by Adolescents," High School Journal, 41 (May, 1958), 326—330.

Stratton, Dorothy C. "Interpretation of the Findings of the National Study of Adolescent Girls," Journal of the National Association of Women Deans and Counselors, 21 (October, 1957), 18—20. (D.38)

Straus, Murray A. "Work Roles and Financial Responsibility in the Socialization of Farm, Fringe, and Small Town Boys," Rural Sociology, 27 (September, 1962), 257—274.

Strauss, Anselm L. "The Development and Transformation of Monetary Meanings in the Child," American Sociological Review, 17 (June, 1952), 275—286.

————, and Karl Schuessler. "Socialization, Logical Reasoning, and Concept Development in the Child," American Sociological Review, 16 (August, 1951), 514—523.

Sullenger, T. E. "Leadership and Leisure-Time Interest of Grade School Boys," Sociology and Social Research, 25 (March—April, 1941), 351—355. (A.26)

Survey Research Center. A Study of Adolescent Boys. A report of a national survey of boys in the fourteen to sixteen age range. Conducted by Survey Research Center, Institute for Social Research, University of Michigan, Ann Arbor, Michigan, for the National Council, Boy Scouts of America, New Brunswick, New Jersey, 1955. (A.31)

Sutherland, Edwin A. "White-Collar Criminality," American Sociological Review, 5 (February, 1940), 1—12.

————. White Collar Crime (New York: Holt, Rinehart & Winston, 1961).

Swanson, G. E. "The Disturbance of Children in Urban Areas," American Sociological Review, 14 (October, 1949), 676—678.

Sweeney, Francis J. "Intelligence, Vocational Interests and Reading Speed of Senior Boys in Catholic High Schools in Los Angeles," California Journal of Educational Research, 5 (September, 1954), 159—165.

Swenson, Clifford H., Jr. "College Performance of Students with High and Low High School Grades When Academic Aptitude is Controlled," Journal of Educational Research, 50 (April, 1957), 597—603.

Swenson, Jean, and Jessie Rhulman. "Leisure Activities of a University Sophomore Class," Educational and Psychological Measurement, 12 (1952), 452—466. (A.27)

Sykes, Gresbam M., and David Matza. "Techniques of Neutralization: A Theory of Delinquency," American Sociological Review, 22 (1957), 664—670.

Symonds, Percival M. "Sex Differences in the Life Problems and Interests of Adolescents," School and Society, 43 (May, 1936), 751—752. (E.27)

————. Adolescent Fantasy (New York: Columbia University Press, 1949).

Taba, Hilda. "The Moral Beliefs of Sixteen-Year-Olds," Adolescent Character and Personality (New York: John Wiley and Sons, 1949), 83—87. (E.28)

————, et al. "School Culture and Group Life," Journal of Educational Sociology, 21 (May, 1948), 497—560.

Taylor, Donald C. "Courtship as a Social Institution in the United States, 1930 to 1945," Social Forces, 25 (October, 1946), 65—69.

Terrell, Glenn, Jr., and Joy Shreffler. "A Developmental Study of Leadership," Journal of Educational Research, 52 (October, 1958), 69—72.

Thayer, Lloyd. "The Junior High School Movement in North Carolina," High School Journal, 41 (March, 1958), 236—245.

Thayer, V. T. "Some Significant Aspects of School Desegregation," School and Society, 87 (November 21, 1959), 469—472.

Thistlewaite, Donald L. "Effects of Social Recognition Upon the Educational Motivation of Talented Youth," Journal of Educational Psychology, 50 (June, 1959), 111—116.

————. "College Press and Student Achievement," Journal of Educational Psychology, 50 (October, 1959), 183—191.

Thomas, Robert J. "An Empirical Study of High School Dropouts in Regard to Ten Possible Related Factors," Journal of Educational Sociology, 28 (September, 1954), 11—18.

Thompson, Muriel. "Students Evaluations of Guidance Services," California Journal of Educational Research, 11 (September, 1960), 167—169.

Thompson, O. E. "High School Students Values: Emergent or Traditional," California Journal of Educational Research, 12 (May, 1961), 132—144.

Thorpe, Louis P., and Virginia Johnson. "Personality and Social Development in Childhood and Adolescence," Review of Educational Research, 28 (December, 1958), 422—433.

Thrasher, Frederic M. "Social Backgrounds and Informal Education," Journal of Educational Sociology, 7 (April, 1934), 470—484.

————. The Gang: A Study of 1,313 Gangs in Chicago, 2nd revised ed. (Chicago: University of Chicago Press, 1936).

Toby, Jackson, "Universalistic and Particularistic Factors in Role Assignment," American Sociological Review, 18 (April, 1953), 134—141.

————. "The Differential Impact of Family Disorganization," American Sociological Review, 22 (October, 1957), 505—512.

Toch, Hans. "A Preliminary Inquiry Into the Learning of Values," Journal of Educational Psychology, 48 (March, 1957), 145—156.

Travers, John F., and R. G. Davis. "A Study of Religious Motivation and Delinquency," Journal of Educational Sociology, 34 (January, 1961), 205—220.

Trent, Richard P. "The Relation Between Expressed Self-Acceptance and Expressed Attitudes Toward Negroes and Whites Among Negro Children," Journal of Genetic Psychology, 91 (September, 1957), 25—31.

Trow, William C., Alvin F. Zander, William C. Morse, and David

H. Jenkins. "The Class as a Group: Conclusions from Research in Group Dynamics," Journal of Educational Psychology, 41 (1950), 322—338. (B.96)

Truax, W. W., Jr., and John P. McQuary. "Locating the Underachiever in the Small Secondary School," High School Journal, 40 (May, 1957), 304—307.

Tryon, Caroline McCann. "Evaluations of Adolescent Personality by Adolescents," Child Behavior and Development (New York: McGraw-Hill Book Co., 1943). (E.29)

———. "The Adolescent Peer Culture," Forty-third Yearbook of the National Society for the Study of Education, Pt. 1 (February, 1944), University of Chicago Press, pp 217—239. (C.54)

Tuddinham, Read D. "Constancy of Personal Morale Over a Fifteen Year Interval," Child Development, 33 (September, 1962), 663—673.

Tuma, Elias, and N. Livson. "Family Socioeconomic Status and Adolescent Attitudes to Authority," Child Development, 31 (June, 1960), 387—399.

Turner, James W. "High School Marriages in Missouri," School and Community, 48 (February, 1962), 9.

Turner, Ralph H. "Moral Judgement: A Study in Roles," American Sociological Review, 17 (February, 1952), 70—77. (E.30)

———. "Self and Other in Moral Judgement," American Sociological Review, 19 (June, 1954), 249—259.

———. "Role-Taking, Role Standpoint and Reference Group Behavior," American Journal of Sociology, 61 (January, 1956), 316—328.

Tyler, Fred T. "Stability of Intra-Individual Patterning of Measures of Adjustment During Adolescence," Journal of Educational Psychology, 48 (April, 1957), 217—227.

Ullmann, Charles A. "Teachers, Peers and Tests as Predictors of Adjustment," Journal of Educational Psychology, 48 (May, 1957), 257—267.

Uthy, Ishmel. "The Slow Learner in the Secondary School," Education, 81 (February, 1961), 341—344.

Valry, J. Richard. "The Importance of Social Class in a Suburban School," Journal of Educational Sociology, 33 (April, 1960), 307—310.

Van Waters, Mariam. Youth in Conflict (New York: Republic Printing Co., 1925).

Vener, Arthur M. Adolescent Orientations to Clothing (Thesis, Michigan State University, 1957).

Vernon, Glenn M., and Robert L. Stewart. "Empathy as a Process in the Dating Situation," American Sociological Review, 22 (1957), 48—52.

Via, Charles S. "Teenage Problems," High School Journal, 41 (May, 1958), 362—365.

Vickery, F. E. "Adolescent Interests in Social Problems," Journal of Educational Research, 40 (1946), 309—315.

Vold, George B. "Discussion of Solomon Kobrin's Paper, 'The Conflict of Values in Delinquency Areas,'" American Sociological Review, 16 (October, 1951), 671—672. (F.21)

Volkart, Edmund H. (ed.). Social Behavior and Personality: Contributions of W. I. Thomas to Theory and Social Research (New York: Social Science Research Council, 1951).

Wagner, Guy. "Toward Better Reading in Our High Schools," Education, 77 (May, 1958), 555—560.

Wagner, John A. "Talented High School Students," Education, 81 (December, 1960), 232—234.

Wall, William D. The Adolescent Child (London: Methuen, 1952).

Waller, Willard. Sociology of Teaching (New York: John Wiley and Sons, 1932).

——. "The Rating and Dating Complex," American Sociological Review, 2 (October, 1937), 727—734. (C.55)

Wallin, Paul. "Cultural Contradictions and Sex Roles: A Repeat Study," American Sociological Review, 15 (1950), 288—293. (C.56)

——. "Marital Happiness of Parents and Their Children's Attitude to Marriage," American Sociological Review, 19 (February, 1954), 20—23.

Wardlow, Mary E., and James E. Greene. "An Exploratory Sociometric Study of Peer Status Among Adolescent Girls," Sociometry, 15 (1952), 311—318. (C.63)

Warnath, Charles F. "The Relation of Family Cohesiveness and Adolescent Independence to Social Effectiveness," Marriage and Family Living, 17 (November, 1955), 346—348. (B.97)

Warner, W. Lloyd, Robert J. Havighurst, and Martin B. Loeb. Who Shall Be Educated? (New York: Harper and Bros., 1944).

Washburn, Wilbur C. "Patterns of Self-Conceptualization in High School and College Students," Journal of Educational Psychology, 52 (June, 1961), 123—131.

——. "Factors Associated with Levels of Self-Conceptualization in High School Students," California Journal of Educational Research, 12 (November, 1961), 200—206.

——. "Patterns of Protective Attitudes in Relation to Differences in Self-Evaluation and Anxiety Level Among High School Students," California Journal of Educational Research, 13 (March, 1962), 84—94.

Washburne, Norman F. "Socioeconomic Status, Urbanism and Academic Performance in College," Journal of Educational Research, 53 (December, 1959), 130—137.

Wattenberg, William W. The Adolescent Years (New York: Har-
Court, Brace, 1955).
————, and James J. Balistrieri. "Gang Membership and Ju-
venile Misconduct," American Sociological Review, 15 (De-
cember, 1950), 744—752. (F.22)
Wax, Murray. "Themes in Cosmetics and Grooming," Ameri-
can Journal of Sociology, 62 (May, 1957), 588—593. (A.28)
Weary, Bettina. "Stay in School Campaign," School Life, 39,
(May, 1957), 13—15.
Weaver, Paul. "Youth and Religion," Annals of the American
Academy of Political and Social Science, 236 (November,
1944), 152—160.
Weber, Louis C. "A Study of Peer Acceptance Among Delin-
quent Girls," Sociometry, 13 (November, 1950), 363—381.
Webster, Harold. "Changes in Attitudes During College," Jour-
nal of Educational Psychology, 49 (June, 1958), 109—117.
Webster, Staten W. "The Influence of Interracial Contact on
Social Acceptance in a Newly Integrated School," Journal of
Educational Psychology, 52 (December, 1961), 292—296.
Weckler, Nora L. "Social Class and School Adjustment in Re-
lation to Character Reputation," in Havighurst and Taba,
Adolescent Character and Personality (New York: Wiley
and Sons, 1949), Chap. 5. (B.98)
Weiland, I. Hyman. "The Psychological Significance of Hot Rods
and Automobile Driving to Adolescent Males," Psychiatric
Quarterly Supplement, 31 (1957), 261—275. (A.29)
Welch, Louise Thompson. "Recent Studies in Adolescence,"
Bulletin of the Maritime Psychological Association (April,
1953), 34—38.
Wellman, Beth. "The School Child's Choice of Companions,"
Journal of Educational Research, 14 (September, 1926),
126—132. (C.57)
Wells, James A. "Junior High School Literature," School and
Community, 45 (January, 1959), 27.
Wertheimer, Rita R. "Consistency of Sociometric Status Posi-
tion in Male and Female High School Students," Journal of
Educational Psychology, 48 (November, 1957), 385—390.
Westley, William A., and Frederick Elkin. "The Protective
Environment and Adolescent Socialization," Social Forces,
35 (March, 1957), 243—249.
Westmeyer, Paul. "Can High School Students Do Research?"
High School Journal, 41 (March, 1958), 258—262.
Whiting, John W. M., and Irvin L. Child. Child Training and
Personality: A Cross-Cultural Study (New Haven: Yale
University Press, 1953).
————, R. Kluckhohn, and A. Anthony. "The Function of Male
Initiation Ceremonies at Puberty," in E. E. Maccoby, T. M.
Newcomb, and E. L. Hartley (eds.), Readings in Social Psy-
chology (New York: Henry Holt and Co., 1958). 359—370.

Whitlow, C. M. "Attitudes and Behavior of High School Students," <u>American Journal of Sociology</u>, 40 (January, 1935), 489—494. (E.31)

Whyte, William Foote. "Corner Boys: A Study of Clique Behavior," <u>American Journal of Sociology</u>, 46 (March, 1941), 647—664. (C.59)

————. "A Slum Sex Code," <u>American Journal of Sociology</u>, 49 (1943), 24—31. (C.58)

————. <u>Street Corner Society: The Social Structure of an Italian Slum</u> (Chicago: University of Chicago Press, 1943).

————. "The Transients," <u>Fortune</u> (May, June, July, August, 1953).

Wilkins, W. L. "Social Peers and Parents," <u>Education</u>, 73 (1952), 234—237.

Williams, Helen L., and Warren H. Southworth. "Stimulating Interest in Public Health Problems Among High School Pupils," <u>Journal of Educational Research</u>, 53 (October, 1959), 53—61.

Wilson, Alan B. "Residential Segregation of Social Classes and Aspirations of High School Boys," <u>American Sociological Review</u>, 24 (December, 1959), 836—845. (D.39)

Wilson, John A. R. "Differences in Achievement Attributable to Different Education Environments," <u>Journal of Educational Research</u>, 52 (November, 1958), 83—93.

————. "Some Results of an Enrichment Program for Gifted Ninth Graders," <u>Journal of Educational Research</u>, 53 (December, 1959), 157—160.

Wilson, Robert C., and W. R. Morrow. "School and Career Adjustment of Bright High-Achieving and Under-Achieving High School Boys," <u>Journal of Genetic Psychology</u>, 101 (September, 1962), 91—103.

Wilson, W. Cody. "Value Differences Between Public and Private School Graduates," <u>Journal of Educational Psychology</u>, 50 (October, 1959), 213—218.

Winbigler, H. Donald. "Creative Potential of College Youth," <u>School and Society</u>, 86 (April, 1958), 194—195.

Winch, Robert F. "Primary Factors in a Study of Courtship," <u>American Sociological Review</u>, 12 (December, 1947), 658—666.

————. "The Relation Between Courtship Behavior and Attitudes Toward Parents Among College Men," <u>American Sociological Review</u>, 8 (April, 1943), 164—174.

Wirth, Louis. "Ideological Aspects of Social Disorganization," <u>American Sociological Review</u>, 5 (August, 1940), 472—482.

Wispe, Lauren G. "Sociometric Analysis of Conflicting Role-Expectancies," <u>American Journal of Sociology</u>, 61 (September, 1955), 133—137.

Witherspoon, Paul. "A Comparison of the Problems of Certain Anglo- and Latin-American Junior High School Students,"

Journal of Educational Research, 53 (April, 1960), 295—299.

Witmer, Helen Leland. "The Influence of Parental Attitudes on the Social Adjustment of the Individual," American Sociological Review, 2 (October, 1937), 756—763. (F.23)

Witryol, S. L. "Age Trends in Children's Evaluations of Teacher-Approved and Teacher-Disapproved Behavior," Genetic Psychology Monographs, 41 (1950), 271—326. (B.99)

Wittenberg, Rudolph M. Adolescence and Discipline (New York: Association Press, 1959).

———. "Young People Look at Society," Child Studies, 37 (1959—1960), 16—20.

———, and Janice Berg. "The Stranger in the Group," American Journal of Orthopsychiatry, 22 (January, 1952), 89—97. (C.60)

Witty, Paul A. "Only and Intermediate Children in the Senior High School," Journal of Experimental Education, 6 (1937), 180—186.

———. "A Study of Pupils Interests, Grades 9, 10, 11, 12," Education, 82 (November, 1961), 169—174.

———, and Paul Kinsella. "Children and TV—A Ninth Report," Elementary Training, 35 (1958), 450—456. (A.30)

Wolf, William T. "The University of North Carolina Experience in Student Self-Government," High School Journal, 41 (October, 1957), 25—30.

Woodcock, Bart L. "Who Should Teach Our Child to Drive?" Education, 77 (April, 1957), 513—515.

Woodring, Paul. "Ability Groupings, Segregation and the Intellectual Elite," School and Society, 87 (April 11, 1959), 164—165.

Woronoff, Israel. "An Investigation of the Relationship of Some Pre-Adolescent Development Factors to Adolescent Social Adjustment," Journal of Educational Research, 56 (November, 1962), 164—166.

Wrenn, C. G., and P. L. Harley. Time on Their Hands: A Report on Leisure, Recreation and Young People (Washington, D.C.: American Council on Education, 1941).

Wright, Charles R. "Mass Communication: A Sociological Perspective (New York: Random House, 1959).

Wrightstone, J. Wayne. "Do Students Benefit From Testing?" High School Journal, 41 (December, 1957), 75—78.

Yablonsky, Lewis. The Violent Gang (New York: The Macmillan Company, 1962).

Yashino, I. R. "The Classroom Teacher and the Pre-Delinquent," Journal of Educational Sociology, 33 (November, 1959), 124—131.

Yinger, J. Milton. "Contraculture and Subculture," American Sociological Review, 25 (October, 1960), 625—635.

Youmans, E. Grant. "Social Factors in the Work Attitudes and

Interests of 12th Grade Michigan Boys," Journal of Educational Sociology, 28 (September, 1954), 35—48. (D.40)

Young, Frederica Y. " Fostering Co-Operative Attitudes in Children Through an Action Program," Dissertation Abstracts, 16 (1956), 1731—1732.

Zachry, Caroline B. Emotion and Conduct in Adolescence (New York, 1940).

Znaniecki, Florian. "Education and Self-Education in Modern Societies," American Journal of Sociology, 41 (November, 1930), 371—386.

Zuk, Gerald H. "Sex Appropriate Behavior in Adolescence," Journal of Genetic Psychology, 93 (September, 1958), 15—32. (C.61)

Zunich, Michael. " The Relation Between Junior High-School Students' Problems and Parental Attitude Toward Child Rearing and Family Life," Journal of Educational Research, 56 (November, 1962), 134—138.